Introduction to WordStar 2000

Introduction to WordStar® 2000

David Kolodney
Thomas Blackadar

With a Foreword by
Seymour I. Rubinstein,
designer of WordStar

SYBEX®

Berkeley • Paris • Düsseldorf • London

Cover design by Judithe Sager
Book design by Sharon Leong

WordStar, WordStar 2000, SpellStar, CorrectStar, StarIndex, TelMerge, MailList, and MailMerge are trademarks of MicroPro International Corporation.

American Heritage Dictionary is a trademark of Houghton Mifflin Co.
Epson MX-80 and Epson RX-80 are trademarks of Epson America, Inc.
Grammatik is a trademark of Wang Electronic Publishing.
IBM, IBM PC, IBM PC-AT, IBM PC-XT, and PC-DOS are trademarks of International Business Machines Corporation.
MS-DOS is a trademark of Microsoft Corporation.
ProKey is a trademark of RoseSoft, Inc.
Punctuation + Style is a trademark of Oasis Systems.
SYBEX is not affiliated with any manufacturer.

Every effort has been made to supply complete and accurate information. However, SYBEX assumes no responsibility for its use, nor for any infringements of patents or other rights of third parties which would result.

Copyright©1985 SYBEX Inc., 2344 Sixth Street, Berkeley, CA 94710. World rights reserved. No part of this publication may be stored in a retrieval system, transmitted, or reproduced in any way, including but not limited to photocopy, photograph, magnetic or other record, without the prior agreement and written permission of the publisher.

Library of Congress Card Number: 85-50616
ISBN 0-89588-270-1
Printed by Haddon Craftsmen
Manufactured in the United States of America
10 9 8 7 6 5 4 3 2

To people who type for a living

In a minute there is time
For decisions and revisions which a minute will reverse.

—T.S. Eliot
from "The Love Song of J. Alfred Prufrock"

Foreword

The first computerized word processors were developed for people with typing skills who could use the added efficiency brought about by electronic storage and command manipulation of text. As new models of these "dedicated" word processors were produced, they became easier to use for a wider variety of user needs and skills. Similarly, when I designed WordStar for the new breed of microcomputers that were available in 1978, improving the efficiency of the touch typist was the primary goal. In those days dedicated word processors cost in excess of $12,000 to $13,000, which is more like $18,000 or $19,000 in 1985 dollars. Thus, in April of 1979, WordStar was born to provide a more economical way to get high quality, comprehensive, efficiency-tuned word processing.

In November 1984, MicroPro introduced a new word processing program, WordStar 2000. We were able to utilize more than six years of WordStar operator experience in designing our new product. We found ways to increase efficiency while making the program easier to learn and use. We found ways of adding many more features without adding to (and, in fact, diminishing) the program's complexity.

Rodnay Zaks, founder and president of SYBEX, and I first met in the spring of 1980 at the Micro Expo Exhibition held at the Palais de Congrés in Paris. We became colleagues and friends, and SYBEX became the first outside publisher to come out with a book on WordStar, *Introduction to WordStar,* by Arthur Naiman. I am very grateful to all our friends and faithful users of MicroPro products. I know you will be pleased with WordStar 2000.

Seymour I. Rubinstein
Chairman of the Board Emeritus
MicroPro International Corp.

May 1985

Acknowledgments

It is a pleasure to be able to thank some of the people who helped us on this book. Dr. R. S. Langer and Karl Ray provided valuable support and advice in developing the project. Our editor, Marilyn Smith, added ease and clarity to the text. Valerie Robbins' careful and intelligent work produced the Command Summary in Appendix A, the Command and Symbol Index, and the bound-in poster. Bonnie Gruen provided skillful editorial assistance at a moment's notice. Jeremy Elliott cheerfully resolved technical difficulties.

We'd especially like to thank the many people in the production department who put so much effort into this book: Sharon Leong, book design and graphics; Janis Lund, typesetting; Sarah Seaver, proofreading; and Elizabeth Thomas, coordination.

And final thanks to Susan Wall at MicroPro, who came up with clear answers to obscure questions.

Contents

Introduction   xxiii

1
Word Processing with WordStar 2000   1

    The Backspace Key   1
    Insertions   2
    Moving Text   3
    Other Features   3
    Help   4
    How to Think About Word Processing   5

2
Some Essentials   7

    What is a Word Processor?   7
    Your Computer   7
    Memory and Disks   9

Files 10
Long Files 11
The Cursor 14
The Cursor Keys 14
The Control Key 14
The Alt Key 16
Function Keys 16

3
WordStar 2000 in 60 Minutes 19

Installation 19
Starting Your System 19

4
Editing with WordStar 2000 25

Entering a File Name 25
Selecting a Disk Drive 27
The File Name Directory 28
Choosing a Format 30
The Editing Menu 31
Moving the Cursor 33
Function Key Commands 34

Word by Word   35
Hard Spaces   35
Inserting and Overtyping   35
Deleting Text   36
Cursor Up and Down   38
Scrolling Text   39
Hard and Soft Carriage Returns   39
The Status Line   39
The Ruler Line   40
Saving a File   41

5

A Quick Tour of the Editing Menus   43

The Editing Submenus   43
Setting the Menu Level   44
The Quit Editing Menu   46
Editing Menu Selections   47
The Repeat Option   50

6

Moving the Cursor   53

Moving Within a File   54
Moving by Screenfuls   56
Moving by Blocks   57

Moving to Specific Destinations 57
Inserting Returns 59
Starter Set 59

7
Removing Text 61

Removing Characters and Words 61
Removing Sentences and Paragraphs 62
Removing Other Portions of Text 62
Joining Paragraphs 63
Starter Set 63

8
Working with Blocks of Text 65

Marking Blocks of Text 66
Moving and Deleting Blocks 67
Copying Blocks of Text 68
Cursor Menu Block Commands 68
Working with Vertical Blocks 69
Block Arithmetic 71
Using Block Arithmetic 72
Vertical Block Arithmetic 73
Starter Set 75

9

Locating and Replacing Text   77

    Locating Text   77
    Options for Locating Text   78
    Spaces and Hyphens   79
    Locating Command Tags   80
    Locating Returns and Tabs   80
    Wild Cards   81
    Replacing Text   81
    Options for Replacing Text   82
    Locating and Deleting Text   84

10

Print Enhancements   87

    Special Effects   87
    Your Printer   88
    Boldface   88
    Deleting Tags   88
    Underlining   89
    Combined Effects   89
    Screen Colors   89
    Print Emphasis and Doublestrike   90
    Strikeout   90
    Subscripts   90
    Superscripts   91
    Overprinting   91
    Word Grouping   92

Line Height   93
Stand-Alone and Variable Tags   94
Print Pause   94
Print Color   95
Paper Change   95
Print Font   96
Proportional Spacing   97
Type Size and Margins   98
Type Size and Tabs   99
Type Size and Line Height   99
Starter Set   99

11

Tabs, Margins, and Formatting Options   101

Page Formatting   101
Tabs   102
Setting Tabs   103
Clearing Tabs   105
Setting Margins   105
Ruler Lines   106
Temporary Margins   106
Centering   108
Justification   108
Hyphenation   109
Page Breaks   110
Assigning Page Numbers   111
Headers   112
Footers   114
Footnotes   115
Comments   116
Starter Set   116

12

Format Files   119

What is a Format File?   119
Predefined Formats   120
Unformatted Files   121
Creating and Modifying Formats   122
Printer Defaults   123
The Decisions Screen   123
Boilerplate in Formats   127

13

Key Glossaries   129

Long and Short Forms   129
The Key Glossary Menu   130
Defining a Short Form   130
Using the Short Form   132
Deleting a Short Form   133
Using Another Key File   133

14

Files and Windows   137

Using DOS Commands   138
The Logged Disk Drive   138
Deleting Files   139

15
Printing Out — 147

The Print Decisions Screen   147

16
The Spelling Checker — 153

Spelling Mistakes   153
Your Dictionary Disk   154
Kinds of Spelling Checks   156
Running a Spelling Check   156
Choosing a Personal Dictionary   157
The Spelling Correction Menu   158
Ending the Spelling Check   163
Spelling Checks from Within Documents   164
Selecting a Personal Dictionary   164
More on Personal Dictionaries   165
Bypassing the Spelling Check   167

17
MailMerge — 169

Merging Documents   169
Creating a Form Letter   171
Variable Names   171
The Data File   172

Creating a Master Document   174
Ending a Master Document   177
Page Numbers   177
Page Breaks   178
Printing Out   179
Messages   180
Samples   181
Master Document   181
Data File   181
Output   182
Asking for Values   183
Conditional Expressions   185
Merging Whole Files   188
Command files   189
Mailing Labels   189
Alternating Letters and Envelopes   190

Appendices

A
Summary of WordStar 2000 Commands
193

B
Installing WordStar 2000
241

C
WordStar 2000 for Former WordStar Users — 255

D
Hard-Disk Systems — 269

Indexes

Command and Symbol Index   272

Subject Index   284

Introduction

What This Book Is About

If you're reading this, it's because you've bought WordStar 2000 or you're at least interested in it. In these pages, you'll learn everything you need to know as you begin working with your word processor.

WordStar 2000 is the latest innovation of MicroPro, one of the leaders in word processing software. This new program is a descendent of WordStar, a program which has dominated the word processing field for more than five years. WordStar 2000 maintains the flexibility of the older program while bringing it up to the standards of today's word processors.

When you bought WordStar 2000, you got a stack of manuals thick enough to rival *War and Peace*. Among this stack, there is a start-up manual, a training guide, and a reference manual— enough to discourage you from ever mastering the program!

MicroPro's manuals are fine for occasional reference, but they aren't the best thing to use when you're first learning the program. The hefty reference manual has so much detail that you'll never be able to weed out what's important, and the training guide really doesn't satisfy the needs of new users.

The good news is that the program is much better than the manuals, and it's not hard to learn if you've got the right book. And that's what we're here for.

Our aim is to give you an introduction to WordStar 2000 in a form that is both entertaining *and* informative. We'll try our best to take you quickly through all the steps while keeping it enjoyable. But we'll stay businesslike about it—we've got a job to do and we don't want to waste your time.

If this is your first time with a word processor, you'll learn how to think about writing on a computer and how to approach a large program such as WordStar 2000. In Chapter 3, for example, you will find a 60-minute tour of WordStar 2000, where you'll write a letter, save it on a disk, and print it out—all in less than an hour. And, at the end of many chapters, you'll get a **starter set** of commands for easy reference to the basic commands that you'll want to use right away.

If you're an experienced user, there's a lot here for you, too. If you're like most WordStar 2000 users, you've probably mastered only one-tenth of the entire program, and you can surely benefit from a clear explanation of the features that can make your life simpler. You may even discover some useful commands that you didn't even know about; WordStar 2000 is a big program, and few people know everything there is to know about it.

Of course, you mustn't throw away your MicroPro manuals. This book is only an introduction, and we would defeat its purpose if we tried to say everything about everything. Although it includes every WordStar 2000 command, this book concentrates on communication rather than completeness. Some of the nitty-gritty details aren't all that important—MicroPro has to tell you all that, but we don't and we won't. If you can't find something here, you'll surely find it somewhere in MicroPro's reference guide.

What's In This Book

You can think of this book as having three parts: a beginning, a middle, and an end. These three parts provide the basic information you'll need as you go from a novice to a WordStar 2000 expert.

The beginning consists of the first three chapters, which serve as a quick orientation course. Here you'll find a lot of important background, such as what a word processor does, how it runs on your computer, and how you should think about writing on a machine. In Chapter 3, you'll get a quick taste of working on your word processor.

The heart of the book is Chapters 4 through 15, which give specific details on the features of WordStar 2000. These chapters are generally organized by **menus**—the small reminder boxes that WordStar 2000 puts at the top of the screen. These menus divide the WordStar 2000 program into manageable groups of commands.

The last two chapters are the third part of the book, which will probably fill a more specialized need than what has gone before. Chapters 16 and 17 are devoted to two special mini-programs that come as a part of WordStar 2000: CorrectStar, a spelling checker and MailMerge, a program to generate repetitive documents (typically used for form letters). Although you use these modules as a part of WordStar 2000, you can think of them as separate programs that perform a specialized function.

After the text, you'll find a series of extensive appendices, which treat special subjects. The first appendix is a summary of all the commands in the WordStar 2000 program grouped into a logical order. Other appendices treat the subjects of installation, hard-disk systems, and WordStar 2000 for former WordStar users.

Don't forget the indexes: one for command symbols and one for general subjects. Once you've learned the program, you can easily refer to information about subjects as you need to, without having to thumb through the book. The boldfaced numbers in the index refer to the page where a key or concept is covered in the greatest detail. The indexes will help you to keep using this book as a reference guide once you've learned the basics of the program.

1

Word Processing with WordStar 2000

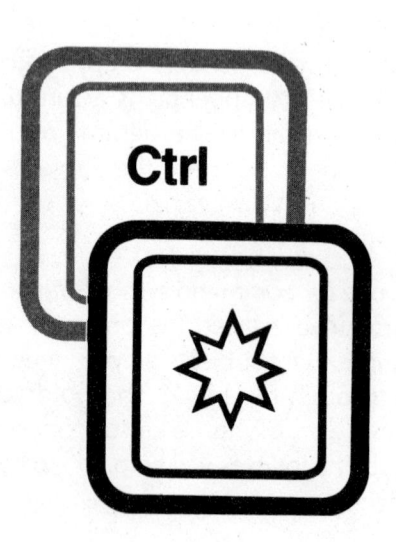

Word processors are great. Anyone who spends their life writing will tell you that. Novelists, newspaper reporters, secretaries—all these people spend hours typing in front of a screen, and all would attest to the hours of work their machine saves them. Many a novelist would rather shiver without heat in a garret than write without a word processor.

So what's so great about this machine? Well, everybody's got their reasons, but a few stand out.

The Backspace Key

You type on a word processor just as you would on a typewriter—until you make a mistake. Then you discover one of the word processor's most important features.

When you make a mistake on most typewriters, you have to stop, reach for the white-out, dab it on the paper, go wash your hands because you dripped white-out all over them, then finally come back and type the right letter.

On a word processor, you press the Backspace key and continue typing.

The key to a word processor is that the words you type never get physically printed until you decide they're ready. As you type, you see your words on the computer's display screen, and you store them in the computer's **memory.** This electronic storage is much easier to change than ink on paper.

The Backspace key tells the computer to back up and delete the last letter you typed. The letter immediately disappears from the screen and from the electronic image of your page in the computer's memory. You are then free to type the correct letter. When you print your document, the correct letter has replaced the mistake.

When you're learning WordStar 2000, it'll take you about a half hour to develop the **backspace key reflex.** Whenever you make a mistake, the pinkie of your right hand will immediately reach up and hit the Backspace key—it's marked by a long left arrow on the IBM keyboard (⬅). This reflex will soon be so strong that you'll never want to type on a typewriter again.

You can, of course, delete text in many other ways as well. WordStar 2000 has commands for deleting words, lines, sentences, paragraphs, even large blocks of text.

Insertions

Besides letting you delete what you don't want, a word processor also lets you **insert** text at any place. If you forgot a word in a sentence that you typed, just go back to the place and type the new word. It will be inserted in the appropriate place, and the rest of the words will be moved around to make room for the insertion. On a typewriter, such an operation would mean retyping the whole page.

Along with this ability to insert text at will, WordStar 2000 contains a feature called **automatic word wrap.** When you type, you just set your margins to the width you want, then begin typing. WordStar 2000 automatically begins a new line when it reaches the right margin. You don't have to push the carriage return bar or Return key at the end of each line. And, if you insert a word in the middle of the text, WordStar 2000 can rearrange the rest of the paragraph so it all fits neatly within the margins you have set. You can even have WordStar 2000 align the right margin as well as the left (called **justification**), automatically hyphenate words, and supply page numbers at the bottom of each page.

WordStar 2000 belongs to the elite class of word processors that have full **on-screen formatting.** This means that what you see on the screen is exactly what you'll get on paper, except in special cases where the program indicates a special print feature, such as boldfacing. As you work, you can constantly see how your text will look when it is printed, adjusting it if necessary before you print it out.

Moving Text

The other thing a word processor can do easily is **move** chunks of text. If you write a sentence and realize it belongs somewhere else, just pick it up and move it. WordStar 2000 will automatically cut the text out of the old place and paste it into the new.

A related feature is **copying** text. When you copy a piece of text, the original remains intact and the copy appears at a location you specify. The result is a duplicate copy of a block of text (which you can leave or alter if you wish). This copy feature is a quick way to churn out repetitive prose.

Other Features

Here are some other things you can do easily on a word processor such as WordStar 2000:

- **Locate and replace.** You can find words or symbols wherever they occur in the text and change them to something else.
- **Print enhancements.** You can mark sections of your text for special treatment when you print them out. With most printers, you can produce many special effects, such as **boldface,** underlines, superscripts ($e = mc^2$), subscripts (H_2O), and strikeout. Some printers also allow other effects, such as emphasized printing and overtyping.

- **Margins and tabs.** In WordStar 2000, you can set margins and tab stops just as you do on a typewriter. On the word processor, however, you can easily change the margins and realign the tabs without having to retype large blocks of text.

- **Key glossaries.** You can give special meanings to certain key combinations, so that you have a shorthand way of typing a frequently used word or phrase or a sequence of commands.

- **Spelling checks.** You can have WordStar 2000 compare the words in your text against the spellings in a dictionary.

- **Boilerplate.** WordStar 2000 contains a special feature called MailMerge that lets you insert varying information into different copies of a standard document. (WordStar 2000 also includes copy commands that produce similar effects.)

Help

On-screen help pages make WordStar 2000 easy to learn. At any time while you are using the program, you can press a key to get one or more screens of information about the command you are trying to perform.

WordStar 2000 also has an elaborate system of menus that list commands at the top of each screen. Once you've worked a little while, these menus should be all you'll need to remember all the commands. And when you become an expert, you can turn off these menus completely to get more space on the screen for your text.

How To Think About Word Processing

Think of a word processor as a fancy typewriter. Your computer's keyboard contains an alphabetic section that is essentially the same as an electric typewriter's. If you just type as you would on a typewriter, you'll have mastered 98 percent of the word processor.

Remember the backspace key reflex. Type as fast as you want and don't worry about mistakes. If you realize that you made a mistake, you can quickly go back and fix it. Or, you can always go back and correct your mistakes later. Professional secretaries, in fact, often type their whole text at lightning speed without thinking about their mistakes, then go back and proofread the entire document when they've finished.

Don't be scared of learning the fancier features of your word processor. WordStar 2000 pays for itself just in its capacity as a typewriter, but it is even more convenient if you use it to its full extent. Some people are initially intimidated by WordStar 2000's many features, but then they discover that even the complex commands can save them lots of time.

Approach using a word processor as an experiment. You can start from the familiar ground of the typewriter, then let your thinking evolve as you learn about WordStar 2000's special features.

2

Some Essentials

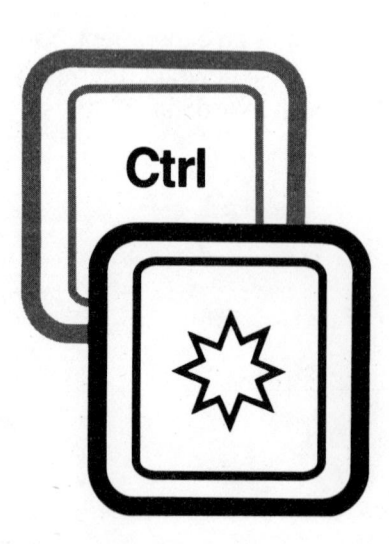

Some Essentials 7

Before we start our guided tour of WordStar 2000, we need to cover the basic ideas and terminology we'll be using throughout this book. If you already know this stuff, skip it and go straight to Chapter 3.

What is a Word Processor?

The modern English language has no less than three different meanings for the term *word processor:*

1. A computer that does word processing
2. A program on a computer that does word processing
3. A person (such as a secretary) who uses a computer to do word processing

It's too late now to separate these three meanings—just try not to let them confuse you.

WordStar 2000 fits the second of these meanings. It is a **program**—a series of electronic instructions that control a computer. All of these instructions are stored on a **floppy disk,** and you load them into the computer when you start the program. Because these instructions are electronic codes rather than physical wiring, they are often called **software.**

Your Computer

The opposite of software is **hardware**—the physical computer that runs the program. In the case of WordStar 2000, that machine must be an IBM PC or another computer that is closely compatible.

When you run WordStar 2000 on your PC, the program takes control of the computer and tells it to work in a particular way. Since you can't use your computer for anything else while you're running WordStar 2000, the machine itself becomes a word processor—as in the first definition. The difference is that you can always stop using WordStar 2000 and use your computer for other tasks.

In addition to the WordStar 2000 program, your computer must be running an **operating system.** The operating system is like a traffic cop that controls everything going on in the system without actively interfering with your particular work. For WordStar 2000 on an IBM PC, you'll want IBM's PC-DOS, version 2.0 or higher. On a compatible computer, you'll want Microsoft's MS-DOS, version 2.0 or higher.

You probably have some other equipment attached to your main computer unit, such as:

- A **keyboard,** which you'll use to type words and give special commands.

- A **screen** or **monitor,** where you'll see the words you type. WordStar 2000 works with either a **monochrome** or a **color monitor.** Most people use a monochrome monitor because it's cheaper and easier to read. If you have a color monitor, WordStar 2000 can use the colors to distinguish among print features, such as green for underlined text.

- A **printer,** which prints out your text when you finally want to see it on paper. WordStar 2000 works with over a hundred standard printers, including **dot-matrix printers** that produce characters as a group of small dots, and **letter-quality printers** that produce text that looks like it came from a typewriter.

You'll need all three of these components: the keyboard to type letters in, the screen to see what you have typed, and the printer to get the information out of the computer and onto paper.

Memory and Disks

Between the time you type your text and the time you print it out, your words are kept in the computer's **memory,** also called **RAM** (for random access memory). The memory is a series of electronic chips that stores characters of information and calls them back when necessary. To run WordStar 2000, you'll need at least 256K (256 thousand bytes) of RAM installed in your computer.

Besides storing your text in the computer's internal memory, WordStar 2000 also stores it on magnetic disks. A disk is like a phonograph record, except that the computer can both **read** information off of it and **write** information onto it.

Disks serve two purposes:

- They maintain a permanent record of your work. Unlike the computer's memory, which is erased every time you turn off the power, the magnetic disks keep all their data until you specifically tell them to erase it.
- Disks have a much larger storage capacity than the computer's internal memory.

With an IBM PC, you may be using either of two types of disks: **floppy disks** or **hard disks.**

A floppy disk is a 5¼-inch vinyl plate enclosed in a plastic sheath, which is covered by a magnetic recording surface. If you have a standard IBM PC, you probably have two floppy **disk drives** built into it. You'll use **double-sided, double-density** disks in these drives because they have the most storage capacity.

You can insert floppy disks into either of these drives. In general, you'll need to keep the WordStar 2000 program disk in the first drive (called drive A:) and your data disk in the second drive (drive B:). You can generally remove your data disk anytime you are not actually working on a document.

Don't worry about the backslash that WordStar 2000 supplies after the drive name. This symbol shows that you are using the **main directory** of the entire disk. This information is important if you have a hard disk. On a floppy-disk system you can ignore it.

A hard disk is a sealed unit that is built directly into your computer. The more advanced IBM models such as the PC-XT and PC-AT come with hard-disk drives built into them. You can also have a hard disk installed in a regular PC.

Hard disks have several advantages over floppy disks:

- They work much faster.
- They hold much more information.
- One hard disk can hold both the WordStar 2000 program and your text.

Since it is sealed permanently inside the computer, you cannot remove a hard disk; however, you can create a **backup** of its stored information by copying it onto a removable floppy disk.

It doesn't make a big difference which kind of disk you are using; both floppy and hard disks store information in essentially the same way. Most of this book is written with floppy disks in mind because they are more common. You can, however, do all the same things on a hard disk. Appendix D gives some hints on using WordStar 2000 on a hard-disk system.

Files

The information on a disk is organized into **files,** which are logical blocks of information stored as a unit. Each document you create becomes a separate file on the disk. You give your text file a unique **file name,** which you'll use every time you need to refer to the information. (The electronic codes for programs such as WordStar 2000 are also stored in disk files.)

When you want to start working with a file on a disk, you **load** it into the computer's memory. This merely copies the information from the disk into the active memory (without erasing the copy of the file on the disk).

When you edit a document, you work with the image of the file in the computer's internal memory. The memory is extremely fast and flexible, allowing WordStar 2000 to insert, delete, and rearrange text much more quickly than it could if it had to write all the changes immediately on the disk.

When you're done editing the file, you **save** it on a disk. This operation copies the information from the computer's internal memory and writes it magnetically on the disk. The information also remains in the computer's memory.

If you save a file with the same name as a file on the disk, you would normally erase the previous version of the file. WordStar 2000, however, automatically preserves the previous version as a **backup file,** in case you didn't intend to replace the old information. The backup file keeps the same file name, followed by **.BAK.**

Long Files

A long disk file may be larger than the available memory in the computer. Rather than restrict a file to what will fit in the memory, WordStar 2000 performs a more complex operation.

When you load a long file, WordStar 2000 reads only the first part of the text into the computer's memory. Then, as you move down through the text, WordStar 2000 reads the later parts of the text into the memory and writes out the earlier portions. At any one time, therefore, the memory will hold only what's displayed on the screen and a few pages before and after. The screen acts as a window into the part of the file currently in memory, and that part of the file is like another window into the entire file as it is stored on a disk. The figure on the next page illustrates this structure.

This complex structure achieves two important goals:

1. It allows WordStar 2000 to make changes to text near your current position quickly, without having to read or write anything on the disk.

2. It lets you work with files that are longer than will fit into the computer's available memory. Since WordStar 2000 automatically takes care of moving the text on and off the disk, it allows you to work with files as long as the capacity of your disks. On a floppy-disk system, you can have files as long as about 30,000 words. (Practically, of course, you'll generally want to keep your files shorter than that to save processing time.)

As far as you're concerned, you should see little difference between a short file and a long file. You load both types in, work with them, then save them on the disk. You usually don't even realize that WordStar 2000 is only loading part of a long file, except when the program pauses briefly while it reads and writes information on the disk.

One rule applies to both short and long files: Your information is not safe until you have written it permanently back on the disk. The computer's internal memory is preserved only as long as its power remains on. If the power goes off, everything in the memory will be wiped out, and you will be left with the last version you saved on the disk.

Wise people save their files frequently! Make a habit of saving every few minutes or after every few paragraphs—start now, before you have to learn by sad experience.

Disk files are discussed more fully in Chapter 14.

Some Essentials

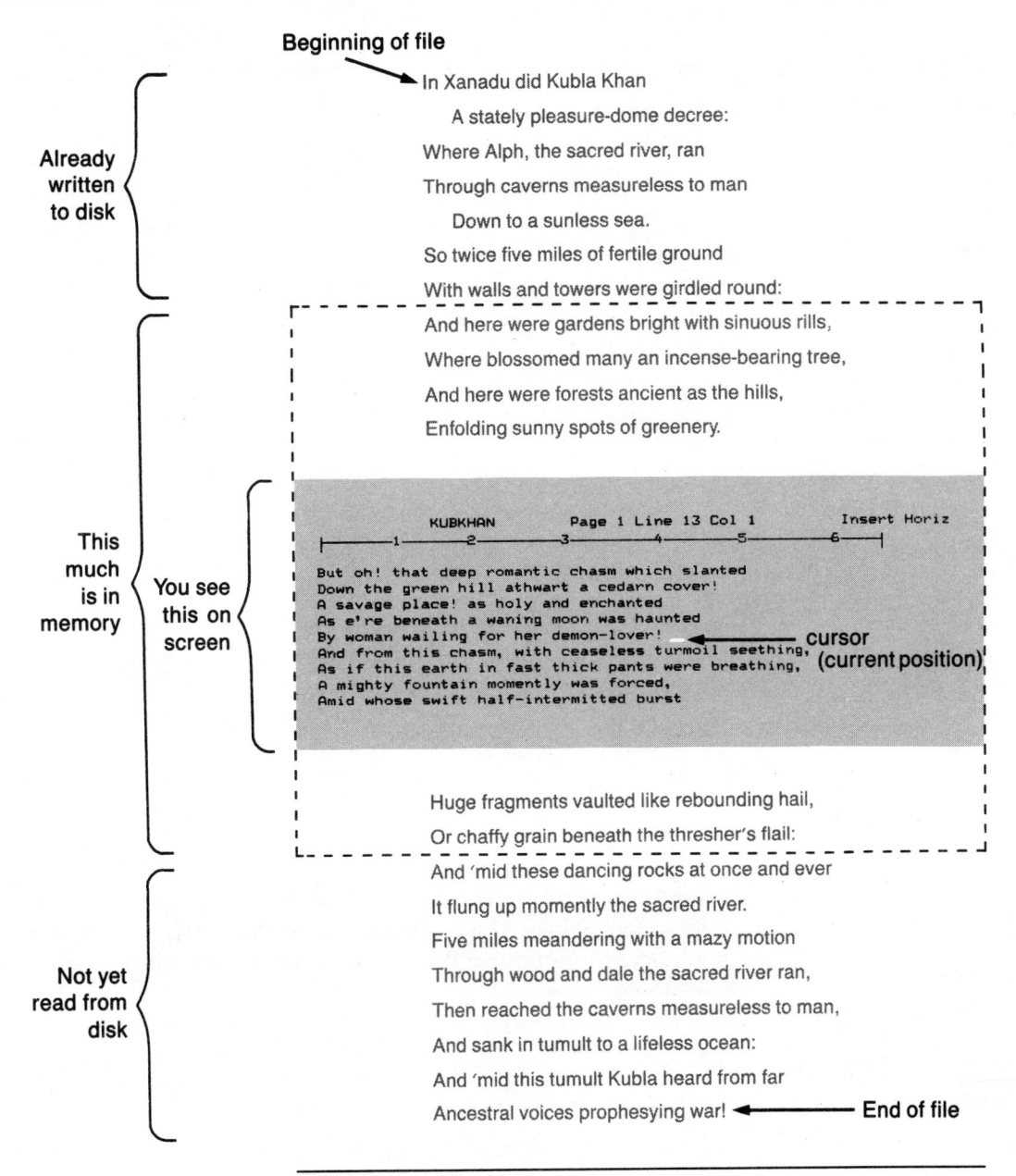

Beginning of file

Already written to disk
- In Xanadu did Kubla Khan
- A stately pleasure-dome decree:
- Where Alph, the sacred river, ran
- Through caverns measureless to man
- Down to a sunless sea.
- So twice five miles of fertile ground
- With walls and towers were girdled round:

This much is in memory / **You see this on screen**
- And here were gardens bright with sinuous rills,
- Where blossomed many an incense-bearing tree,
- And here were forests ancient as the hills,
- Enfolding sunny spots of greenery.

```
         KUBKHAN         Page 1 Line 13 Col 1          Insert Horiz
    |-------1-------2-------3-------4-------5-------6-------|
    But oh! that deep romantic chasm which slanted
    Down the green hill athwart a cedarn cover!
    A savage place! as holy and enchanted
    As e're beneath a waning moon was haunted
    By woman wailing for her demon-lover!           ───── cursor
    And from this chasm, with ceaseless turmoil seething,  (current position)
    As if this earth in fast thick pants were breathing,
    A mighty fountain momently was forced,
    Amid whose swift half-intermitted burst
```

- Huge fragments vaulted like rebounding hail,
- Or chaffy grain beneath the thresher's flail:

Not yet read from disk
- And 'mid these dancing rocks at once and ever
- It flung up momently the sacred river.
- Five miles meandering with a mazy motion
- Through wood and dale the sacred river ran,
- Then reached the caverns measureless to man,
- And sank in tumult to a lifeless ocean:
- And 'mid this tumult Kubla heard from far
- Ancestral voices prophesying war! ◄───── **End of file**

The structure of a WordStar 2000 document (The text is from "Kubla Khan" by Samuel Taylor Coleridge.)

14 Introduction to WordStar 2000

The Cursor

Somewhere on the display screen, you will see a flashing underline character or solid box. This is called the **cursor,** and it shows you where you are in your text.

As you type, the cursor moves along. The cursor always marks the point where the next character you type will go—normally the space after the last letter you typed. The cursor also marks the point where other commands, such as delete, will take effect.

The Cursor Keys

On the right side of the IBM PC keyboard is a **numeric keypad.** These keys include all ten digits, a decimal point, and the plus (+) and minus (-) symbols.

In WordStar 2000, these keys normally have a different set of meanings as **cursor keys.** The four number keys marked with arrows each move the cursor one step in the indicated direction. Other keys, such as PgUp and PgDn, move the cursor by larger increments such as an entire screen. These are the basic keys you'll use to move from one part of your text to another. You'll learn about the other cursor keys in Chapter 6.

You can also use the cursor keys as a numeric keypad. Press the key marked NumLock once, and the keypad changes to its numeric meanings. This might be handy if you're typing lists of numbers in a document. Press the NumLock key again to switch back to cursor keys.

The Control Key

The IBM PC keyboard has another special key marked Ctrl just to the left of the letter A. You'll use this **Control key** every time you want to give a command to WordStar 2000.

The Control key works like the Shift key on a typewriter (on the PC keyboard, the Shift keys are marked by hollow up-arrow symbols). When you press the Shift key on a standard typewriter, it changes the meanings of all the other letter keys; the small letter a becomes the capital letter A. Likewise, when you hold down the Control key and press the letter a, you get a different character, called *Control-A*. To produce this special computer character, you must hold the Control key down while you press the letter A. (You don't need to type the A as a capital letter; *Control-A* and *Control-Shift-A* mean the same thing.)

Control characters do not show up directly on the screen. Instead, they give a **command** that tells WordStar 2000 to do something to your text. Control-A, for example, tells it to move the cursor backwards one word. WordStar 2000 has meanings for all 26 Control-letter keys, as well as a few others such as Control-hyphen.

WordStar 2000 uses Control-letter key commands so often that it's useful to have an abbreviation for them. Instead of writing out Control-A, it is customary to use a caret symbol (^): ^A. This book uses this abbreviation consistently. Whenever you see this symbol before a letter, hold down the Control key and press the letter key. Don't type the actual caret symbol—WordStar 2000 would treat that as a caret that you want to insert in your text.

WordStar 2000 has more than 26 commands, so it has to split some of them into **two-letter-key commands.** The first key is a Control-key **prefix** such as ^C, which tells WordStar 2000 that the command is going to be one of a dozen or so related commands. You then follow this prefix by a second key that specifies which of those commands you want to use; ^C followed by U, for example, is the command ^CU, which means Cursor Up. You can type the second of these keys with or without the control key: WordStar 2000 treats ^C^U, ^CU, ^Cu, and ^cu the same.

The CorrectStar and MailMerge modules within WordStar 2000 have some commands that require three keystrokes: ^OMS, for example, means *Control-O,* followed by *M* and then by *S.*

The Alt Key

WordStar 2000 provides alternate ways of giving some common commands, which involve the **Alt key,** located just below the Control key.

The Alt key works just like the Control key: you hold it down while you press another key. To give the command *Alt-1,* for example, you would hold down the Alt key while you press the number 1. To WordStar 2000, this key combination happens to mean the same thing as the Control-key command ^QS (for saving files on a disk).

To reduce the confusion, this book generally avoids the alternate keys. Once you become an expert, you can save yourself a few keystrokes by learning some of them—they are all listed in the command summary of Appendix A. While you are learning, however, you should stick to the Control-key sequences.

Function Keys

The function keys along the left side of the keyboard are another alternate way of giving certain commands. These ten keys, alone and in combination with the Shift key, give a series of one-key equivalents for other Control-key sequences.

About six of these function keys are useful. Those six are mentioned as alternates when their commands are described in this text, and they are displayed as keys in the margin.

The rest of the function keys are not terribly useful until you are an expert. Don't worry about the ones not mentioned in the text—you'll spend more time in trying to remember them than you would save by using them. If you're interested, you'll find them all listed in Appendix A.

You can, by the way, redefine these Alt and function keys as other commands when you install WordStar 2000. Appendix B gives details on how to do this and suggestions for useful redefinitions.

3

WordStar 2000 in 60 Minutes

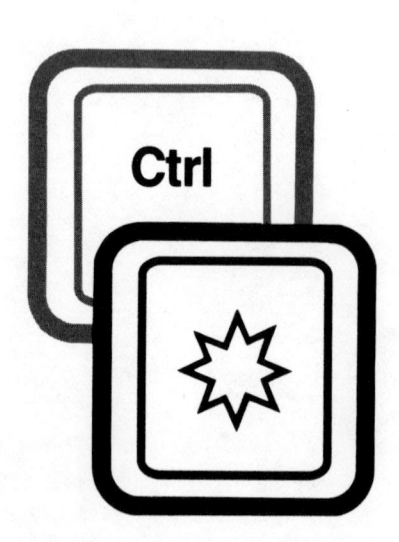

Now that we've got the background out of the way, let's give WordStar 2000 a quick trial. The idea of this chapter is to see what we can do in 60 minutes, without getting bogged down in all the details.

Installation

The first hurdle is to **install** your WordStar 2000 program disk so it will run on your system. If you haven't done this already, read Appendix B now and get your program disk set up.

The installation isn't as hard as it sounds. It really boils down to three basic steps:

1. Copy all of your MicroPro disks and put the originals away in a safe place.

2. Run the first part of MicroPro's **autoinstall program** on the disk you use to start your system.

3. Run the second part of MicroPro's installation program on your copy of the program disk. Answer the three or four questions the program asks, then exit from the installation program.

Starting Your System

Once you have your program disks installed, you can start up your system to run WordStar 2000. Put your start-up disk (such as the IBM PC-DOS disk) in the first floppy-disk drive, then turn on the computer's power. If the power is already on, press the Control, Alt, and Del keys all at once. After a moment, the machine should beep, the drives should clack for a bit and then stop, and perhaps you'll be asked to supply the current date and time. If you wish you can just press Return twice instead of answering the date and time questions.

Finally, you should get a line that looks like this:

A>

This **DOS prompt** shows you that the IBM operating system has been loaded correctly and that you are ready to run WordStar 2000.

Replace the start-up disk with your installed WordStar 2000 program disk. Then type the letters **ws2** and press the Return key (it's the large key to the right of the keyboard marked with a crooked arrow pointing left). These letters are the computer's name for the WordStar 2000 program. When you pressed Return, you told the computer to look for the program on the disk and run it.

The disk drive will clack again for about 30 seconds. Then it will stop, and you'll see a menu on the screen. This display, titled Opening menu, shows a series of commands that you can use at this point.

Type the letter *E* to choose the first of these commands, Edit/Create. The display will again shift, this time to a screen titled Choose a Name.

The cursor is flashing at the end of this line:

Document to edit or create? _

Put a blank work disk into your second disk drive and type:

B:SILLY.LTR

The *B:* indicates a file on the second disk drive. The name of the file is SILLY.LTR. If you make a mistake while typing the response, use the Backspace key to erase the mistake and type the letter over.

After you press Return to give this response, WordStar 2000 will ask you another question:

Format to use?

Below this question, there should be a table of seven **format files** that you can choose to define the page layout for the letter. Use the arrow keys to move the highlighting bar to the name NORMAL.FRM and press Return.

Now the screen changes again, and the Editing Menu appears. Below the menu, you'll see the flashing cursor. Just start typing the letter shown below. Use the Spacebar to get over to the right side of the first line to type the date.

                                                July 26, 1985(RETURN)
(RETURN)
Dear Julius,(RETURN)
(RETURN)
(RETURN)
   I just wanted to let you know I have enrolled in the Association of Silly People (ASP). I am really quite excited about the possibilities for extending the range of my silliness, an area in which I have been sorely lacking.(RETURN)
(RETURN)
(RETURN)
   I understand that ASP also has a chapter in Cleveland, where you are living. Perhaps you might also want to investigate this wonderful organization, since I know you too are afflicted by overbearing seriousness.(RETURN)
(RETURN)
(RETURN)
   I remain, as always, your devoted servant,(RETURN)
(RETURN)
(RETURN)
(RETURN)
(RETURN)
                                             Theodore J. Ludicrum(RETURN)
(RETURN)
(RETURN)
(RETURN)
(RETURN)
P.S. I hope this letter finds your wife Gertrude and your daughter Brunhilde in good health. (RETURN)

Type the letter just as you would on a typewriter, except don't press the Return key at the end of each line. WordStar 2000 will automatically fit the text into even lines (the automatic line breaks won't necessarily match the breaks shown on the letter). Don't press Return until you get to the end of each paragraph, at the places marked (RETURN).

As you get near the bottom of the letter, the text will start moving up, and the top will disappear under the menu. Don't worry—it's still stored in the computer's memory even though it isn't displayed. You can get back to that part of the text by pressing the up arrow key.

As you're typing, you'll probably make a few mistakes. If you catch them immediately, just press Backspace and correct them. If you let one go by, use the cursor keys to position the cursor over the error, and press the Del key (it's the period key of the numeric keypad). The erroneous character under the cursor will disappear, and you can type a new one.

When you're satisfied with the letter, turn on your printer and put a sheet of paper in it. Then press ^QP (remember, this means to hold down the Control key and press the letter Q followed by the letter P). This tells the program to quit editing, save the file on your work disk, and print the letter on your printer. WordStar 2000 will ask you another question:

Begin printing on what page? 1

Press ^Q (Control-Q) to accept this default answer. Then do as WordStar 2000 asks:

Prepare the printer and press Return.

If all has gone right, you should be able to watch your letter roll out of your printer.

That's it for the quick trial. You've started up the WordStar 2000 program, opened a document, typed a letter, saved it, and printed it. Not bad for 60 minutes!

4

*Editing with
WordStar 2000*

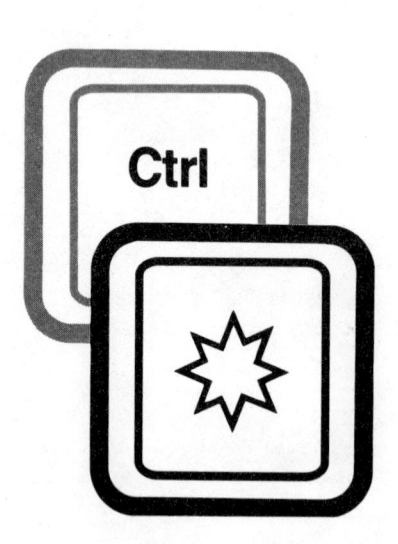

Now we are going to start over, but this time we will take things a bit more slowly. Boot up your computer with your DOS disk and dispose of the DATE and TIME questions as explained in the first section of Chapter 3. When you type **ws2** and press **Return** a screen will show briefly giving your WordStar 2000 version number, serial number, and copyright information. Then the **Opening menu** will appear.

```
                    OPENING MENU – 1 of 2

      Edit / create          Print                Get help
      Remove                 Copy                 Quit

      Directory / drive      Key glossary
      Move / rename          Typewriter mode
      Spelling correction    Format design

      Press a highlighted letter or Spacebar for more choices.
```

The Opening Menu

You choose a command from the menu by typing the highlighted letter, usually the first letter of the command. Most of the commands on the Opening menu deal with whole files as a unit—copying them, renaming them, removing them, and so on. These commands are covered in Chapter 14. **Edit/create** allows you to edit an existing file or create a new one, so type **E.**

Entering a File Name

The **Choose a Name screen** now appears, with the cursor prompting you

Document to edit or create?

```
                    CHOOSE A NAME

  ┌─────────────────────────────────────┬──────────┐
  │ Type or highlight name.  Press Return. │          │
  │                                      │ ^Get help │
  │   Move highlighting with cursor keys.│          │
  │   Erase errors with Backspace.       │ Escape   │
  │   Transfer highlighted letters to answer line with ^T. │
  └─────────────────────────────────────┴──────────┘

        ^G means hold down Ctrl key and press G.

  Document to edit or create?




  JUSTIFY.FRM    MEMOFORM.FRM    MSCRIPT.FRM    NORMAL.FRM
  RAGGED.FRM     UNFORM.FRM      WS2.BAT        WS2.KEY
  WS2LIST.FRM
```

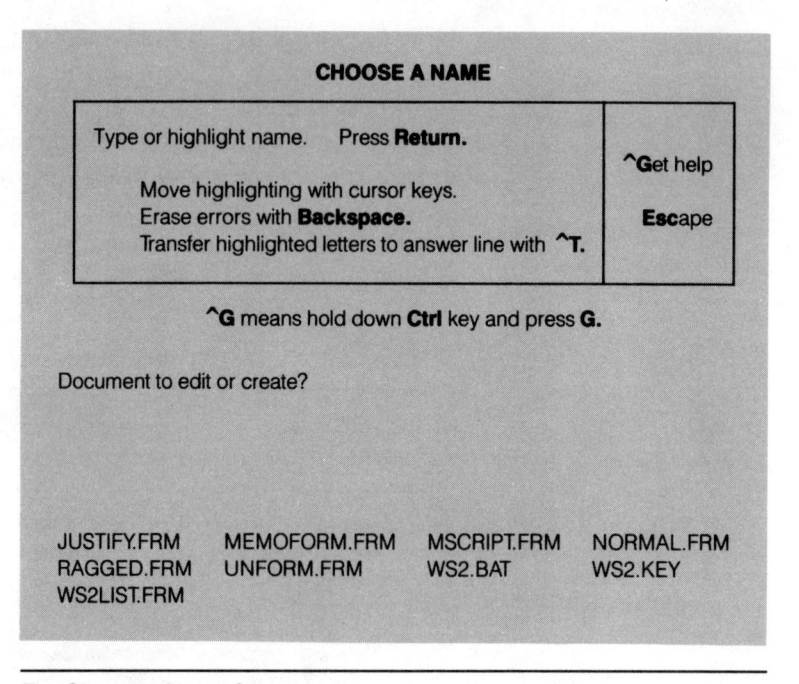

The Choose a Name Screen

WordStar 2000 has to know which file you want to work on. If it is an existing file, you have to enter its name. If it is a new file, you have to give it a name so you can refer to it in the future.

The file name should help you to remember what is in the file. It is a common experience to look at a long list of old file names and not recall what the files contain.

You can give a file just about any name you like. A file name has two parts, but the second part is optional. The main part can contain up to eight characters. If you want to add a **file name extension,** set it off from the main part of the file name with a period (no spaces). The extension can be up to three characters long.

The extension usually identifies the type of file, for example DOC (DOCument), BAK (BAcKup), TXT (TeXT), LET (LETter), and LST (LiST). Extensions can also be time savers because some DOS commands, including COPY, RENAME, and DELETE, can be applied simultaneously to all files on a disk that share an extension.

The characters in a file name can include any letter or number, as well as any of these characters:

$ & # @ ! % ' ' ( ) - { } _ /

There are a few names that DOS uses to refer to devices like printers, so you can't use them as file names:

CON, AUX, COM1, COM2, PRN, LPT1, LPT2, LPT3, and NUL

These are examples of valid file names:

CH4.WS2
CH4.BAK
CH4
4
1985.TAX
TAXES.85

Selecting a Disk Drive

Besides knowing the name of your file, WordStar 2000 has to know which disk it is on, or will be on. The disk on drive A: is nearly full just from the WordStar 2000 program, so the files you create should go on drive B:. However, if you look at the upper left of your screen you will see

A:\

This means that if you don't specify otherwise, WordStar 2000 will assume that you want your files to go on drive A:—it is currently the **logged** or **default** drive. In Chapter 14, we will talk about changing that; in the meantime, specify the drive by typing B: just before the file name (no spaces).

The answer to "Document to edit or create?" will consist of B: and the main part of the file name, followed, if you like, by a period and a file name extension.

    B:*filename.ext*

For simplicity, we will call this whole unit the file name.

The File Name Directory

The most straightforward way to enter the file name is just to type it and press Return. If you make a mistake typing the name, use the Backspace key to erase it.

There are three other ways to choose a file name. One way is to specify an existing file by highlighting its name on the list or **directory** at the bottom of the screen. Press Return to enter the highlighted name. Be sure the answer line is empty, or you will be entering whatever name is there.

Since you are logged onto drive A:, the directory shows the names of files from your program disk. To see the directory for your work disk, type B: Return. ^V turns the directory display off. Use it a second time to restore the directory. When the same command switches something back and forth like this, WordStar 2000 calls it a **toggle**.

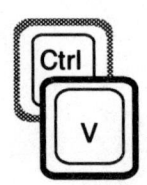

The main use of the four arrow keys at the right of the keyboard in WordStar 2000 is to move the cursor, but on the Choose a Name screen, the arrows move the highlighting bar around the directory. The highlighting bar starts out showing the file name you chose last time you used this screen in this session. This **default name** appears on a line by itself, just above the first name in the directory. If this is the first time you are entering a file name this session, the first file name itself is highlighted.

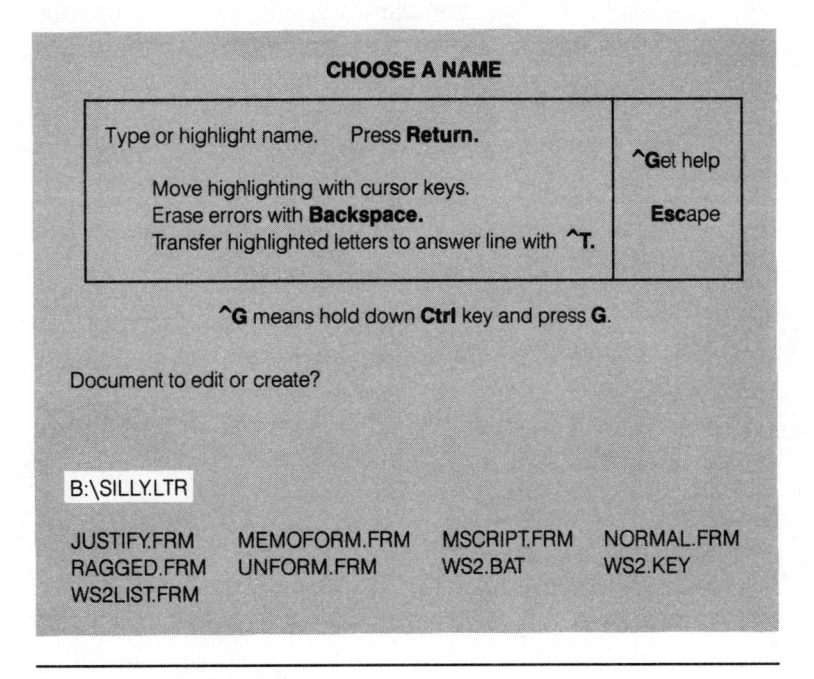

CHOOSE A NAME

Type or highlight name.   Press **Return.**

^**Get** help

Move highlighting with cursor keys.
Erase errors with **Backspace.**   **Esc**ape
Transfer highlighted letters to answer line with ^**T.**

^**G** means hold down **Ctrl** key and press **G**.

Document to edit or create?

B:\SILLY.LTR

JUSTIFY.FRM	MEMOFORM.FRM	MSCRIPT.FRM	NORMAL.FRM
RAGGED.FRM	UNFORM.FRM	WS2.BAT	WS2.KEY
WS2LIST.FRM			

The Highlighted Default Name

A long directory may not fit on the screen all at once. To see the next line down, press ^Z; for the next line up, use ^W.

On a very long directory, it may be tiresome to move the highlighting bar with the arrow keys. Another way to find a file name in the directory is to type the first one or two letters of the name instead. The highlighting bar will move to the first file name on the list that starts with those letters, and that portion of the directory will be brought to the screen. You can keep typing letters until the bar is on the name you want, or type just enough letters to get the name within arrow distance.

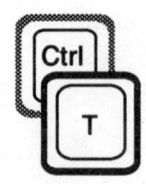

When the highlighting is where you want it, press ^T to move the file name to the answer line, then press Return to enter it.

Sometimes you want to create a file whose name is a slight variant of an existing one. To do this, highlight the old file name and use ^T to move it up to the answer line. Now you can create a variant and enter it as the name of the new file. For example, you might have a series of files called WS2CHAPT.1, WS2CHAPT.2, and so on.

If you change your mind about a file name, you can always rename the file later on.

Let's create a file to play with and call it PLAY.DOC. When you enter the file name, a new question appears on the screen.

Document to edit or create? PLAY.DOC
Format to use?

Choosing a Format

More than fifteen decisions go into the format of a WordStar 2000 document as it appears on the printed page. You determine the size of the left, right, top, and bottom margins; you choose single or double spacing, justified or ragged right margin, and so on. WordStar 2000 could be tedious and ask you to make all of the these decisions every time you create a new file. Instead, it offers you a selection of seven standard formats. You can add to the selection by preparing standard formats of your own. Once you have selected a standard format for a document, you can override any of its decisions for that document. Chapter 12 discusses formatting.

When the format question appears, the directory display shifts to a list of the formats available.

```
                    CHOOSE A NAME

  Type or highlight name.    Press Return.
                                                      ^Get help
       Move highlighting with cursor keys.
       Erase errors with Backspace.                   Escape
       Transfer highlighted letters to answer line with ^T.

           ^G means hold down Ctrl key and press G.

  Document to edit or create?    PLAY.DOC
  Format to use?


  A:\JUSTIFY.FRM

  JUSTIFY.FRM    MEMOFORM.FRM    MSCRIPT.FRM    NORMAL.FRM
  RAGGED.FRM     UNFORM.FRM      WS2LIST.FRM
```

The Format Directory

Use the highlighting bar to select RAGGED.FRM, and press Return to enter your choice. You are done with the Choose a Name screen for now.

The Editing Menu   The **Editing menu** now appears.

EDITING MENU

^Blocks	^Tabs and margins	^Print enhancements	
^Cursor	^Locate text	^Remove ^Undo	^Get help
^Options	^Next locate	^Key glossary	^Quit

^G means hold down **Ctrl** key and press **G**.

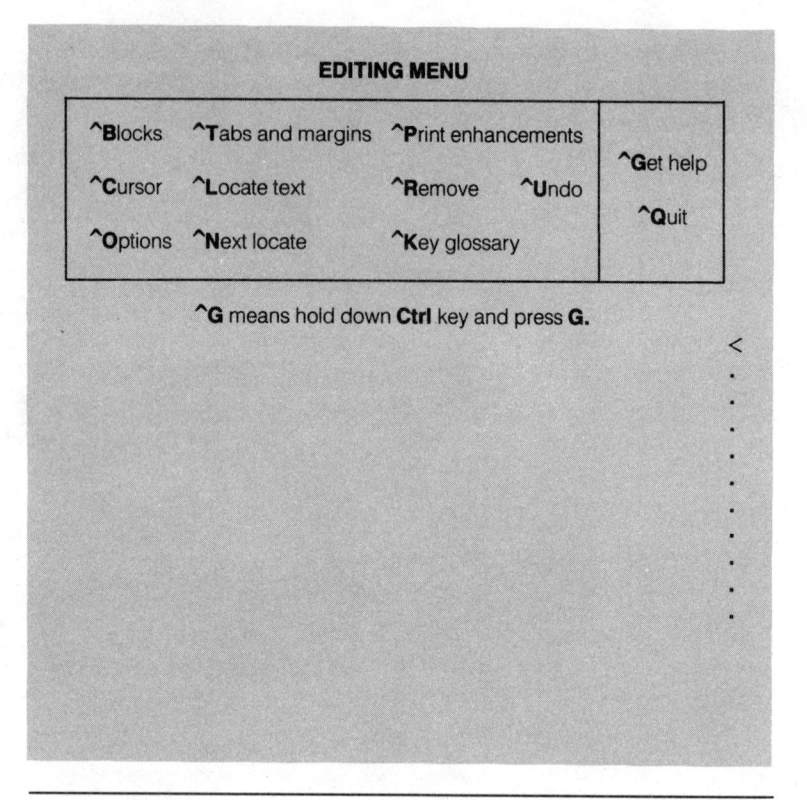

The Editing Menu

    This is not so much a menu of commands as a menu of about ten submenus. We will take a quick tour of these submenus in the next chapter and then discuss them in separate chapters.

    Below the menu the screen is blank. This is the electronic page on which you will write. You will need to have some text on the screen for this chapter. It doesn't matter what it is: make something up; hold a key down to use the **auto-repeat** feature to make nonsense words (broken up by occasional spaces), use one of the sample files that came with WordStar 2000, or type in the text we are using, the first stanzas of "The Tiger" by William Blake.

Tiger, tiger, burning bright
In the forests of the night,
What immortal hand or eye
Could frame thy fearful symmetry?

In what distant deeps or skies
Burnt the fire of thine eyes?
On what wings dare he aspire?
What the hand dare seize the fire?

And what shoulder and what art
Could twist the sinews of thy heart?
And, when thy heart began to beat,
What dread hand and what dread feet?

To begin with, let's work with one line. Type just this much:

Tiger, tiger, burning bright

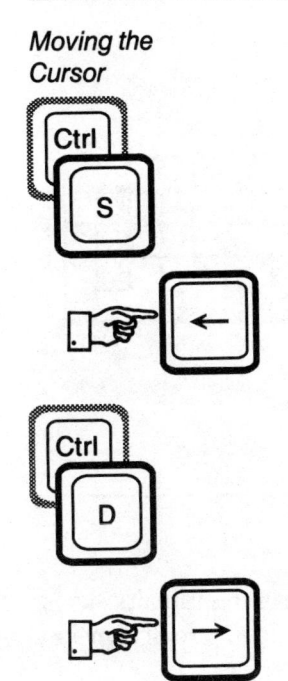

Moving the Cursor

Use the left and right arrow keys to move the cursor back and forth along the line. The arrow keys move the cursor over existing text without changing it (unlike the Backspace key).

Now try the key combinations ^S and ^D. They have the same effect as the Arrow keys because they are just different forms of the same commands. WordStar has alternate forms for many of its commands.

We will generally use the letter-key form to refer to commands. The letter keys will also appear in the left margin where the main explanation of each command appears in the book (that won't always be where the command is first mentioned). Sometimes the equivalent non-letter keys will also be shown in the margin, like the arrow keys on this page (identified by the pointing hand). We'll do this only when we think the alternative form is especially convenient to use. We recommend that you try these out, even if you otherwise keep your hands in normal typing position. All of the alternative forms can be found in Appendix A: WordStar 2000 Command Summary.

Function Key Commands

Every editing command can be given by pressing Control (Ctrl) and one or two letter keys. Most of the letter key commands were selected to sound like what they do, as you can see from the Editing menu itself. About fifty commands have a second form as well, given by one of the following:

- The function keys at the left of the keyboard (F1, F2, etc.), either alone or in combination with the Shift key;
- The keys on the numeric keypad at the right of the keyboard (you have already been using the arrow keys there), either alone or with Control;
- The regular number keys at the top of the keyboard in combination with the Alt (Alternative) key located below the Shift key on the left.

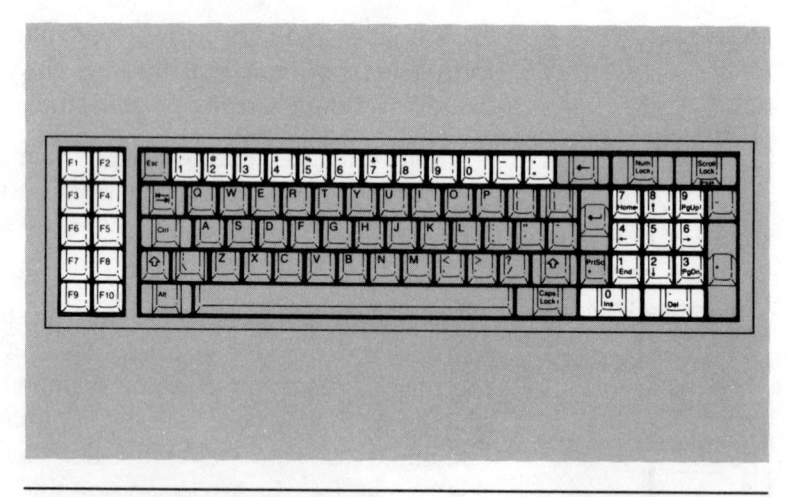

The Function Keys

Although only the first group actually use the function keys, we will be calling all of these alternate forms **function key commands.**

Word by Word

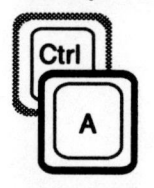

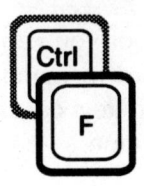

As you move the cursor left and right, notice that the auto-repeat feature works here too. Hold the key or keys down, and the cursor keeps moving. Even this can be too slow in normal editing, and there is also the problem of overshooting the character you want. To move the cursor left or right a word at a time instead of a space at a time, use ^A and ^F. These keys were selected as directional extremes because A is more leftward than S on the keyboard and F is more rightward than D. Using Control with the right and left arrow keys also moves the cursor word by word.

Hard Spaces

The cursor stops just past the last character you typed. The cursor control keys will move the cursor around existing text, but they will not break new ground. Type a few blank spaces at the end of the line on your screen. Now the cursor does move. But bear in mind that the Spacebar moves the cursor in the same way that typing letters does, by creating text as it goes along; the characters, called **hard spaces** just happen to be invisible at the end of a line.

Move the cursor so it is on the *b* in *bright* and type some spaces. The spaces are more apparent here because you are inserting them in the middle of a line, rather than adding them on to the end. Use the Backspace key to erase the extra spaces.

Inserting and Overtyping

Now type the word *very.* You are in **insert mode,** so the letters you type do not cover over what is already there, they are added to it and space is made to accommodate them.

Tiger, tiger, burning [b]right
Tiger, tiger, burning v[b]right
Tiger, tiger, burning ve[b]right
Tiger, tiger, burning ver[b]right
Tiger, tiger, burning very[b]right
Tiger, tiger, burning very [b]right

WordStar 2000 starts you out in insert mode, but you can change it. Use the Backspace key to erase the word *very,* and press the **Ins** (Insert) key at the bottom right of the keyboard. Now start typing *very* again just as you did the first time.

Tiger, tiger, burning [b]right
Tiger, tiger, burning v[r]ight
Tiger, tiger, burning ve[i]ght
Tiger, tiger, burning ver[g]ht
Tiger, tiger, burning very[h]t
Tiger, tiger, burning very [t]

You can stop as soon as you get the idea. You have switched to **overtype mode,** in which new text replaces what was there before. Backspace over the letters you just typed.

Ins is a toggle; press it again to return to insert mode. Now you can retype the letters that were lost.

Deleting Text

To take full advantage of the WordStar 2000 editing commands you will want to stay in insert mode most of the time. Although it may seem like a bother to have an error remain on the screen after you have typed a correction; it is easy to get rid of it. Just start the correction where you would have for overtyping. This pushes the error on ahead of the cursor. Then erase the characters you don't want with the **Del** (Delete) key, which swallows them up nicely. If you prefer to correct with overtype, you can just toggle between modes as needed.

The Del key erases the character the cursor is on, and any text beyond the cursor moves back to fill in the space. The cursor is stationary on the screen, but a new character is under it.

The Backspace key erases the character to the left of the cursor. Any further text, including the character the cursor is on, moves left. The cursor stays with the character it was on and moves left with it.

To see the difference between erasing with the Backspace and Del keys, insert *very* again and erase it both ways. With Backspace, you start on the right, one column past the text you will erase. So move to the space after *very* and begin.

Tiger, tiger, burning very☐bright
Tiger, tiger, burning ver☐bright
Tiger, tiger, burning ve☐bright
Tiger, tiger, burning v☐bright
Tiger, tiger, burning ☐bright
Tiger, tiger, burning☐bright

With Del, you start on the left, with the cursor on the first character to be erased.

Tiger, tiger, burning ⟦v⟧ery bright
Tiger, tiger, burning ⟦e⟧ry bright
Tiger, tiger, burning ⟦r⟧y bright
Tiger, tiger, burning ⟦y⟧ bright
Tiger, tiger, burning ☐bright
Tiger, tiger, burning ⟦b⟧right

Cursor Up and Down

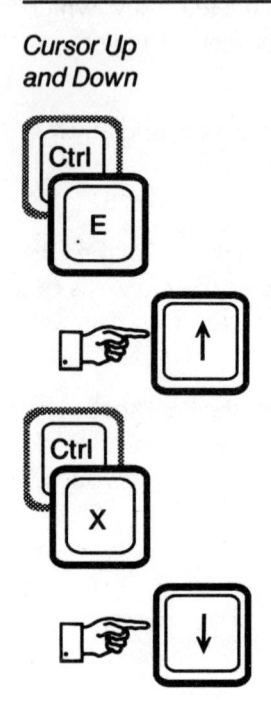

We are now ready to start working on more than one line at a time. Move the cursor as far as it will go to the right and press Return to start a new line.

If you had pressed Return at a character before the last of those hard spaces that you typed, some of the spaces would have been pushed onto the new line, and inevitably they would turn up somewhere as an unexplained gap in your text. So avoid using the Spacebar to move the cursor.

Keep typing the poem up to the end of the second stanza, pressing Return at the end of each line to start a new line. When you are done, use the arrow keys to move up and down the text. When you move the cursor up and down, it stays in a straight vertical line if possible. However, when the cursor reaches lines that are too short, it jumps to the left temporarily. The letter command for the up arrow is ^E; for the down arrow it is ^X. The letter keys that move the cursor make a pattern on the keyboard like the points of the compass.

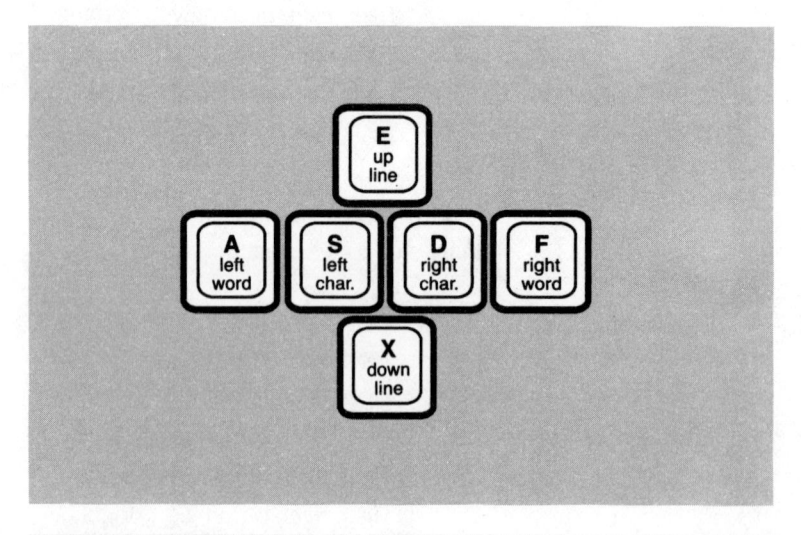

The Cursor Movement Diamond

Scrolling Text

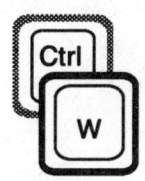

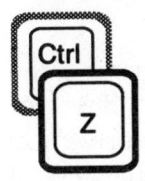

As with the directory display, you can **scroll** your text up or down. ^W lets you see the next line of text above what is showing on the screen, and ^Z lets you see the next line below. The cursor remains on the same character and moves up or down the screen with the text.

As you type more text than will fit on the screen, WordStar 2000 scrolls the text up automatically to make room for the new lines at the bottom.

The cursor movement commands won't take the cursor further down the screen than the last line of text. You can move it down by adding blank lines with Return, just as you can move it right by adding spaces with the Spacebar. You can't move down in the text with Return, because it pushes down the text below, and the cursor never reaches it.

Hard and Soft Carriage Returns

Pressing Return inserts a **hard carriage return** in the text, marked by the < at the right of the screen. The carriage returns that WordStar 2000 inserts when there is no more room on the current line are called **soft carriage returns.** You use a hard return to insert blank lines or to end a paragraph. WordStar 2000 allows a line ending in a hard return to stay blank at the end, instead of filling it out with words from the text below. We will usually refer to hard carriage returns simply as carriage returns.

The Status Line

The highlighted line at the very top of the screen is called the **status line.** As you move the cursor, notice that the center portion of the status line keeps track of what page you are on, how many lines you are down from the top of the page, and how many columns (or spaces) you are over from the left.

> PLAY.DOC   Page 1 Line 1 Col 1   Insert Horiz

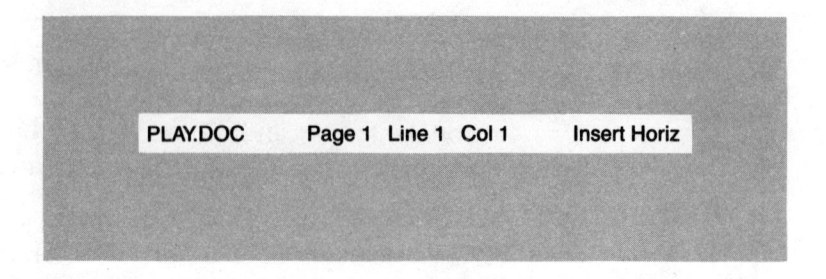

The Status Line

To the left of the cursor-tracking information, the name of the file you are working on is shown. Over to the right, insert or overtype mode is indicated, along with horizontal or vertical mode. You will stay in horizontal mode except when you want to work with text in columns (see Chapter 8).

The Ruler Line

Just below the menu is the **ruler line.** The numbers here indicate ten spaces or columns each. The little pointers mark the tab stops, which fall every five columns unless you reset them. The highlighting shows the margins, starting with 0 on the left. Adjustments to tab stops and margins are discussed in Chapter 11.

The Tab key, shown at the left here, types a **tab character** that is not normally printed out with the document or seen on the screen. To see the tab characters and other invisible **command tags,** use the command ^OD.

A tab character makes the spaces from itself to the next tab stop impossible to occupy. The cursor shoots over tab characters to the next stop. If there is text in those spaces when the tab character is typed, the text slides over to the right. For cursor movement and backspacing, the next tab stop is treated as the next space over.

In overtype mode, the Tab key and Return move the cursor without affecting text. The Tab key promises something it doesn't deliver: it looks like Shift with the Tab key makes a backwards Tab, but it doesn't.

As you keep typing lines of text, you will reach a line of dashes going across the screen. This marks a **page break.** When the document is printed, the text following this line will appear at the top of a new page. The number of lines between page breaks is specified in the format you choose. If the text is double spaced, you won't see it that way on the screen, but there will be only half as many lines between page breaks.

Saving a File

The current form of what you have typed and revised is now being held in the computer's memory. When the computer is turned off, its memory goes blank, so your work is lost unless you make a permanent copy of it. To **save** your file is simply to make a recording of it on the disk. So when you are done with your work, use ^QS to quit editing the file and save it before you switch the power off. It is also a good idea to save your document as it changes and grows, even though you are not yet finished working on it. Then, if something goes wrong with the document in memory, a recent version will be safely stored away. To save the current version and continue working, use ^QC. The screen may change as you type in these last two commands. For now, just ignore it.

^QS brings you back to the Opening menu. If you are done with word processing for now, press **Q** to leave the program. With that done, you can remove your disks and put them away.

5

A Quick Tour of the Editing Menus

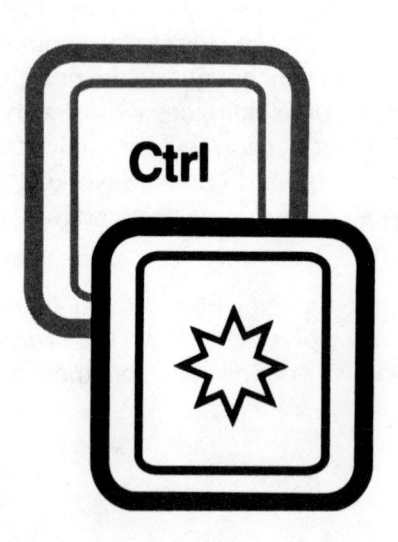

So far, almost all of the letter-key commands we have used have been one letter long. That is because we have kept to the basic commands, like the six commands of the cursor control diamond: ^A, ^S, ^D, ^F, ^E, and ^X. These are used so frequently that each is allotted a letter key of its own. But there are only 26 letters to go around, and the cursor movement commands alone number more than 30. Obviously, many commands will have to double up with others and share a letter key—most are two letters long.

The Editing Submenus

WordStar 2000 commands are set up so that related commands all start with the same letter, usually one that reminds us what that group of commands is about. There are 9 two-letter commands that begin with ^R, all of which provide various ways of removing text: ^RW removes a word, ^RS removes a sentence, ^RP removes a paragraph, and so on.

Open up a file to work with, and when the Editing menu appears, type ^R. This by itself does not give a command, but it narrows things down. WordStar 2000 shows you the **Remove menu,** which lists the nine choices available for completing your ^R command. When you type the second letter, the letter combination flashes at the left of the status line, the Editing menu reappears, and the command is executed. (You don't have to hold down Control while typing the second letter.)

Press the Esc key to get back to the Editing menu without completing a ^R command. The Esc key returns you to the Editing menu from any of the Editing submenus.

The menus are there to help you remember the commands; they are not essential to giving the command. If you type the second letter fast enough, the command will execute immediately without ever displaying the submenu.

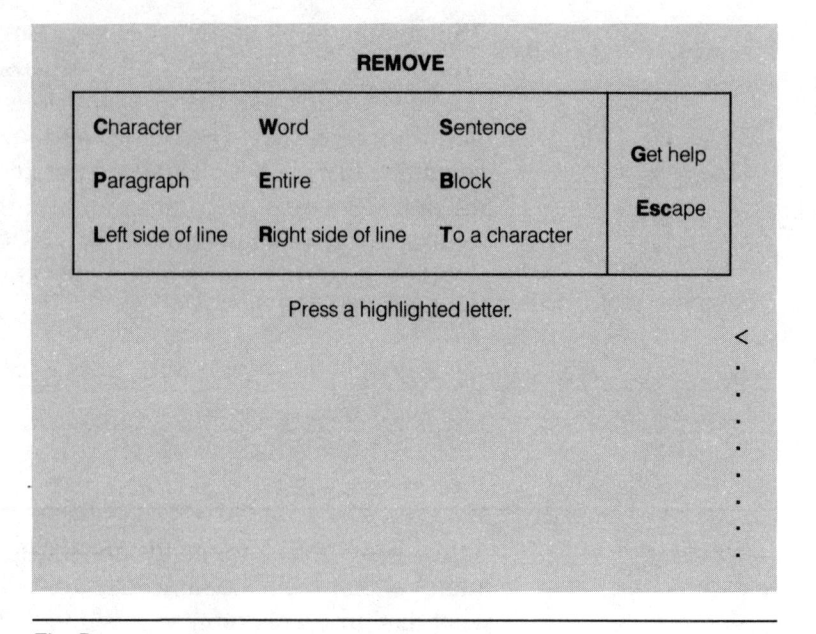

```
                          REMOVE
    ┌─────────────────────────────────────────┬──────────┐
    │  Character      Word         Sentence   │          │
    │                                         │ Get help │
    │  Paragraph      Entire       Block      │          │
    │                                         │ Escape   │
    │  Left side of line  Right side of line  To a character │
    └─────────────────────────────────────────┴──────────┘
             Press a highlighted letter.
```

The Remove menu

Setting the Menu Level

If you would rather not be shown the submenus, type ^**GG**. You will see this screen:

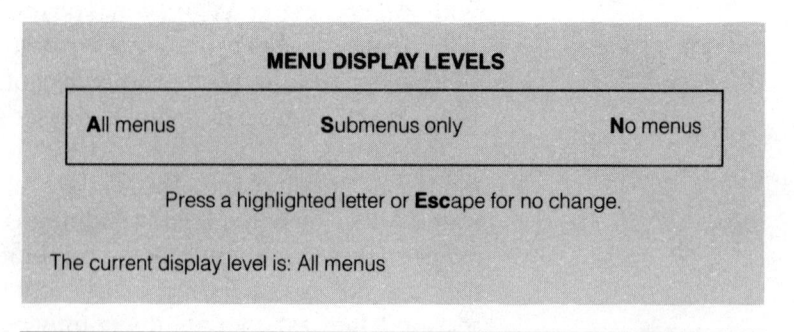

```
                    MENU DISPLAY LEVELS
    ┌──────────────────────────────────────────────────┐
    │  All menus        Submenus only       No menus   │
    └──────────────────────────────────────────────────┘
      Press a highlighted letter or Escape for no change.

    The current display level is: All menus
```

The Set Menu Level Screen

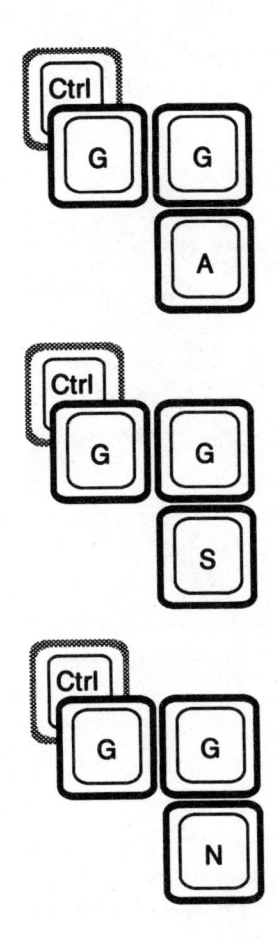

All menus is the level that you have now. If you have seen enough of the Editing menu but still want the submenus to appear when called, type **S**. To eliminate the submenus too, type **N**. Even with N, you will still see the Choose a Name and Decisions screens required in using certain commands.

If you need to consult a submenu after you have typed N, you have two options:

- Turn the submenus back on for as long as you like by pressing ^**GGA** or ^**GGS**.
- Leave the menus off and type ^G followed by the letter for the submenu you need to refer to. You will see a Help screen showing all the choices from that menu, along with a brief description of each one. Try this with ^GR. Press the Esc key to return to the Editing menu from any of the submenu Help screens. All the submenu Help screens can also be called by typing the menu letter before the G— ^RG and ^GR both get you the Help screen for the Remove commands. For some commands, the Help screen information runs to more than one screen. You can quickly page through them by pressing the Spacebar.

You can also just leave the submenus on and head off their appearance by quickly typing the second letter of the commands you know. Then, the submenus will only appear when you are stuck and really need them. If this is your strategy, you might want to reinstall your program disk so you have more time to type the second command letter before the menu is triggered. You can also change the default setting for the menu display so that WordStar 2000 starts out each session with the menus off. See Appendix B for details on reinstalling a program disk.

Along with the submenus and Help screens, the grouping of related commands by their first letter helps you to remember

46 Introduction to WordStar 2000

and make sense out of the tremendous variety of WordStar 2000 editing commands. As an example, type ^Q to call up the Quit Editing commands.

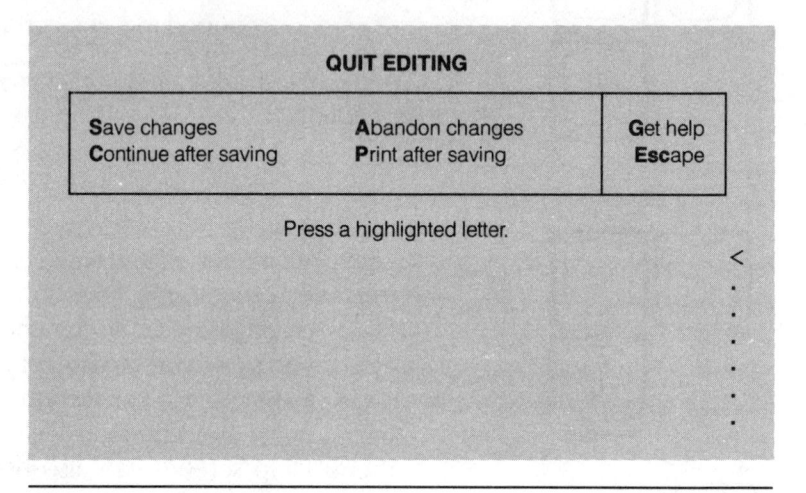

QUIT EDITING

| **S**ave changes | **A**bandon changes | **G**et help |
| **C**ontinue after saving | **P**rint after saving | **Esc**ape |

Press a highlighted letter.

<

.
.
.
.
.

The Quit Editing Menu

The Quit Editing Menu

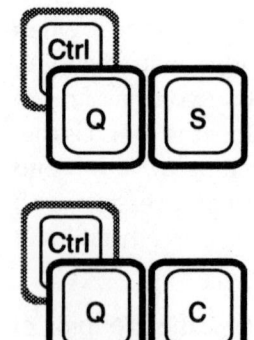

These four commands logically go together. We have used **^QS** to quit and save documents in Chapters 3 and 4. ^QS returns you to the Opening menu. Both **^QC** and **^QP** do what ^QS does plus something extra. ^QP goes on from there to give the Print command from the Opening menu and prints the file you just saved. This is a nice shortcut, since saving a file and then printing it is a very common sequence of commands. ^QC gives the Edit command from the Opening menu and reopens the same file so that you can continue to work on it.

Using ^QC is the most crucial safety precaution you can take to prevent the loss of valuable work. You can't hurt your computer by pressing odd combinations of keys, but sometimes you can make it **crash** so it won't respond any more until you reboot it. This blanks out its memory, and you lose all the work you've done since you last saved the document on disk. Having a single command for the Quit, save, and reopen sequence is like having a well-designed seatbelt in your car. So buckle up! This is one lesson you don't want to learn from experience.

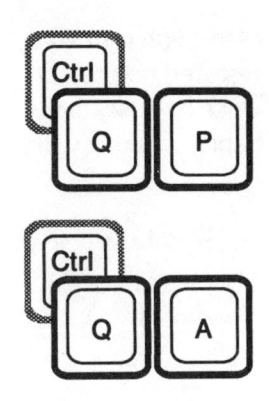

You use the fourth quit command, **^QA,** when you like the file as you last saved it better than the revision you are working on now. ^QA gets you out of the editing session without saving the most recent changes. You may have made an inadvertent deletion or, as in our practice sessions, you were just using the text to play around. Remember, ^QA leaves the file exactly as it was when it was last saved, so be sure you aren't throwing out some useful work along with the errors. (This is not a problem if you used ^QC to save your most recent work before you made the error.) The backup files that WordStar 2000 automatically creates are discussed in Chapter 14, along with other safety measures and some problems (especially with long files) that can lead to a loss of editing work.

Editing Menu Selections

Besides ^G for getting help and ^Q for quitting, there are ten other selections that can be made from the Editing menu. Three are commands that do not call up a submenu for execution. These are:

    ^L   Locate Text command
    ^N   Next Locate command
    ^U   Undo command

^L and ^N go together. ^L locates pieces of text that you specify and, if you choose, replaces them with other text. Pressing ^L opens up a screen that requests you to make further decisions. ^N allows you to repeat the last ^L command without retyping the decisions each time. Locating and replacing text is the subject of Chapter 9.

The ^U command restores the last piece of text you removed that was larger than a single character. The restored text can be inserted in its original position or elsewhere once or many times over. The Undo command is discussed in Chapter 7, along with the Remove commands.

The other selections from the Editing menu are submenus:

^C	Cursor menu
^R	Remove menu
^B	Blocks menu
^P	Print Enhancements menu
^T	Tabs and Margins menu
^K	Key Glossary menu
^O	Options menu

The **Cursor menu** (discussed in Chapter 6) offers a variety of powerful ways to get around in your text. For example, one command takes you directly to the beginning of the file, and another takes you to the top of any page you specify.

The **Blocks menu** (discussed in Chapter 8) allows you to mark a chunk of text and then work with it as a unit. It includes commands for making multiple copies of the block, for moving the block to a new location or to another file, and so on.

The **Print Enhancements** menu (discussed in Chapter 10) includes commands for boldfacing, underlining, subscript, and superscript. From this menu, you can call for just about any variation your printer can produce, and probably several that it cannot produce. If your printer can change colors or paper size in midstream, this menu will order it for you. Actually you may be surprised at what your printer can do. The standard IBM dot matrix printer sold with the IBM PC can print in four type sizes as well as in italics.

The **Tabs and Margins menu** (discussed in Chapter 11) allows you great flexibility in adjusting the text format, either throughout a file or just in specified portions.

The **Key Glossary menu** (discussed in Chapter 13) allows you to create a kind of short hand code in which one or two letters can stand for a long string of text or commands.

The **Options menu** is the only one whose name tells you almost nothing about its contents. It is a great catchall submenu, which gives you access to 33 assorted commands.

Fifteen of these commands are actually tucked away in *sub-submenus*. Eleven are devoted to MailMerge, the facility that produces automated personalized letters and boilerplate texts built up of standard paragraphs that you combine in different ways. When you press ^O for the Options menu, one of the choices is M, and this opens the menu of MailMerge commands. You select from this menu by typing another letter, so these are actually three-letter commands. MailMerge is covered in Chapter 17.

^OS calls up a second sub-submenu of the Options menu that contains four commands related to the spelling correction facility, covered in Chapter 16. ^OB is also a spelling-check command.

^OI leads to an indexing sub-submenu available only with the optional program IndexStar; it is outside the scope of this book.

That leaves 14 selections on the Options menu proper:

^OJ	Justify text on/off
^OC	Center text
^O-	Insert discretionary hyphen
^OU	Unprinted comment
^OP	Page break
^OK	Keep lines together on page

^OA   Assign page numbers
^OD   Display tab characters, tags, place markers on/off
^OF   Footer
^OH   Header
^ON   Footnote
^OO   Overtype on/off
^OW   Open window
^OR   Repeat commands or text

The first 11 commands on this list fall roughly into the category of formatting the text; they are discussed along with tabs and margins in Chapter 11.

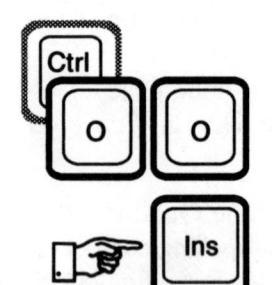

^OO is the letter-key command that turns overtype on and off, just like the Ins key. Overtype mode was discussed in Chapter 4.

^OW opens up a **window** on the screen in which you can view and work with a second file. (The window actually looks like a second ruler line in the middle of the text display.) This very useful feature will be discussed with file handling in Chapter 14.

The Repeat Option

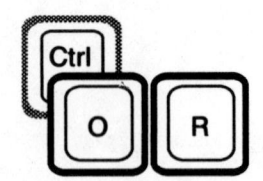

The only command on the Options menu that is not described in another chapter is **^OR, (Repeat Commands or Text)**. This command can be used to repeat any other command over and over until you stop the process by pressing the Spacebar or any other key.

To see this work, type ^OR. You will see a prompt at the top of your screen:

Type the keystrokes or command to repeat. (Press ^Q to end.)

Type ^A here, pressing the caret on top of the 6 key rather than Control. Then press ^Q in the usual way. The cursor will move back through your text word by word until you press a key to stop it. Press the number 1 along the top of the keyboard to speed up the repetition of a command, or a number up to 9 (the slowest) to slow it down. The starting speed of ^OR is 3. Use ^OR to bring the cursor to the end of the file with a repeated ^F command. To see plain text repeated, type your name at the ^OR prompt, leave a space and press ^Q.

Your repeated text or commands can be up to seven lines long. You can include carriage returns (try repeating your name and address typed on three lines) and you can mix text with commands; for instance, you can type a word and then move the cursor so it can write the word again elsewhere.

While you type an item to be repeated, the cursor diamond, Backspace, and Del keys work normally. However, ^R by itself works here to remove an entire line.

6

Moving the Cursor

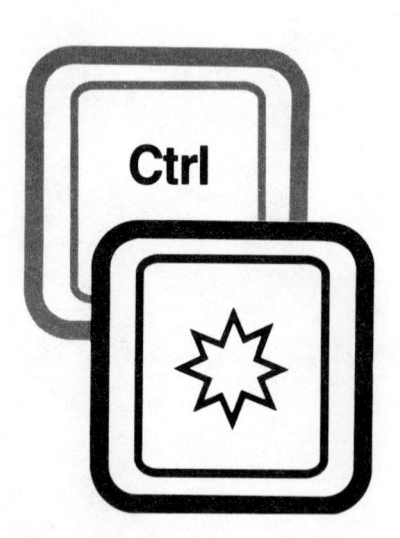

The Cursor menu offers you eighteen choices, not counting Get Help and Escape. When it first comes up, you see only nine of these.

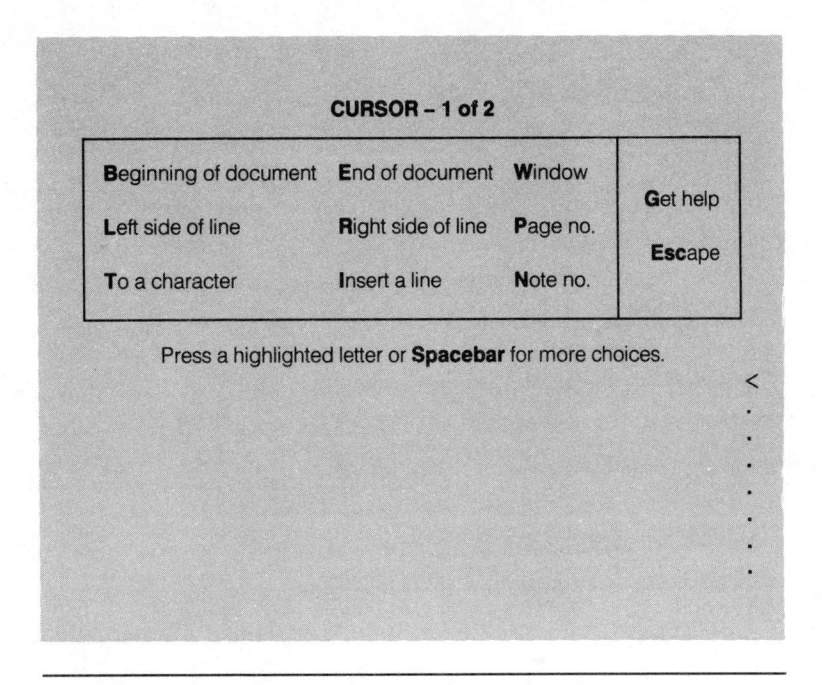

CURSOR – 1 of 2

Beginning of document	**E**nd of document	**W**indow	**G**et help
Left side of line	**R**ight side of line	**P**age no.	**Esc**ape
To a character	**I**nsert a line	**N**ote no.	

Press a highlighted letter or **Spacebar** for more choices.

The Cursor Menu–Screen 1

The other nine are on a second screen that you get to by pressing the Spacebar. Pressing the Spacebar again returns you to the first screen.

These eighteen selections do not include the six commands on the cursor diamond or the two scrolling commands ^W and ^Z. Instead, the Cursor menu commands allow you to move the cursor on a larger scale and provide new ways to specify a destination.

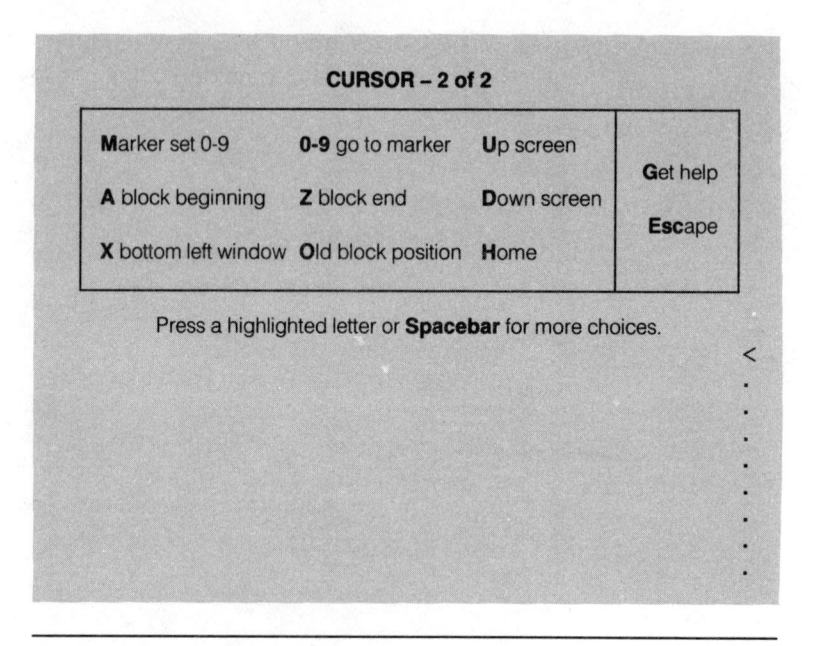

```
                    CURSOR – 2 of 2

Marker set 0-9    0-9 go to marker    Up screen
                                                      Get help
A block beginning    Z block end       Down screen
                                                      Escape
X bottom left window  Old block position  Home
```

Press a highlighted letter or **Spacebar** for more choices.

The Cursor Menu–Screen 2

Moving Within a File

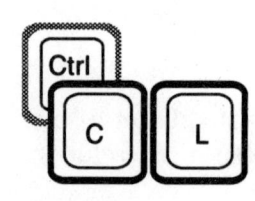

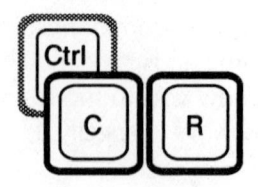

^CL (**Cursor Left**) and ^CR (**Cursor Right**) move the cursor all the way left or right on the line it is on. If the text extends all the way to the right margin, ^CR sends the cursor there. If the text is short of the margin, the cursor will go one column past the last character in the line, ready for the next character you type. (^CL always sends the cursor to the left margin.)

^CL and ^CR are handy because they move the cursor faster than ^A and ^F, and they avoid overshooting the end of the line. On the reprogrammed function keys recommended in Appendix B, ^CL and ^CR occupy F5 and F6 respectively.

^CH (**Cursor Home**) brings the cursor "home" to the top left of the screen. ^CX (**Cursor lower left**) moves the cursor to the bottom left, either at the start of the last line of text showing or, if that line ends in a hard carriage return, at the start of the next line.

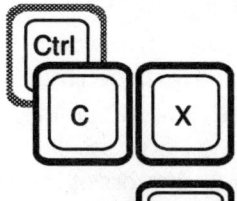

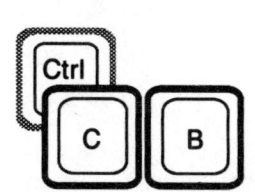

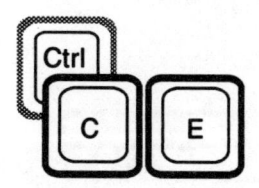

Commands like ^CH and ^CX are not indispensible by any means, and you can lead a long and happy life word processing without them. But as you use WordStar 2000 over a period of time, you will develop strategies for moving the cursor that appeal to you and are adapted to the editing maneuvers most typical in your work. You may find, for example, that you like to use ^CH and ^CE to get the cursor to the general neighborhood you want, then use the cursor diamond commands to position it exactly.

The Starter Set at the end of this chapter contains only four of the eighteen commands on the Cursor menu. These four commands, together with the commands on the cursor diamond, are all you need to work quite competently with your text. But the other fourteen comands are there because experience has shown them to add considerable convenience in one situation or another. When the Starter Set commands have become more or less second nature to you, it is a good idea to branch out and try some new ones.

^CB (Cursor to Beginning of file) takes the cursor all the way to the beginning of the document, and **^CE (Cursor to End of file)** takes it to the end. As the file gets longer, these two commands take a while to execute (long enough to make you wonder if something has gone wrong). Also, in a long file that is getting too big for the disk, you might get this message on the screen:

> **The disk is full—you must delete one or more files to continue or press Escape to abandon current document.**

Problems with long files and what to do about them are discussed in Chapter 14. The best safety rule is to keep enough space on your work disk for three copies of the file you are working on.

You can also move the cursor to the beginning of a file by saving the file with ^QS and reopening it. This may be quicker than using ^CB if the cursor has a long way to go. (^QC won't help because it leaves the cursor where it was.)

When you are adding text to a document, you often go back to correct or revise something and then want to resume writing where you left off. ^CE is probably the most convenient way of getting there, even over short distances.

Moving by Screenfuls

You can move the cursor up or down your text by screenfuls with **^CU** (**Cursor Up**) and **^CD** (**Cursor Down**). When the Editing menu is on the screen, the cursor will move 13 lines each time; without the menu, it will move 20 lines. These commands first move the cursor to the new line in the text, then they move the text up or down on the screen so the new cursor line appears on the screen just where the old one was. So if the cursor was on line 10 of a page and line 10 is at the top of the screen, ^CD moves the cursor to line 23 (or 30) and moves that line to the top of the screen.

The function key equivalents of ^CU, ^CD, ^CH, and ^CE have some special attractions:

- They do not require you to press Shift or Control, and they are only one "letter" long.
- The keys are more or less labeled for the commands.
- They are arranged logically on the keyboard.

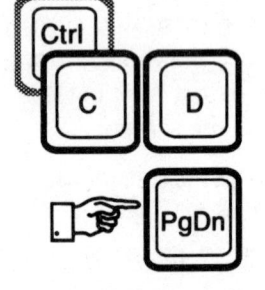

The keyboard with Home, End, PgUp, PgDn highlighted

Moving the Cursor 57

Moving by Blocks

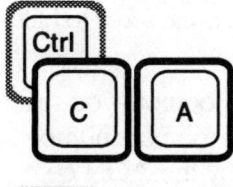

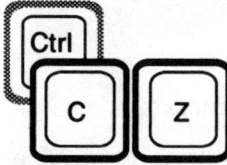

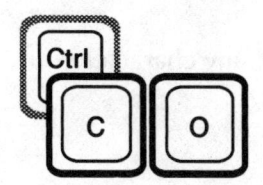

If you have marked a block of text on the screen for use with the Block commands (discussed in Chapter 8), ^**CA** (**Cursor to beginning of block**) and ^**CZ** (**Cursor to end of block**) move the cursor to the beginning or end of the block from anywhere in the document. If you have moved a block to a new place in the text, you may want to go back to where it came from and resume work.

^CA and ^CZ are useful when you want to return to a block of text and add to it or revise it periodically as you continue to write the main text. For example, you might use the block to enumerate points that are to follow, then you can return to the block as new points occur to you later on.

^**CO** (**Cursor to block's Old position**) takes the cursor to the old position of the last block you moved.

Moving to Specific Destinations

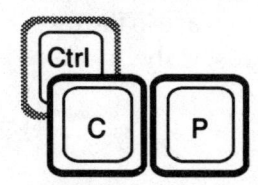

^**CP** (**Cursor to Page**), ^**CN** (**Cursor to Note**), and ^**CT** (**Cursor To**) ask you to specify a destination for the cursor and then move it there. ^CP moves the cursor to the beginning of any page you specify. When you choose this command, you see this message:

Go to which screen page number?
(Press + for next page or − for previous page.)

Type the number you want, then press Return.

WordStar 2000 allows you to print your document with page numbers that are different from those that appear on the status line (see ^OA, Chapter 11). However, ^CP always goes by screen page numbers.

Instead of typing a number you can use + and − to move forward or back a page. Or you can type +5 or −5, for example, to move the cursor ahead or back five pages. You might also try using the Repeat command ^OR and specifying ^CP+ or ^CP− as the command to repeat. This will take you through a document a page at a time until you press a key to halt the process.

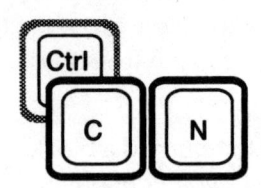

^CN works like ^CP, except it goes to any footnote you specify, or rather to the place in the text where the footnote number appears. This works with footnotes created by the ^ON command (see Chapter 11). The ^CN message is:

> Go to which footnote number?
> (Press + for next footnote or − for previous footnote.)

You can specify footnote numbers in the same ways as page numbers.

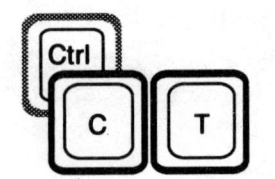

^CT takes you to the next occurrence of any character you specify. It gives the message:

> Character to go to?

You can type any letter, number, or punctuation mark. Typing a period gets you to the end of a sentence. ^CT distinguishes between capital and lowercase letters.

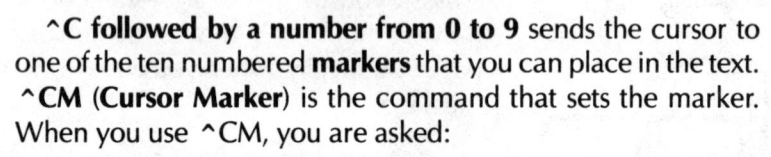

^C followed by a number from 0 to 9 sends the cursor to one of the ten numbered **markers** that you can place in the text. **^CM (Cursor Marker)** is the command that sets the marker. When you use ^CM, you are asked:

> Set which marker (0–9)?

The marker looks like this:

> <3>

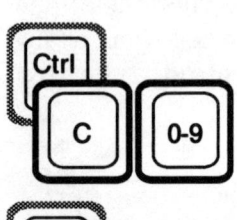

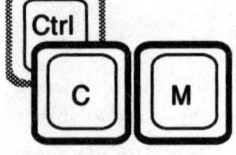

Although the marker seems to occupy a space in the text, it is just an imaginary space that the cursor can't land on. When you press ^C3, for example, the cursor lands on the space to the right of marker 3. You can't delete a marker with Backspace or the Del key. Instead, you place the same marker again in the same place, and it disappears. If you set marker 3 elsewhere in the text, it moves to that location. Markers remain visible on the screen even when other command tags are not displayed.

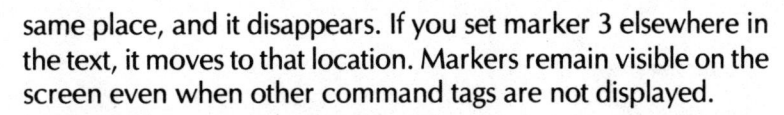

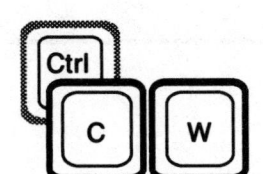

You can set markers anyplace you might want to return to, for example, at a fact you need to check or at a name you will fill in later.

^CW (**Cursor to Window**) moves the cursor to the next open window on the screen; the cursor lands wherever it was the last time it was in that window.

Inserting Returns

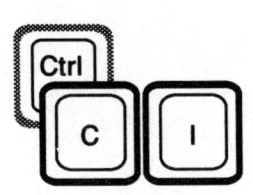

^CI (**Cursor Insert**) is kind of a ringer among the cursor commands because it doesn't actually move the cursor; instead, it inserts a hard carriage return. When you use ^CI, the text to the right moves down to start a new line. The difference between using ^CI and Return is that with ^CI, the cursor remains on the line above, but when you use Return, the cursor goes to the new line along with the text. In overtype mode, ^CI works as usual, but Return just moves the cursor without affecting the text. If you want the new line indented to start a paragraph, press the Tab key, then the left arrow (to get the cursor behind the tab character), before you use ^CI. To place a blank line between two lines of text, use ^CI at the left margin on the second line.

Starter Set – Cursor Commands		
^CB		Cursor to Beginning of file
^CE		Cursor to End of file
^CU	PgUp	Cursor Up one screen
^CD	PgDn	Cursor Down one screen

7

Removing Text

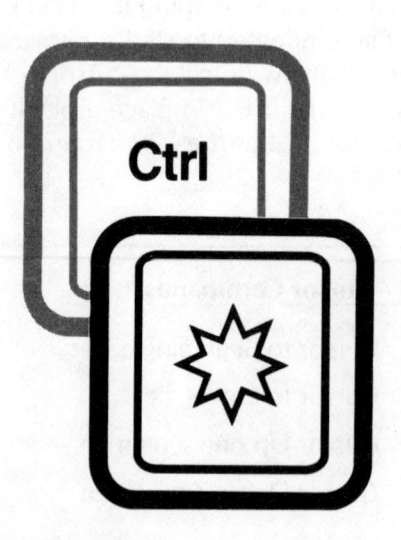

The Remove menu commands allow you to delete text by various units ranging from individual characters to large blocks of text. There are nine different units in all. When you delete any unit larger than a single character, you can restore it with the ^U (Undo) command from the main Editing menu, but only the last deletion can be restored this way. Since ^U will insert the deleted text anywhere you like and as many times as you like, it provides a quick way to move or copy text in any of the units on the Remove menu.

Removing Characters and Words

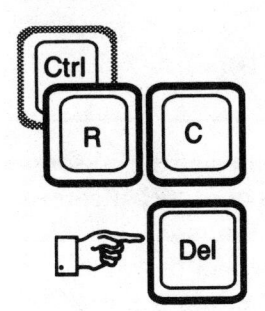

^RC (**Remove Character**) erases the character the cursor is on; it is equivalent to the Del key.

You can remove a whole word with ^RW (**Remove Word**), as long as the cursor is on any letter in the word. If the cursor is on a space, ^RW deletes the space along with any other spaces up to the beginning of the next word.

When you remove a word with ^RW, a space is erased at the same time—otherwise two spaces would be left behind. When you insert the word in text with ^U, place the cursor over the first letter of the word that follows, since the removed word already has a space tacked on to the end. If the word you remove ends with a period or other punctuation mark, the punctuation and the space after it are deleted, and both are restored where you use ^U.

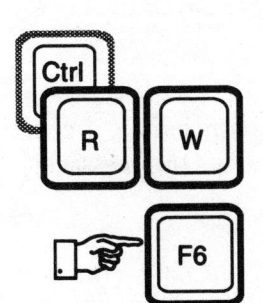

When you use ^RW repeatedly, it works like a Del key for words, erasing one after another and pulling the text back toward the cursor. The function key for this command, F6, is very convenient for this kind of repetition since it only requires a single keystroke. The combination of ^A to move the cursor back a word and ^RW to delete it, removes the word to the left of the cursor. Used repeatedly, it is like a Backspace key for words. A function key can be reprogrammed to do this, as recommended in Appendix B.

Removing Sentences and Paragraphs

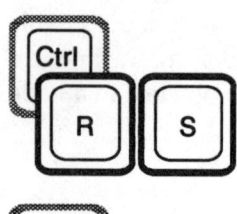

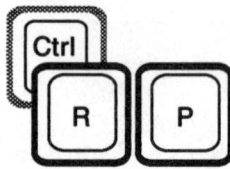

^RS (**Remove Sentence**) deletes a sentence when the cursor is anywhere within the sentence or on the space in front of it. In fact, ^RS deletes all characters and spaces from the last period (or carriage return) up to and including the next one. The removed sentence has a space tacked on *in front,* so to insert the sentence elsewhere, place the cursor on the space separating the two sentences that you want the inserted sentence to come between. You can also use this command to cut a sentence short by typing a period where you want it to end and then pressing ^RS.

^RP (**Remove Paragraph**) deletes the entire paragraph that the cursor is on. The hard return and any indentation go with the paragraph, so to insert it elsewhere, place the cursor at the left margin of the line that will follow it.

Removing Other Portions of Text

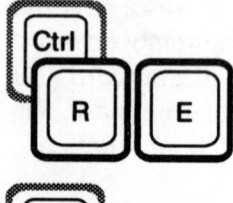

^RE (**Remove Entire line**) deletes the entire line the cursor is on, including the carriage return if there is one. ^RL (**Remove Left**) removes the text to the left of the cursor, and ^RR (**Remove Right**) removes the text to the right of the cursor, as well as the character the cursor is on. ^RR does not affect carriage returns.

If you have marked a block of text with the Block commands, you can remove it with ^RB (**Remove Block**), with the cursor anywhere in the file.

^RT (**Remove To**) deletes the character the cursor is on together with all further text up to, but not including, a character you specify. When you press ^RT you get this message:

Remove from cursor to what character?

^RT works with any letter, number, or punctuation mark. It distinguishes between capitals and lowercase letters. If you

Removing Text 63

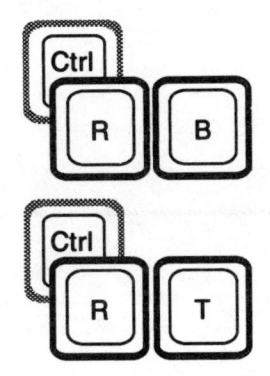

answer the message by pressing the Spacebar, the remainder of the word you are on is erased. Answer with a period to remove the remainder of a sentence, and with Return to remove the remainder of a paragraph (the period or Return remains intact). ^RT will not go on removing past a Return or page break, even if it has not yet reached the character you named. Instead, ^RT stops and gives this message:

> Couldn't find that character in this paragraph [page].
> Press ^U to restore removed text. Press Esc.

If you want to restore the text, press the Esc key first or the computer will beep at you. If you want to continue deleting, use ^RT again.

Joining Paragraphs

To join two paragraphs, remove the carriage return that separates them: move the cursor as far as it will go on the last line of the paragraph above, and then press the Del key. If the paragraph is indented, you will have to remove the indentation too.

Starter Set – Remove Commands

^RW	F6	Remove Word
^RS		Remove Sentence
^RE		Remove Entire line

8

Working with Blocks of Text

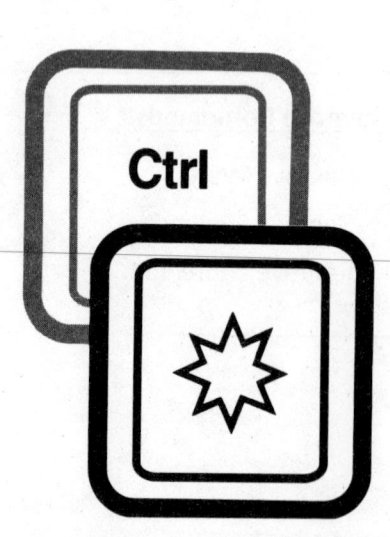

The **Block menu** includes commands for moving, deleting, and copying blocks of text.

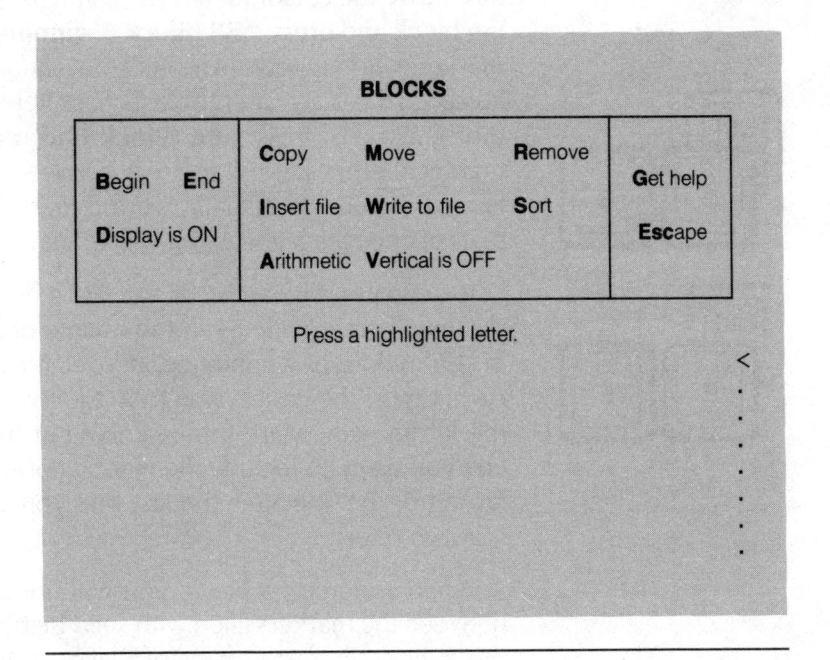

```
                         BLOCKS

              Copy      Move       Remove
  Begin  End                                  Get help
              Insert file  Write to file  Sort
  Display is ON                                Escape
              Arithmetic  Vertical is OFF

              Press a highlighted letter.
```

The Block Menu

A block can be as short as a single character. The maximum length depends on the disk space available. If the block you want to work with is too big, WordStar 2000 will let you know. You can then break the block into chunks and work with the smaller pieces.

Although in many cases you can delete, copy, or move blocks of text with a combination of the Remove commands and ^U (Undo), there are limitations to this. For one thing, ^U only works for the most recent Remove command. Also, you will often want to work with text that does not come in the units specified on the Remove menu. To manipulate a block of text that can be in any unit, use the commands from the Block menu.

Marking Blocks of Text

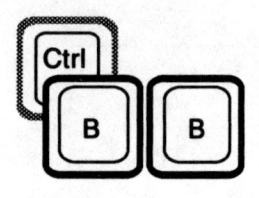

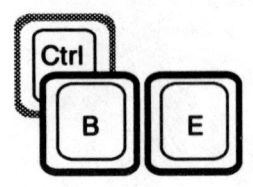

The first step in manipulating a block of text is to **mark** it. To do this, move the cursor to the first character you want included in the block and press ^**BB** (**Block Beginning mark**). A beginning marker <B> appears in front of that character. Then, move the cursor to the space after the last character you want included in the block and press ^**BE** (**Block End mark**). The beginning marker disappears and the text between the markers is highlighted. You never actually see the marker <E>. Neither the markers nor the highlighting will appear in your printed text.

You can use ^BB and ^BE to mark a block beginning or ending anywhere on a line—in the middle of a paragraph or even in the middle of a sentence. If your block consists of whole paragraphs, the easiest way to mark it is to keep the cursor at the left margin. Mark the beginning at the far left of the first line you want (to include the indentation). Mark the end at the far left of the line *after* the last one you want (to include the carriage return).

When you mark a block, you will not always see the space between the markers filled with solid highlighting. For instance, this is how the first stanzas of Blake's "The Tiger" look when marked as a block

> Tiger, tiger, burning bright
> In the forests of the night,
> What immortal hand or eye
> Could frame thy fearful symmetry?
>
> In what distant deeps or skies
> Burnt the fire of thine eyes?
> On what wings dare he aspire?
> What the hand dare seize the fire?

"The Tiger" marked as a block

Notice that the highlighting does not cover areas after carriage returns where there is no text. Marking a block is a good way to see where you have or have not typed hard spaces that are otherwise invisible.

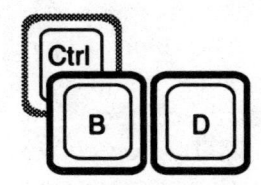

If you don't want to see the highlighting on the screen, use ^BD (**Block Display on/off**). This is a toggle command that restores the highlighting when you press it again. When you turn the block display off, the markers are not deleted, but they are deactivated. So the highlighting must be on if you want to use the other block commands.

There actually isn't any way to delete the markers short of using a Quit command. (Even then, if you select ^QC, Quit and Continue, the markers are retained.) However, you can turn off the block display and forget about the markers, or you can move them by setting them elsewhere. You can only mark one block at a time. If you ^BB or ^BE when you already have a <B> or <E>, the new mark will replace the existing one.

If you insert text between the markers, the block expands. If you delete text, the block shrinks.

Moving and Deleting Blocks

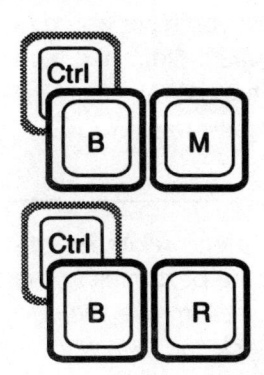

Once you have marked a block, the other commands on the menu are available to you. To move a block, place the cursor on the character you want the block to come before and press ^BM (**Block Move**). When a block is moved or copied, any numbered cursor markers (0–9) that you may have set are left behind at the block's old location.

^BR (**Block Remove**) deletes the entire block. This works the same as the ^RB command on the Remove menu. ^BR is a powerful command, and having two ways to type it is a hazard as well as a convenience. If you hit ^BR by mistake, you might not notice it since the block could be out of sight elsewhere in the file. As a safety measure, you can leave the block display off to deactivate the block commands whenever you are not actually using them.

Copying Blocks of Text

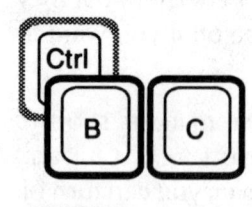

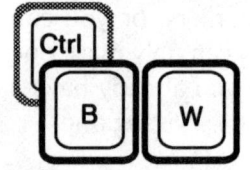

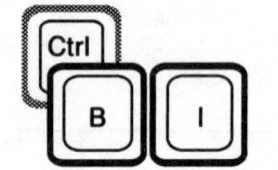

If you want the same block of text to appear in another part of the file, as well as where it already is, use ^**BC** (**Block Copy**). This leaves the block intact at its present location, but makes a copy of it elsewhere. Just place the cursor on the character you want the block to come before and press ^BC. The new copy is now the marked block. It is reproduced exactly, including such features as boldfacing.

^**BW** (**Block Write to file**) makes a copy of the block in a new file you create. When you use ^BW, the Choose a Name screen appears, and you name the new file for the copy of the block as you would name any file (see Chapter 4). Files created in this way are unformatted.

^**BI** (**Block Insert file**) copies the entire contents of another file into the document you are editing. This is not a true block command since no block has to be marked; however, the text is inserted at the cursor position just as when you are working with blocks. When you use ^BI, the Choose a Name screen appears, and you select the existing file that you want to insert in the document you are editing. The text in that file takes on the format of the file you are working on. You can use ^BI to create a composite document out of chunks of text you have stored in various files. To insert just part of another file in your text, you have to open a window for that file (see Chapter 14).

Cursor Menu Block Commands

Three of the commands on the Cursor menu relate specifically to blocks. ^CA moves the cursor to the beginning of the marked block from anywhere in the text. ^CZ moves the cursor to the end of the block. If you move a block and then want to resume work at its old location, ^CO will get you there.

Working with Vertical Blocks

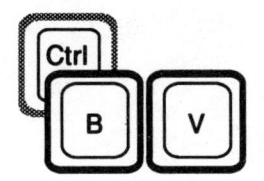

WordStar 2000 starts you out in **horizontal block mode,** which means that in the text between the markers, the entire line is automatically included in the block. ^**BV** (**Block mode Vertical**) switches you to **vertical block mode.** In this mode, the block includes only the text in the columns to the right of the <B> and to the left of the <E>. The two examples below have the markers in the same places, but the first highlights the block they would create in horizontal mode, and the second shows the block in vertical mode.

Horizontal Block Mode

	FRUIT	CALORIES	GRAMS
	Grapefruit (one half)	48	18
<B>	**Apple**	**76**	**18**
	Orange	**70**	**17**
	Pear	**95**<E>	**24**
	Banana	88	35

Vertical Block Mode

	FRUIT	CALORIES	GRAMS
	Grapefruit (one half)	48	18
<B>	**Apple**	**76**	18
	Orange	**70**	17
	Pear	**95**<E>	24
	Banana	88	35

Vertical mode is particularly useful for tables. When you're working with tabular material, it is best to use overtype mode rather than insert mode so that the Tab key moves the cursor without pushing text around.

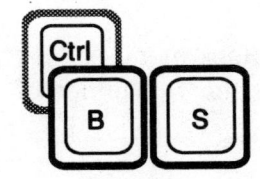

When you are in vertical mode, you can take advantage of ^**BS** (**Block Sort**). ^BS sorts all the lines between the markers into alphabetical and numerical order. The sorting places numbers ahead of letters, and spaces ahead of both.

If the vertical block begins at the left margin, the sorting is based on the first 20 characters in each line. If the block begins further to the right, sorting is based on the first 20 characters within the block. In either case, the whole line is moved as a unit—even if the lines are sorted on the basis of a column over to the right. Up to 150 lines can be sorted by ^BS. When you use ^BS you are asked to choose

    Sort orders:
    Ascending Descending

Type A unless you want the lines sorted in reverse alphabetical and numerical order.

This is how the table above would be sorted based on two different vertical blocks:

List Sorted by First Column

FRUIT	CALORIES	GRAMS
<B>**Apple**	76	18
Banana	88	35
Grapefruit (one half)	48	18
Orange	70	17
Pear <E>	95	24

List Sorted by Second Column

FRUIT	CALORIES	GRAMS
Grapefruit (one half)	<B>**48**	18
Orange	**70**	17
Apple	**76**	18
Banana	**88**	35
Pear	**95**<E>	24

The only remaining command on the Block menu is ^BA (Block Arithmetic). It is the subject of the remainder of this chapter.

Block Arithmetic

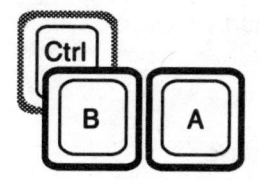

^BA (Block Arithmetic), one of WordStar 2000's fancier features, lets you use your word processor like a calculator. It can be quite handy for calculations in financial reports and in other documents.

Performing basic arithmetic operations with WordStar 2000 is simple. Whenever you press ^BA, WordStar 2000 scans through the marked block and performs calculations on all the numbers it finds inside. It then types the answer starting from the current position of the cursor.

WordStar 2000 can perform any standard arithmetic operation. You tell it which operations to perform by inserting **operator** symbols between the numbers. These are the operations WordStar 2000 can perform and their symbols:

Operation	Symbol	Examples
Addition	+	10+14 = 24
	space	50 62 = 112
	other characters	5 and 10 = 15
Subtraction	–	54–40 = 14
	< > surrounding	54 <40> = 14
Multiplication	*	2*1.4 = 2.8
	@	3@1.98 = 5.94
Division	/	2/3 = 0.67
Exponentiation	^	5^2 = 25
Grouping	( )	5*(3+1) = 5*4 = 20

For the most part, these are standard arithmetic symbols used by computer programming languages and spreadsheets. The brackets < > for subtraction are a common financial symbol used to mark debits. The @ sign for multiplication makes sense if you think of phrases such as:

3 lb mushrooms @ $1.98 per lb

The marked block may contain words and other symbols. However, when you use ^BA, WordStar 2000 treats any characters it doesn't recognize in the calculation as spaces, which imply addition. Thus, the phrase:

3 plus 2

would yield the result 5. Of course, the phrase:

3 minus 2

would yield the same result because the word *minus* is not the operator for subtraction.

Using Block Arithmetic

Using ^BA requires three steps:

1. Type the numbers and symbols that you want to use in your calculation.
2. Mark the numbers as a block, using ^BB and ^BE.
3. Move the cursor to the place where you want the answer to appear and press ^BA.

^BA does not do anything to the contents of the marked block. The answer doesn't replace the numbers from which it was calculated—it simply appears wherever you have put the cursor. If you started with the block:

3 plus 2 equals □

and pressed ^BA with the cursor at the end of the line, WordStar 2000 would complete the phrase:

3 plus 2 equals 5□

You must be careful where you put the cursor for the answer because ^BA inserts the answer at that exact spot. For example, if the cursor is over the q in *equals,* you get:

3 plus 2 e5quals

Probably not what you intended.

Vertical Block Arithmetic

So far, these examples have all been showing the use of ^BA in horizontal block mode. Frequently, you will want to use ^BA in vertical block mode, to add up a column of numbers. To do this, press ^BV before you press ^BA. The ^BA command works exactly the same on vertical blocks as it does on horizontal blocks.

Suppose you were writing a financial report for your company. You might have a section that looks like this:

Assets:

Fixed capital	$2,143,276.13
Accounts receivable	785,942.54
Deferred taxes	< 173,190.31 >
	- - - - - - -
Total	$_

The space between the first and second items shows that they should be added, and the brackets around the third item show that it is a deficit to be subtracted.

To get the total, press ^BV, ^BB, and ^BE to mark the column as a vertical block, then move the cursor to the proper column. WordStar 2000 will fill in the answer:

Assets:

Fixed capital	**$2,143,276.13**
Accounts receivable	785,942.54
Deferred taxes	< 173,190.31 >
	- - - - - - -
Total	$2756028.36

Note that WordStar 2000 does not automatically fill in the commas in the answer. If you want commas to appear, you have to go through and insert them yourself. (WordStar 2000 just ignores the commas in the numbers inside the marked block.)

You can use decimal tabs to align the answer with the other numbers (see Chapter 11). If you have set a decimal tab stop to type this column of numbers, just tab to it on the total line before you press ^BA. WordStar will align the answer just as it would if you typed it from the keyboard.

On the other hand, you don't have to line up the decimals if you don't want to. The ^BA command will come up with the correct answer even if you use it on a disorganized column such as this:

452.1
.1523
4

So you can use ^BA to perform calculations and have the answers appear as part of your text, or you can use it instead of a calculator to do quick calculations.

Starter Set – Block Commands

^BB	Block Beginning marker
^BE	Block Ending marker
^BC	Block Copy
^BM	Block Move
^BR	Block Remove
^BD	Block Display on/off

9

Locating and Replacing Text

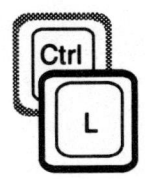

WordStar 2000's search feature lets you find any piece of text—words, numbers, or phrases—everywhere it occurs in a document and change it to something else. The ^L (**Locate and Replace**) command searches through your document for whatever sequence, or **string,** of characters you specify and, if you like, replaces it with another string.

^L can be used simply to find a word in the file and move the cursor to it. Or you can use ^L to locate and delete a string of characters. The replacement feature comes in handy for correcting a consistent error and for tailoring a document to a new purpose by changing names, dates, and so forth. Also, if a long name or phrase appears often in your document, you can type an abbreviation for it, and then locate and automatically replace the abbreviation with the full expression when you are done.

First, We'll explain how to use ^L for just locating a string of characters.

Locating Text

When you type ^L, you are prompted with the question:

Text to locate?

Type the string of characters you are looking for, and press Return. The string can be up to 40 characters long, counting spaces. You can include any of the characters on the keyboard: letters, numbers, punctuation, and special characters like **$** and **%.** You can also include special WordStar 2000 command tags like the ones that mark boldfaced or underlined text—we'll get back to the command tags later.

If you make any mistakes when entering the text to locate, you can correct them in the same way you make corrections in a document—by using the left and right arrow, Backspace, and Del keys. You can also use ^R to erase the whole line, and ^T to restore it.

When you have entered the string you want, a second question appears below the first one:

Locate only/Replace? (L/R)

Since right now we are only interested in locating text, type L, and press Return. You are now prompted to choose from an options menu.

```
Text to locate? ......................... win
Locate only/Replace? (L/R) ..... L
Options? ...................................
```

n th occurrence	**W**hole words only	**^G**et help
Backwards search	**C**ase match	
		Escape

Options for Locating Text

You have four options to select from when locating text. You can choose the options in any sequence, or press Return to choose none of them. It doesn't matter if you type a capital or lowercase letter for the option.

[n]

Use the *n* (**nth occurrence**) option when you want to locate only certain occurrences of the string rather than all of them. To select this option, type a number (not the letter *n*). The number that you specify tells WordStar to go to that occurrence of the string. For example, if you type in 5, the search skips over the first four occurrences and locates the fifth.

[B]

Type **B** (**Backwards search**) if you want to search backward through the document from the present cursor position; otherwise, the search progresses from the cursor forward to the end of the document. If you want to search the entire file, press ^CB to move the cursor to the beginning before using ^L.

Use **W** (**Whole words only**) to match the string with whole words only. Otherwise, *win* would be found wherever those three letters appear together, such as in *wind, twin,* and *Winnemucca.*

Select the **C** (**Case match**) option if you want an exact match of capital and lowercase letters. For example, use C if you don't want *win* matched with *Win* or *WIN*. You might use C to locate a word only when it is at the beginning of a sentence.

With no options selected, ^L locates the next occurrence of the string after the cursor position, even when it appears as a part of other words, and does not distinguish between capital and lowercase letters.

When you are done choosing options, press Return. Word-Star 2000 reads through the file until it finds the string. Then the ^L display disappears, and the cursor is left on the first character of the string in the document.

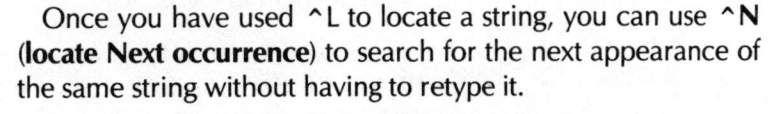

Once you have used ^L to locate a string, you can use ^N (**locate Next occurrence**) to search for the next appearance of the same string without having to retype it.

If there are no occurrences of the string to be found, the cursor won't move and you will see a message like this:

Can't find "win". Press Escape.

Once you have used ^L in an editing session, your previous answers become the default answers to the series of questions. You can use any default answer by just pressing Return.

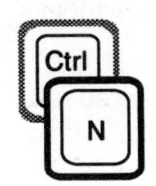

Spaces and Hyphens

When you identify the string of characters you want to locate, make sure the spaces and any hyphens appear the same as they do in the document. If you type the spaces incorrectly, say two spaces between words in the string and there was only one space in the text, no match will be found.

If you want to find a word with a hyphen, put a hyphen in that word in the string. However, if the word has a hyphen that WordStar 2000 added to justify the right margin, don't include the hyphen in the string. If the word has a **discretionary hyphen** that you added with ^O- (see Chapter 11), include a hyphen in the string only if you have the Option Display (^OD) on (see Chapter 4), otherwise, omit it.

Locating Command Tags

You can use ^L to locate the command tags that WordStar 2000 adds to the text when you issue various formatting commands. These tags, which do not appear in the printed text, are only visible on the screen when you have the Option Display on. With the display on, you can search for command tags by typing them in the string just as they appear on screen (although you can type them in lowercase).

For example, to search for the next piece of boldfaced text, type **[B]** (see Chapter 10). To search for *win* only where it is boldfaced, type **[B]win[B]**. To search for a page break that you created with the ^OP command (see Chapter 11), type **[PAGE]**. (We will cover the other command tags as they come up in connection with the commands that create them.)

When ^L finds a tag, it places the cursor on the first bracket. To search for the next occurrence of a tag, move the cursor past the tag before pressing ^N, or WordStar 2000 will keep locating the same one.

Locating Returns and Tabs

To search for a carriage return, type **[R]**; for a tab character, type **[T]**. If you want to find the places where there are two returns together, type [RR]; for three returns, type [RRR]; and so on. The same is true for finding tab stops in text—type [TT] for two tabs together or [TT] for three. But you don't mix Rs and Ts within brackets.

If you used a hard carriage return to create a new line within the text you want to find, then type [R] where the return occurs when you identify the string of characters to be located. If the text you want to find includes a page break you created with ^OP, then type [PAGE] at the same point in the identifying string.

Wild Cards

WordStar 2000 allows you to use a kind of wild card in your string that stands for any character. [?] stands for any letter, and [#] for any numeral. So, for example, the string *win[??]* will match with *wines* or *wined*. The string *198[#]* will match with *1981* or *1987*.

If you type a backslash (\) in front of the special characters [R], [T], [?], or [#], ^L searches for just that string of three characters, rather than what they usually represent. So *[R]* will locate a left and right bracket with an R in the middle, rather than a carriage return. You can locate a backslash by typing another backslash in front of it.

Replacing Text

To use ^L for replacing text, start out just as before by entering the string you want to locate and replace. But this time, when you are asked:

Locate only/Replace? (L/R)

type R and press Return. You will be prompted with:

Replacement text?

Like the search string, the replacement string can have up to 40 characters and can include command tags for commands you want executed, like boldfacing, underlining, and line breaks. For example, if you wanted to change the word *win* to boldface in your text, you would use *[B]win[B]* as the replacement string. To change from having one line between paragraphs to two, replace *[R]* with *[RR]*. [?] and [#] don't work as wild cards in the replacement string.

After you supply a replacement string and press Return, you will see an options menu slightly different from the one you saw before.

```
Text to locate? ........................ win
Locate only/Replace? (L/R) ..... R
Replacement text? .................. firmly hold our ground
Options? ...............................
```

no. of times to search and replace	**W**hole words only	**^G**et help
Backwards search	**C**ase match (locate)	
Don't ask approval **S**how onscreen	**P**reserve case (replace)	**Esc**ape

Options for Replacing Text

You have seven options to choose from when replacing text. Just as with the locating options, you can choose options in any sequence, type either a capital or lowercase letter to select the option, or press Return to choose none of them.

Three of the replacement options—B, for replacing backwards from the cursor position to the beginning of the document; W, for replacing only complete words; and C, for distinguishing between capital and lowercase letters—make the same distinctions for locating text for replacement as they do for just locating it. The other four options are specific to replacing text.

Use the **no.** (**number of times to search and replace**) option to tell WordStar 2000 how many occurrences of the string you

Locating and Replacing Text   83

want replaced. To select this option, type a number (not *no.*). If you enter a *5,* for example, the next five occurrences of the string will be replaced (not just the fifth one). If you don't supply a number, all occurrences will be replaced.

Use the **P** (**Preserve case**) option if you want the replacement string to always appear just as you typed it. For instance, in our example, you would use P if you want *firmly hold our ground* to start with a lowercase *f* even when it is replacing a capitalized *Win.* Without P, the replacement string is adjusted to match the case of each particular occurrence it is replacing. So P preserves the case of the replacement string as you entered it, but may change the case in the document itself.

When you use ^L to replace text, it stops at each instance and asks for your approval before carrying out the substitution. The candidate for replacement is highlighted in the text, and a prompt appears at the right of the ^L display:

Replace? (Y/N)N

(The N is provided as the default answer because WordStar 2000 tries to err on the side of caution.) To go ahead with the replacement, type Y; to skip this instance and go on to the next one, just press Return.

If you are sure that you want all the instances replaced, use the **D** (**Don't ask approval**) option. When you select D, you have a further choice. You can have the whole process take place without seeing the substitutions on the screen, or you can have it stop for a moment each time to show what is happening. Use **S** to view the changes as they are made. S has no effect if you haven't chosen D.

If you press Return without typing any options, ^L searches forward from the cursor position, locates the search string regardless of case and even when it appears as a part of other words, and asks your approval before replacing text in each instance. The replacement string will start with a capital letter only when the text that it replaces does.

Locating and Deleting Text

To use ^L for deleting a string of characters, proceed as if you're going to replace it, but when you are asked for the replacement text, just press Return. This way, you have replaced the string with *nothing,* so you have deleted it.

You can interrupt the locate or locate and replace process at any time by pressing the Esc key. Don't be surprised if ^L takes quite a while to run in a long file, since it reads through the whole file as it does its search.

10

Print Enhancements

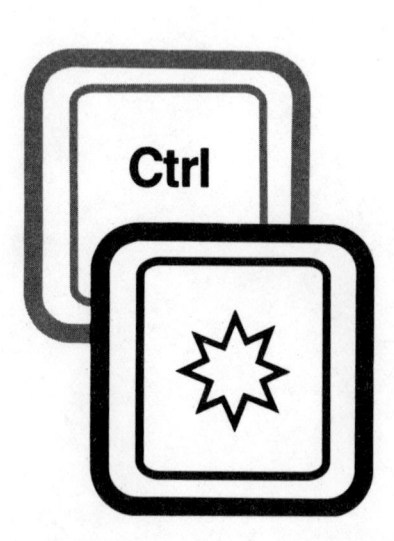

Special Effects

WordStar 2000 allows you to print your text with a wide variety of special effects that would be difficult or impossible to achieve on a typewriter. The two-screen Print Enhancements menu offers 14 selections, including boldface, underline, subscripts, superscripts, and changing the size or color of the text. On many printers, italics are also available.

It's easy to make changes and print out fresh copies of your text, so feel free to experiment with the various effects to find out which ones you like and which work best for different purposes.

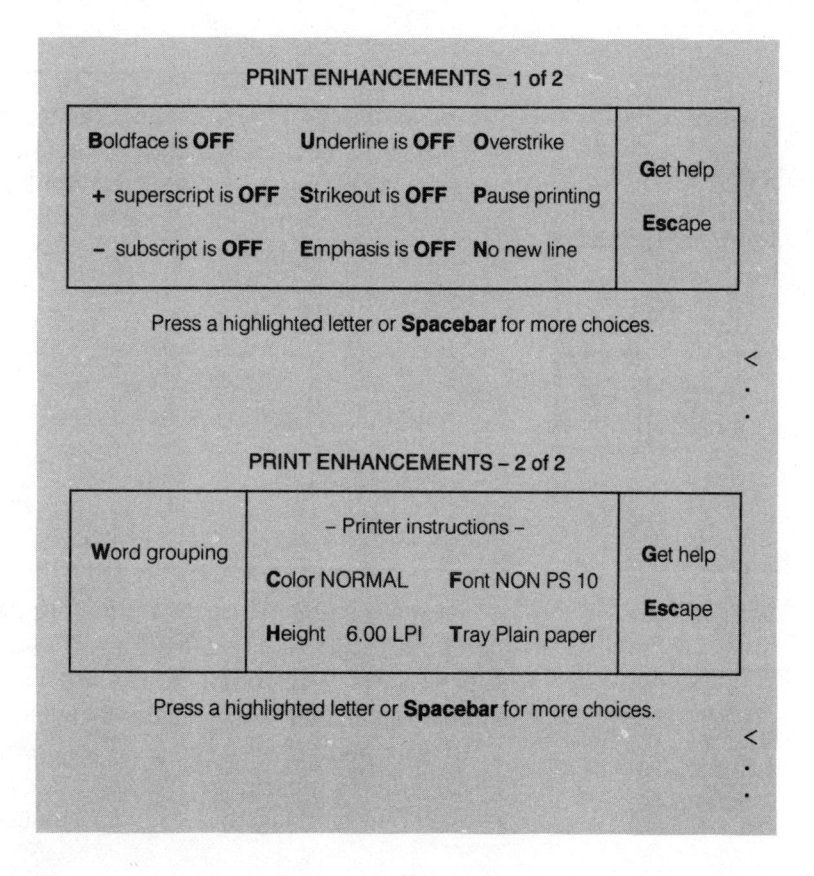

```
                    PRINT ENHANCEMENTS – 1 of 2

  Boldface is OFF       Underline is OFF   Overstrike
                                                            Get help
  + superscript is OFF  Strikeout is OFF   Pause printing
                                                            Escape
  – subscript is OFF    Emphasis is OFF    No new line
```

Press a highlighted letter or **Spacebar** for more choices.

```
                    PRINT ENHANCEMENTS – 2 of 2

                        – Printer instructions –
  Word grouping                                             Get help
                    Color NORMAL     Font NON PS 10
                                                            Escape
                    Height  6.00 LPI  Tray Plain paper
```

Press a highlighted letter or **Spacebar** for more choices.

88 *Introduction to WordStar 2000*

Your Printer

Some of the print enhancements may not work on your printer. To see which ones do work, print the PRINT.SPL file from your copy of the installation disk. (Just place the disk in drive B: like a work disk, Press P from the Opening Menu, and follow the printing instructions at the end of Chapter 3.) Then press E to look at the file on the screen. With the option display (^OD) on, you can see the various tags inserted by the commands described in this chapter. Compare them with the printed text to see what effect, if any, each one produced.

Boldface

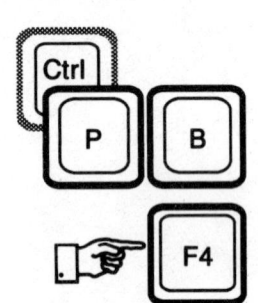

Most of the print enhancement commands are used in pairs: at the beginning of the text that will get special treatment and at the end. When you use ^**PB** (**Print Boldface**), for instance, you are issuing an instruction: Print in boldface all text from here until I use ^PB again. If you use ^PB only once, the entire document from that point on will be boldfaced. WordStar 2000 highlights the text that will appear in boldface, so it's easy to see if you forgot to press ^PB again to mark where the boldfacing should end.

Deleting Tags

If you use ^OD to turn the option display on, you will see the command tags that direct the printer to start or stop printing in a specified way. The command tag inserted by ^PB is **[B]**, and it appears at the beginning and the end of the text to be boldfaced. With the option display on, you can use the Del or Backspace keys to delete these tags. Without the option display, you can delete command tags by removing the text that contains them or by pressing ^RW to remove the word to which the tag is "attached" (as long as there is no space in between).

Underlining

To underline a piece of text, use **^PU (Print Underline)** before and after it. The command tag for underlining is **[U]**. All the WordStar 2000 prepared formats cause ^PU to underline the spaces between words, as well as the letters themselves, but you can change this, either for a format or just for a particular document (see Chapter 12).

Combined Effects

You can combine print enhancements if you like, although some combinations do not work on certain printers even though the features work separately. If you want text to be both underlined and boldfaced use ^PB and ^PU together to mark the beginning and the end. You can type the commands in any order.

Screen Colors

Like boldface, underlined text appears highlighted on the screen whether the option display is on or not. (On some monitors an actual underline appears on the screen as well.) On a color monitor, the print enhancements are color-coded. Underlined text is green; boldface is white; combined underlined and boldfaced text is yellow. Subscripts, superscripts, strikeout, and print emphasis all appear in the same color as boldface. You can reset the three colors as you like when you install or reinstall your program disk (see Appendix B).

Print Emphasis and Doublestrike

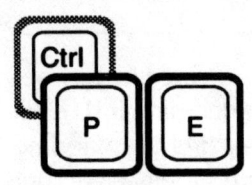

The effect produced by ^PE (**Print Emphasis**) varies from printer to printer. Sometimes it is the same as boldface, but the most common effect is **doublestrike** text. Boldface is produced by printing each character three times, each strike offset just a tiny bit from the last. So boldfaced characters are not only darker, but they are also a little thicker than normal type. Doublestrike hits only twice, and there is no offset or thickening of the lines. You may choose to print an entire document in doublestrike, either to obtain sharper looking copy or to type through clearly on multiple forms. If your printer does not do boldface, you might try print emphasis as an alternative. Doublestrike combined with boldface is useful for headings, warnings, etc. The command tag for print emphasis is **[E]**.

Strikeout

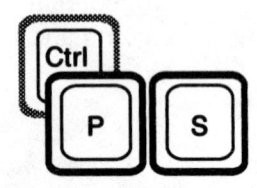

^PS (**Print Strikeout**) prints text in which each character is crossed out with a hyphen. This is used mainly for legal documents to show text that has been deleted in the process of revision. The command tag for strikeout is **[S]**. When you use ^PS, the text on screen looks like this:

The full assets of the company [S]and my personal assets[S] are pledged to secure this loan.

In the printed text, this reads:

The full assets of the company and my personal assets are pledged to secure this loan.

Subscripts

Subscripts are used frequently in scientific and mathematical notation. You produce them in WordStar 2000 just as you do the other print enhancements, by marking the beginning and

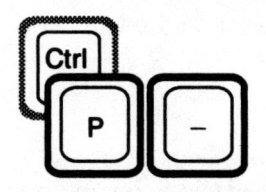

Print Enhancements 91

end of the text you want included. ^P– (**Print subscript**) inserts a tag with a minus sign, [–], to indicate that the text will go below the normal line. On the screen, it looks like this:

CO[–]2[–]

and like this on paper:

CO_2

Superscripts

Superscripts are also common in mathematical and scientific text. The command ^P+ (**Print superscript**) inserts a tag with a plus sign, [+], to indicate that the text will print above the normal line. Text marked with ^P+ looks like this on screen:

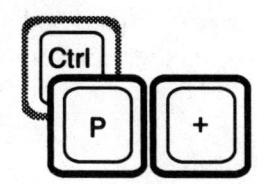

πr[+]2[+]

and like this on paper:

πr^2

On some printers, subscripts and superscripts are in smaller type than the rest of the characters on the line; on other printers, they are the same size. Also, some printers that offer both boldface and subscript and superscript will not accept them in combination.

Overprinting

^PO (**Print Over**) causes a character to print in the same space as the previous character. You would use this to add an accent mark to a letter, for example. Unlike the other print enhancement commands, ^PO applies just to the character that follows the tag, [O], and does not have to be used twice. So your text would look like this on screen:

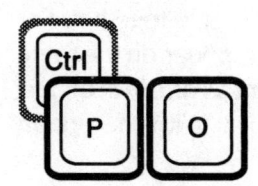

Rene[O]′

and would print like this:

René

If you find that the accent is cutting into the top of the letter it is on, use ^P+ together with ^PO:

Rene[O][+]'[+]

^PN (**Print No new line**) does with entire lines what ^PO does with single characters—it causes a line of text to be printed on top of the preceding line. To use this command, simply type ^PN instead of pressing Return at the end of the first line. Instead of a command tag, you will see a - at the right of the screen in place of the usual <.

You can use ^PN to strike out text with characters other than the hyphens created by ^PS, with slashes (/), for example.

You can also use ^PN to produce doublestrike or underlined text on printers that otherwise do not allow for them. If you wanted to create both of these effects with ^PN, your text on screen would look like this:

    Save your text frequently!!   -
    Save your text frequently!!   -
    _____   <

and print like this:

Save your text frequently!!

Word Grouping

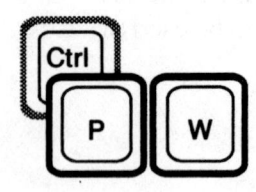

Ordinarily, when WordStar 2000 sees a space between two words, it considers that a legitimate place for a line break. In some cases, however, you want the words to stay together. For example, you would want *Henry* and *VIII* to appear on the same line. You can ensure this by using ^**PW** (**Print as one Word**). Just type ^PW instead of pressing the Spacebar. With the option display on, you will see the tag [**W**]:

Henry[W]VIII

Without the display on, it looks like an ordinary space.

Print Enhancements 93

Line Height

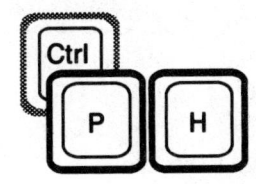

The amount of line spacing, or **line height,** that will appear between lines in your printed text is determined by the format you choose. You can revise the format (see Chapter 12), but the line height you choose will apply to the entire document. If you want to change the line height in just part of a document—for instance, to single-space an extended quote within double-spaced text—use ^**PH** (**Print line Height**).

To do this, move the cursor to the left margin of the first line you want printed with a different amount of space below it and type ^PH. A display appears showing you the choices available. The choices were tailored to the capabilities of your printer when you installed the program disk, but these are typical:

Line height (spacing)?
6.00 LPI

2.00 LPI   3.00 LPI   4.00 LPI   6.00 LPI
8.00 LPI

The highlighted choice is the one currently in effect. Move the highlighting and press Return to choose a different one.

WordStar 2000 gives line heights in lines per inch (LPI). In more familiar terms:

- 8.00 LPI is half-spaced text
- 6.00 LPI is single-spaced text
- 4.00 LPI is one-and-a-half-spaced text
- 3.00 LPI is double-spaced text
- 2.00 LPI is triple-spaced text

If you want to change back to the previous line height, use ^PH again at the far left of the first line you want followed by the old line spacing. You can also use ^PH at the very beginning of the text to change the line spacing of the entire document without changing the format setting.

Stand-Alone and Variable Tags

^PH creates a **stand-alone tag,** meaning that it appears on a line by itself rather than in the midst of the text. If you use ^PH in the middle of a line, it creates a line break at that point with a hard carriage return. To delete a stand-alone tag, use ^RW or ^RE, and then delete the carriage return that was created.

^PH command tags are not only different from other tags because they stand alone, but also because the information they contain varies depending on the choice of line height you made. These are called **variable command tags,** and they cannot be used as replacement text in a locate and replace operation.

Print Pause

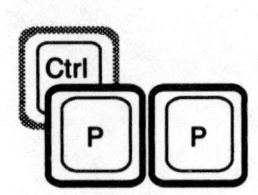

Sometimes you want the printer to pause at a certain point in the text so that you can change ribbons, change print elements such as *daisy wheels,* or perform some other manual alteration. To do this, use ^**PP** (**Print Pause**) at the place where you want the printing to halt. You can use ^PP at any line in the document, but it must be at the first space following a carriage return. When the printer reaches that point, it stops and a message appears on the screen:

Printing is paused.

Press any key to continue.

If you are editing while the printing is going on (see Chapter 15), the message asks you to press the Esc key rather than any key. Like ^PH, ^PP creates a stand-alone tag, **[PAUSE]**.

Print Color

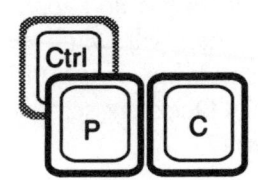

On many printers, if you have a two-color ribbon or some other method of changing print colors, you may be able to use ^PC (**Print Color**) to switch colors automatically instead of ^PP to change them manually. To use ^PC, place the cursor on the first character you want to have printed in the new color and type the command. The new color will remain in effect until you use ^PC to change it again. The tags inserted by ^PC, for example **[RED]**, can be removed with the Backspace or Del keys. Like ^PH, ^PC creates variable command tags that cannot be used as replacement text in a locate and replace operation.

When you type ^PC you see a menu of color choices that was tailored to your printer during installation. On printers that cannot switch colors automatically, you may see other choices, such as a choice between normal and italic type.

Paper Change

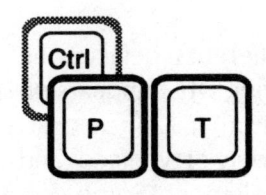

A printer with a **sheet feeder** uses separate sheets of paper as opposed to continuous perforated paper that you must tear apart after printing. On some printers, the sheet feeder can pick up paper from either of two paper trays. Usually one contains letterhead paper and the other plain paper, making it easy to print out multiple page letters in which only the first page goes on letterhead. If your printer is capable of switching paper trays, you can use ^PT (**Print Tray**) to tell the printer which page of text goes on which kind of paper.

To have the first page printed on letterhead, place the cursor at the left on the first line of the file and type ^PT. You will see this prompt:

Paper tray to use?

Plain paper

Letterhead   Plain paper

with the tray currently in use highlighted. Move the highlighting bar to *Letterhead* and press Return. The stand-alone tag **[LETTERHEAD]** will appear in the text. To switch to plain paper after the first page, move the cursor to the far left of the last line on the page and use ^PT again, this time selecting *Plain paper,* which produces a **[PLAIN PAPER]** tag. The printer will switch to the correct tray at the appropriate time, even when you print many copies of the letter, either using the Print Decisions screen (see Chapter 15) or MailMerge (see Chapter 17).

Print Font

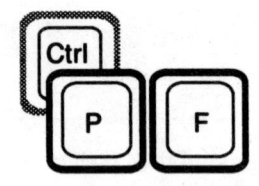

The last print enhancement command, ^**PF** (**Print Font**), allows you to change the type font in which your text is printed. Fonts can differ in three ways:

- Typeface
- Size
- Proportional versus nonproportional spacing

The text in this book is printed in two different typefaces: the main text is in Optima, and the lines showing what appears on screen are in Helvetica. Daisy-wheel and other formed character printers allow you to select from a variety of typefaces and sizes by inserting the appropriate print element. Some dot-matrix printers also have print modules that you can change manually. To change fonts with these types of printers, you use ^PP to halt the printing, change the print element, and then resume printing. But, you may also have to use ^PF to tell WordStar 2000 to adjust its spacing accordingly.

Many dot-matrix printers switch type sizes automatically. An automatic choice of typefaces is not typical, but will probably become more common in the next few years.

When you use ^PF, you see a menu of the fonts available on the printer for which your program disk was installed. The items may include entries like this:

GOTH15-12CPI   GOTH15-15CPI   GOTH15-20CPI

The first part of the entry, *GOTH15*, tells you the typeface. In this case, it is a Gothic type. The number 15 indicates a particular variety of Gothic. The second part of the entry—12CPI, 15CPI, 20CPI—tells you the characters per inch, or size of the characters. For example, 12 CPI means that 12 characters will go into each inch of text.

Proportional Spacing

The other kind of entry you are likely to see looks like this:

NON PS 5   NON PS 6   NON PS 10   NON PS 12

NON PS is not the name of a particular typeface; it stands for any **NON P**roportional **S**pacing typeface that your printer uses. *Nonproportional spacing* means that skinny letters like *I* are printed with just as much space as wide letters like *M* and *W*— the width of the space is not proportional to the width of the letter. In a proportional font, different letters take up different amounts of space on the printed page. On the screen, both fonts look the same, but you may notice a difference in the status line at the top. The anorexic *Is* and *Is* may not advance the cursor a full column, so the column indicator may not change with every letter.

The numbers 10, 12, 6, and 5 in the NON PS entries again indicate the number of characters per inch. These are the four

NON PS fonts available on the Epson RX-80:

NON PS 12

NON PS 10

NON PS 6

NON PS 5

Type Size and Margins

The entry *ECS* indicates an extended character set. You have to look in your printer manual to see what is included in the set and how to use it.

The numbers on the ruler line above your text on the screen measure the length of the line on the assumption that there will be 10 characters per inch. So, if your margins run from 1 to 60, the lines will cover 6 inches on the paper. When you change to a font that is different from 10 characters per inch, the ruler line does not adjust to this; a 6-inch margin is still marked at column 60, and the size of the letters on the screen does not change either. But let's say your font only fits 6 characters in each inch. Now you can only get 36 characters on a 6-inch line, instead of 60. WordStar 2000 shows you this by creating line breaks at column 36, and the text on the screen appears in a relatively narrow strip down the left-hand side. The lines break at the correct words, but you have to imagine those words stretched out in larger type across the paper.

If your font has more than 10 characters per inch, you can fit more than 60 of them on a 6-inch line. A 12-character-per-inch font (elite type on a typewriter) puts 72 characters in 6 inches. WordStar 2000 shows you this by allowing you to type 72 characters before making a line break. On the screen, it looks like you are typing out beyond the right margin, even though the lines will fit just fine on the printed page.

Type Size and Tabs   WordStar 2000 sets tabs in inches as it does margins. When you tab twice with the standard 5-column setting, you are really tabbing over 1 inch (which is column 10 in a 10-character-per-inch font). When you change the font, you are still tabbing 1 inch. But 1 inch in a 12-character-per-inch font takes the cursor over to the twelfth character instead of the tenth, even though the tab appears in the same place on the paper. Tabbing 1 inch in a 6-character-per-inch font takes the cursor only as far as column 6.

Type Size and Line Height   If you use a large font without using ^PH to make a larger line height, you might expect the letters to overlap at the top and bottom. However, WordStar 2000 does not allow this; it automatically increases the line height to accommodate the letters. If you want extra space between the lines, use ^PH to make the adjustment. Also, don't forget to use ^PF to change the horizontal spacing, even if you are going to use ^PP and change the print element manually.

Starter Set – Print Enhancement Commands

Print Boldface	F4	^PB
Print Underline		^PU

11

Tabs, Margins, and Formatting Options

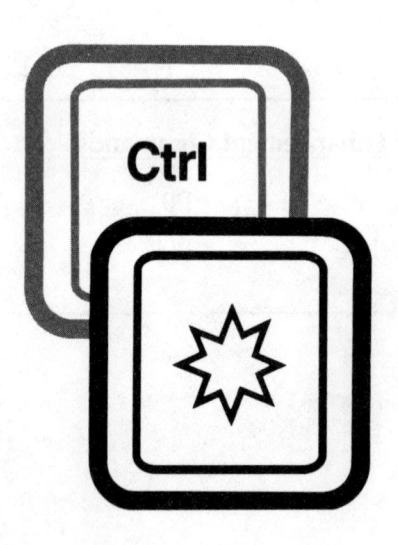

WordStar 2000 has many fancy features that let you format your page in almost any way you want. Some of these, such as tab stops and margins, are familiar from a typewriter; others are neat tricks that you'll only find on the most advanced word processors.

Most of WordStar 2000's formatting commands are on the Tabs and Margins menu:

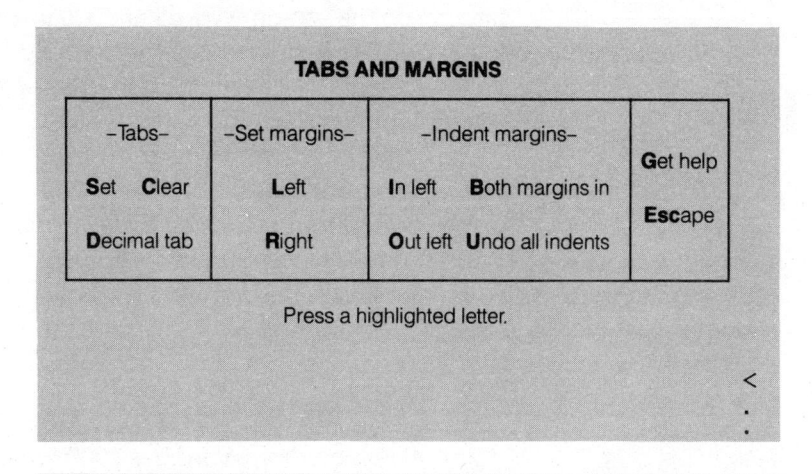

TABS AND MARGINS

–Tabs–	–Set margins–	–Indent margins–	
Set **C**lear	**L**eft	**I**n left **B**oth margins in	**G**et help
Decimal tab	**R**ight	**O**ut left **U**ndo all indents	**Esc**ape

Press a highlighted letter.

Tabs and Margins Menu

In addition to these commands, this chapter also describes the 11 commands on the Options menu that deal with page formatting.

Page Formatting

The basic layout of a printed page is defined by a **format file**. A format file is a template for the document; it defines the page size, text justification, margins, and tab stops. In Chapter 12, you'll learn more about format files and learn how to create your own.

Insofar as possible, WordStar 2000 tries to make the page format on the screen look like the final printed output. When you make any changes that will affect the page layout, WordStar 2000 adjusts the text on the screen so that the change will be reflected there. When you insert a word, for example, the program automatically reformats the paragraph so that it fits neatly between the margins.

When you give a command whose effect cannot be shown directly on the screen, WordStar 2000 inserts a command tag to mark the change in the text. For example, when you use a print enhancement, WordStar 2000 inserts a command tag to show how the printout will be altered. Most of the formatting commands described in this chapter also insert command tags. You will probably want to use ^OD to turn on the option display while you're setting up a format since there is often no other way to see what's going on without looking at the command tags.

Tabs

As on a typewriter, WordStar 2000 lets you set and clear **tab stops** at certain points, or columns in your text, and use the Tab key to skip straight to those columns. Tabs are useful for various formatting functions, such as indenting whole paragraphs, creating columnar tables, and writing outlines, as well as for indenting first lines of paragraphs.

In most of the standard formats, tab stops are set every fifth column across the page—at columns 6, 11, 16, 21, and so forth. Tab stops are marked as downward-pointing wedges in the ruler line at the top of the screen. If you open a document and press the Tab key repeatedly, the cursor will skip five spaces each time you press the key.

The Tab key doesn't actually insert five spaces in the text. Instead, it inserts a special **tab character,** which tells WordStar

2000, "move to the column where the next tab stop is located." When the option display is on, these tab characters appear as dark triangles.

The difference is important if you insert characters between the tabs. Type a series of tab characters on a line and press ^OD. Type a letter at the end of the line so that you have a frame of reference, then use ^S to move the cursor back to one of the earlier tab characters. Each time you move the cursor one space to the left, it skips back *five columns* because each tab is a single character, not a set of five spaces.

Now insert a character between two tabs. Note that the tabs to the right do not change their positions. The character is simply inserted at that place, and the tab next to it is reduced to four spaces—all that remains between it and the next tab stop. Type some more characters at that point. Nothing moves until you have typed five characters. Then, the whole line suddenly jumps over five spaces all at once. Why? Because the tab character has been pushed far enough that "move to the next tab stop" means to skip to the stop beyond where it used to be.

At first, you might think that this behavior is arbitrary, but you'll soon appreciate it as one of the nicer aspects of WordStar 2000. If you set up a two-column table, for example, you want the right column to line up no matter what you put in the left column. With WordStar 2000, you can go back and add characters to the left column without pushing the right column over.

Setting Tabs

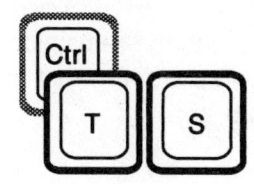

You can set new tab stops on the ruler line with ^TS (**Tabs and margins Set**). When you give this command, WordStar 2000 asks:

Set tab in what column?

As a default response, it suggests the number of the column where you currently have the cursor. Just press Return to use that column, or type another number. However, if you have the option display on and use ^TS on a line that has a command tag, the default column may be not be the exact page column because WordStar 2000 takes the default response from the column where the cursor is displayed on the screen, not the column where it will be on the page. You'll probably want the tab stop set on the page column, so either press ^OD to turn off the display before you use ^TS or replace the default number with the column number from the status line at the top of the screen.

When you get back to your text, notice that an additional wedge has been added to the ruler line at the top of the screen, marking a new tab stop at the column number that you specified. This new stop becomes effective immediately, starting with the current line of text. If you have any tab characters already on that line, they will be adjusted to fit the new tab stop.

You can set a special kind of tab stop by pressing ^TD (**Tabs and margins Decimal**). Unlike a normal tab stop, which lines up the initial characters of the column, a **decimal tab stop,** lines up the column along its decimal points. This is a very useful feature if you're creating a table of numbers that have decimals.

You set a decimal tab in the same way that you set a normal tab: press ^TD, type the column number, and press Return. On the ruler line, the decimal tab stop is marked by a number sign (#).

You use the Tab key to skip to a decimal tab, just like a normal tab, and WordStar 2000 inserts a normal tab character in the line. However, when you start typing numbers at the tab, the difference becomes apparent. The numbers begin appearing to the *left* of the stop, and they keep moving to the left until you type a period for a decimal point. After this decimal point, the remaining numbers are inserted normally. The result is a column that is aligned with its periods directly under the tab stop.

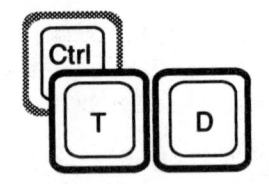

Clearing Tabs

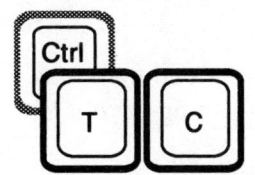

To clear tab stops, use ^TC (**Tabs and margins Clear**). Once again, WordStar 2000 asks you to type the column number where you want to clear the stop, but this time it adds another option:

Clear tab in what column? (A for ALL)

If you type the letter A instead of a number, it will clear all the tab stops from the ruler line. This is handy when you want to set a whole new group of stops.

Setting Margins

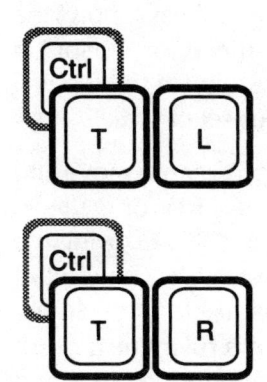

In addition to tab stops, you can also reset the margins on the page with the ^TL (**Tabs and margins Left**) and ^TR (**Tabs and margins Right**) commands. When you press ^TL, WordStar 2000 asks:

Left margin in what column?

Type the number of the column where you want the left edge of your text to begin. WordStar 2000 moves the left edge of the ruler line to show where the text will be aligned. ^TR works the same way for resetting the right margin.

You can set the margins anywhere you want, with just a few restrictions:

- You can't make the left margin number greater than the right margin number (that would put the left margin to the right of the right margin).
- You have to keep at least 10 characters between the two margins, so that you have at least a bit of a line.
- You have to set the left margin at less than 70 and the right margin at less than 240.

Ruler Lines

If you set some tabs or margins and press ^OD, another ruler line will appear above the line in your text, something like this:

L----!-!--!----!----!----!----!----!----!----!----R

You cannot edit this line—it's a special kind of command tag—but it's helpful to look at it to see what's happening in your text.

Every time you change a tab or a margin, you change the **ruler line tag** in the line above the cursor. If there isn't a ruler line tag there, WordStar 2000 automatically creates a new one.

The ruler line tag controls the tabs and margins of all the text below it, all the way down to the next ruler line tag in the text. What comes above the ruler line tag is controlled by the previous ruler line tag, or by the default margins and tabs if there isn't one. The ruler line at the top of the screen always shows the tabs and margins that are in force. If you move the cursor up above the ruler line tag in the text, the ruler line at the top will automatically change to reflect the previous set of tabs.

Although you cannot edit ruler line tags, you can remove and copy them. To remove a ruler line tag, use ^RW or ^RE. To move or copy a ruler line tag, use ^BM or ^BC. Copying the ruler line tag is particularly useful if you establish a new set of tabs and margins for a table, then want to go back to the old settings for the remainder of your text. To copy a ruler line tag, just create a new one at the top of the table, then go back and copy the original ruler line tag to appear at the point just below the table.

Temporary Margins

The Tabs and Margins menu also has four commands that create temporary indentations from the established margins. These commands do not create new ruler line tags; they merely move the effective margins, creating a kind of **hanging indent,** which is especially useful for numbered lists and outlines.

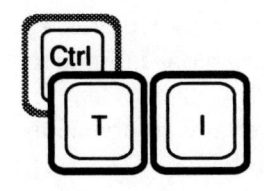

The simplest of the temporary margin commands is ^**TI** (**Tabs and margins Indent**), which indents the left margin to the first tab stop. When you give this command, the ruler line at the top of the screen changes so that only the area to the right of this temporary left margin is highlighted. If you have display on, you will see the command tag **[TI]** appear in your text.

The ^TI command:

1. Takes effect on the current line of your text, if you have the cursor at the beginning of the line, or
2. Takes effect on the next line of your text, if you have the cursor anywhere inside the current line.

This double standard makes it easy to create numbered lists like the one above. At the beginning of the first line of this list, you would use ^TL or ^TI to set the place for the *1*, then type the number and press ^TI again. This sets a temporary left margin for all the following lines, and they will be aligned under the text to the right of the number.

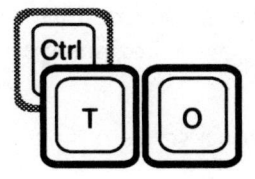

The opposite of ^TI is ^**TO** (**Tabs and margins Out**). If you have moved your margins in, this command moves them back out one tab stop. Press it repeatedly to move multiple stops. If you have the option display on, you will see a [TO] command tag appear each time you give this command. If you press ^TO at a point where you have already put a ^TI marker, the two command tags cancel each other out and both disappear.

In the numbered list above, you might use ^TO at the beginning of the second item to move the left margin back out for the number 2. Then, you would use ^TI again to indent the text of that item.

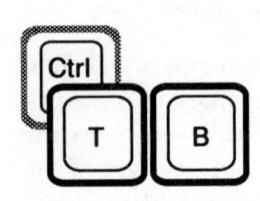

You can also move the left and right margins at the same time, using ^TB (**Tabs and margins Both**). This command creates a temporary left margin one tab stop in, just as if you had pressed ^TI. In addition, it sets a temporary right margin one tab stop to the left of the permanent right margin. ^TO leaves this temporary right margin where it is, so you can get any combination of temporary left and right margins by combining ^TI, ^TO, and ^TB.

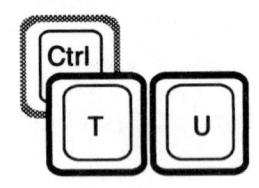

You can cancel a temporary right margin by using the ^TU (**Tabs and margins Undo indentation**) command. This command cancels all temporary indentations and restores the margins on the permanent ruler line. ^TU does not remove the [TI], [TO], and [TB] command tags from the text; it simply cancels their effect from that point on.

In addition to the Tabs and Margins menu, there are a number of commands on the Options menu that affect page formatting. These commands are described in the remainder of this chapter.

Centering

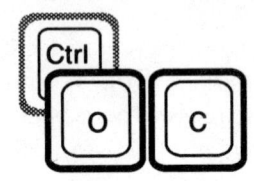

The ^OC (**Option Center**) command centers the text in a line. To use it, you place the cursor anywhere on the line you want to center, then press ^OC. WordStar 2000 will automatically center that line, including any characters you insert later on. ^OC places the command tag [CENTER] at the beginning of the line.

Centering affects only one line. To center a series of lines, press ^OC for each one.

Justification

Most WordStar 2000 formats call for full justification, which means that both the left margin and the right margin of a paragraph are straight. As it prints the document, WordStar 2000 automatically pads the lines with spaces so that they line up on both sides. Justification is not shown in the text, but it is used when you print the document. A few formats do not use justification, but leave a ragged-right margin, just like a typewriter.

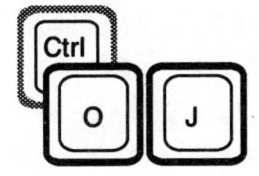

With **^OJ (Option Justify),** you can tell WordStar 2000 to turn justification on or off within a document. ^OJ is a toggle command. In a justified format, the first ^OJ puts a [JUSTIFY OFF] tag in the text, and the next puts in a [JUSTIFY ON] tag. In a ragged-right format, the first ^OJ inserts [JUSTIFY ON].

Hyphenation

Another automatic feature in many formats is **hyphenation.** With this feature, WordStar 2000 automatically divides a word when it is too long to fit at the end of a line. When it divides a word, WordStar 2000 automatically inserts a hyphen at the end of the line. If you reformat the paragraph so that the word no longer needs to be divided, the automatic hyphen disappears.

WordStar 2000 uses the standard rules of hyphenation, but it cannot divide all words correctly. It has special trouble with foreign and technical words, since they often do not follow the standard rules of English.

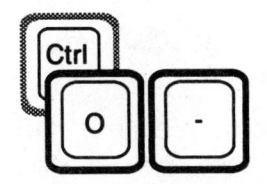

To get around this problem, WordStar 2000 lets you insert a **discretionary hyphen** in a word by pressing **^O-** (**Option hyphen**). This special kind of hyphen overrules the program's automatic hyphenation.

To insert a discretionary hyphen, move the cursor to the place where you want to divide the word and press ^O-. The paragraph will rearrange itself so that the word is divided correctly. If it doesn't, it means that the word won't fit on the line with the hyphenation you have picked, and you'll have to place the hyphen at an earlier syllable division or at the beginning of the word so that it won't be hyphenated, as explained below.

The discretionary hyphen is like a regular hyphen, except that it is printed and displayed only at the end of a line. If you insert a discretionary hyphen in the middle of a line, or if the paragraph gets rearranged so the word isn't divided between lines, the hyphen will disappear. It remains in the file, however, so that the word can be divided correctly if it again falls on a line break. ^O- inserts a [HYPHEN] command tag in the word.

You can also use the ^O- command to make sure a word is *not* divided between two lines. This is useful for names or other sets of words that would look odd if they were separated. You tell WordStar 2000 to keep a word in one piece by typing ^O- before the first letter in the word.

Page Breaks

As it prints your document, WordStar 2000 formats the file into pages. Unless you tell it differently, it will start a new page whenever you type enough lines to reach the bottom of the current page. This page break is displayed on the screen as a line of dashes with a P in the right margin:

------------------------------P

If you insert text in an earlier page, the later page breaks are automatically rearranged. With most WordStar 2000 formats, you can fit 54 single-spaced lines on one page.

You can insert your own page breaks by pressing **^OP** (**Option Page break**). This is useful, for example, when you start a new chapter and want it to begin on a fresh page. When you use ^OP, WordStar 2000 inserts the line:

[PAGE]-------------------------P

on the screen. This command tag starts a new page no matter how few lines there were on the preceding page.

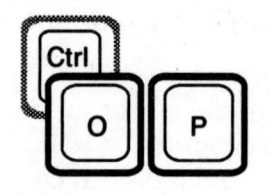

There are times when don't want a page break to fall in the middle of a block of text. Say you've got a table that's 12 lines long, and you don't want to have it split between two pages. You could use ^OP, but that would start a new page even if the table does fit on the previous page. What you want is a **conditional page break,** which will happen only if the table won't fit.

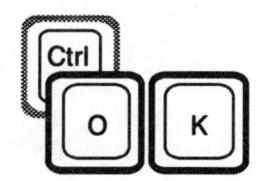

To do this with WordStar 2000, use **^OK (Option Keep lines together).** Move the cursor to the line before the text you want to keep as a unit, and then press ^OK. The program will ask you:

How many lines to keep together?

Type the number 12 and press Return. WordStar 2000 will place a command tag in your text, like this:

[KEEP NEXT 12 LINES TOGETHER]

When it reaches this tag, WordStar 2000 counts the lines that remain before the bottom of the page. If there are fewer than 12, it generates a page break so that the table begins on a fresh page. If there are 12 lines or more left, it ignores the command tag.

Assigning Page Numbers

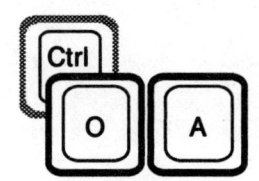

With most formats, WordStar 2000 automatically numbers the pages starting from 1. If you want to number them differently, you can use **^OA (Option Assign page number).** To change the numbering, go to the page where you want to change the sequence, and press ^OA. WordStar 2000 will ask:

Page number to assign?

Type the number that you want printed at the bottom of that page. When you press Return, WordStar 2000 inserts a command tag with that page number.

^OA affects only the numbers on the printed page. It does not change the Page field on the status line at the top of the screen. ^OA also doesn't affect the ^CP (Cursor to Page) command. To use this feature, you will have to keep track of the screen page numbers, which remain sequential from the beginning of the file.

Headers

You can use the **^OH (Option Header)** command to have WordStar 2000 create a **header** at the top of every page. The header can contain one or more lines of text. Many people use headers to provide identification for each page of a manuscript. Book writers, for example, often use a header such as this:

INTRODUCTION TO WORDSTAR 2000 Chapter 11 First Draft

That way, they can quickly identify where a page came from and what version it belongs to.

When you press ^OH, WordStar 2000 will bring up a special menu:

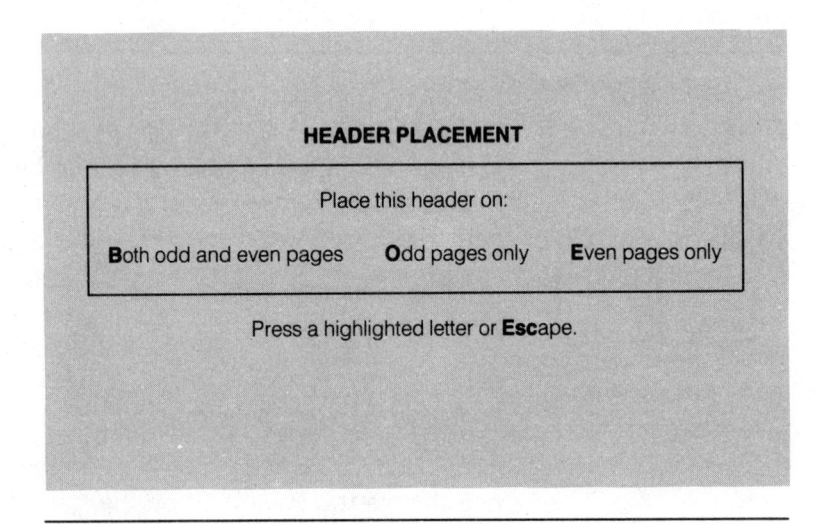

HEADER PLACEMENT

Place this header on:

Both odd and even pages   **O**dd pages only   **E**ven pages only

Press a highlighted letter or **Esc**ape.

Headers Menu

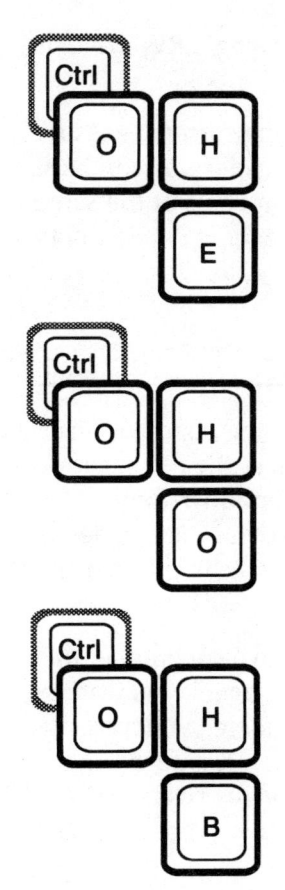

^OHE (Option Header Even) creates a header for even pages, and **^OHO (Option Header Odd)** creates one for odd pages. These commands are useful in a document that you're going to reproduce on front and back sides of the paper, like the pages in a book. If you choose an even or odd header, you may also want to go back and create a header of the other type. If you want the same header to appear on every page, use **^OHB (Option Header Both)**.

If you have turned your menus off with ^GGN, you have to answer which kind of header you want without seeing the Headers menu. The full Option Header command is really a series of three letters: ^OHB, ^OHE, or ^OHO. If you stop at ^OH with the menus off, it will seem WordStar 2000 has gotten hung up and can't finish the command. It's actually just waiting for you to type the third letter of the command.

Once you have specified which of the three types of headers you want, WordStar 2000 opens up a double command tag and puts the cursor inside:

[HEADER]

_
[HEADER]

For even and odd headers, the command tags read [EVEN HEADER] and [ODD HEADER]. If you previously used ^OD to turn off the option display, ^OH automatically turns the display back on so that you can see the command tags.

The command tags mark the beginning and the end of the header in the text. The cursor appears inside so that you can type the text of your header. When you're done, use the arrow keys to move the cursor beyond the second command tag.

If you later want to go back and edit the header, just move the cursor back inside and make your changes. To delete the header, use the Remove commands to delete the text inside—the [HEADER] markers will then automatically disappear. You cannot delete a header marker just by pressing ^RW on it, as you can with most other command tags.

The header goes into effect starting with the current page and remains in effect until you create another header. You can have both an even header and an odd header in effect at the same time. However, if you later add a both header, it cancels both the even and odd ones.

Footers

You can also define a **footer** to appear at the bottom of each page. When you press ^**OF** (**Option Footer**), the menu shows ^**OFE** (**Option Footer Even**), ^**OFO** (**Option Footer Odd**) and ^**OFB** (**Option Footer Both**). Like headers, you can define footers for even, odd, or both pages, and you can put as many lines as you want inside the command tags.

When you define a footer, you replace the page number that automatically appears at the bottom of the page. If you want to include the page number as a part of your footer, you must ask for it specifically. To do that, type the symbols **&%page&** at the place you want the number to appear. When it prints the document, WordStar 2000 replaces this variable name with the current page number. For example:

[FOOTER]

                        Page &%page&

[FOOTER]

would produce the following at the bottom of the first page:

                        Page 1

To get rid of this page number, create another footer that doesn't use &%page&. You will find more on variables in the description of MailMerge in Chapter 17.

Tabs, Margins, and Formatting Options 115

Footnotes

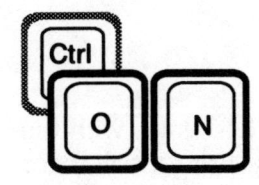

WordStar 2000 also lets you create **footnotes** within your text. More correctly, they should be called **endnotes,** since they are printed after the end of the text rather than at the bottom of each page. WordStar 2000 can't automatically print footnotes at the bottom of each page.

You create a footnote by typing ^**ON (Option Note)** at the place you want the reference to appear in the text. If this is the first note in your document, WordStar 2000 will respond by opening a matched pair of command tags with the cursor between them:

. . . as Niedermeyer has shown.[FOOTNOTE 1]

[FOOTNOTE 1]

You can type as much as you want between the [FOOTNOTE 1] tags. Use the arrow keys to move the cursor outside the command tags when you're done.

You can create as many footnotes as you want. They will all be numbered in the correct order (if you go back and insert a note earlier in the document, all the later notes will be renumbered). You can use the ^CN (Cursor to Note) command to move the cursor directly to a specific footnote reference (see Chapter 6).

When you print the document, all you'll see in the text is a superscript number 1:

. . . as Niedermeyer has shown.[1]

The footnotes appear at the end of your document, numbered and in the proper order.

Comments

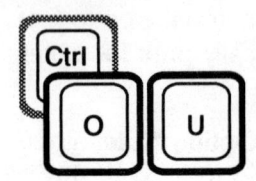

WordStar 2000 also lets you insert an **unprinted comment,** which isn't printed at all. To do this, press **^OU** (**Option Unprinted comment**). WordStar 2000 will open a pair of command tags:

[COMMENT]

[COMMENT]

You can type anything you want inside these tags, with the assurance that it won't appear when you print the file. For example:

Dear Boss:
   I understand and respect your reasons for denying me my raise.
[COMMENT]
You lousy &.%@$*! May you choke on your stinginess!
[COMMENT]

would not get you fired.

Starter Set – Tabs and Margins

^TL	Reset Left margin
^TR	Reset Right margin
^TS	Set tab stop
^TC	Clear tab stop

Starter Set – Formatting Options

^OJ	Justify text
^OC	Center text

12

Format Files

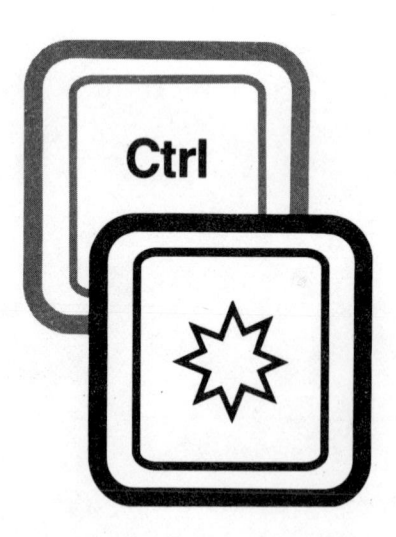

What is a Format File?

Over the last few chapters, you've been reading a lot about page formatting and format files. This chapter reviews WordStar 2000's standard format files and shows how you can design your own.

A format file is a template that WordStar 2000 uses to create each file. You specify the format you want when you first create your document. From then on, WordStar 2000 uses that preset template for all formatting of that document. However, as we'll explain later in this chapter, you can modify the format of a document.

The format file contains a variety of information about the way you want to print and display the document:

- Line spacing and font (how high to space the lines and how wide to make each character)
- Page formatting (how much space to leave on each margin around the text)
- Default tab stops
- Text justification and hyphenation
- Printer options such as automatic form feeds
- On-screen display of page breaks
- Options for printing page numbers at the bottom of each page

The format file settings apply to the whole document, although you can change some of them with commands on the Print Enhancements and Options menus.

A format may also include boilerplate text, which is a copy of the same piece of text to be included in every file you use it with.

Predefined Formats　　　WordStar 2000 comes with a set of six or seven predefined formats that you can use in creating files. These predefined formats are all you'll need for most purposes.

Three of these formats are set up for automatic justification and hyphenation, so that you can print documents that are aligned evenly on both the left and right margins:

- **NORMAL.FRM** A general-purpose justified format with standard margins and single spacing. Tab stops are set every five columns.
- **JUSTIFY.FRM** Same as NORMAL.FRM, but with just a few tab stops near the beginning of the line.
- **MEMOFORM.FRM** Same as NORMAL.FRM, but containing a standard memo heading with spaces for *From, To, Date,* and *Subject.*

You may also have an additional justified format on your program disk: **WS2LIST.FRM.** This format is used with the optional program MailList, which comes as a part of WordStar 2000+. This feature is beyond the scope of this book.

Two other formats print the document with a ragged-right margin:

- **RAGGED.FRM** A general-purpose format like NORMAL.FRM, but without automatic justification and hyphenation.
- **MSCRIPT.FRM** A special ragged-right format for manuscripts, set up with thinner margins and double-spaced text.

The chart below compares the features of these five format files.

	NORMAL	JUSTIFY	MEMOFORM	RAGGED	MSCRIPT
Line spacing	Single	Single	Single	Single	Double
Top margin	6	6	6	6	1
Bottom margin	6	6	6	6	2
Right margin	65	65	65	65	69
Columns per tab	5	*	5	5	5
Lines per page	66	66	66	66	33
Even page offset	10	10	10	10	8
Odd page offset	10	10	10	10	8
Justification?	Yes	Yes	Yes	No	No
Auto hyphenation?	Yes	Yes	Yes	No	No
Use form feeds?	Yes	Yes	Yes	Yes	Yes
Underline between words?	Yes	Yes	Yes	Yes	Yes
Display page breaks?	Yes	Yes	Yes	Yes	Yes
Print page numbers?	Center	None	None	Center	Center

*Tabs at columns 6, 11, 16, 41

Chart of format settings

The final predefined format, **UNFORM.FRM,** is really not a format at all. It creates an unformatted file without word wrap or print controls.

Unformatted Files

UNFORM.FRM is useful for typing computer programs; address lists; and files to be used with special WordStar 2000 features, such as key glossaries (Chapter 13) and MailMerge (Chapter 17). The ^BW command (Chapter 8) also creates an unformatted file when it writes out a block of text as a new file.

In an unformatted file, you can type lines that are as long as you want. Each line continues until you type a hard carriage return. When you print an unformatted file, it comes out exactly as you typed it—lines are never reformatted or justified. Unformatted files are not printed in pages.

You can't use most of the special print enhancements and options while you're editing an unformatted file. In fact, none of the commands on the Print Enhancements and Tabs and Margins menus will work. The only commands on the Options menu that you can use with an unformatted file are ^OO (Option Overtype), ^OR (Option Repeat), ^OS (Option Spelling), and ^OW (Option Window). You cannot use any commands that create command tags in text; an unformatted file contains nothing but straight text.

Creating and Modifying Formats

If you don't like the predefined formats that come with WordStar 2000, you can modify them or create your own using the **F (Format design)** command on the Opening menu.

If you're editing a document, use one of the ^Q commands to get back to the Opening menu. Then press F. WordStar 2000 will respond by asking you:

Format or formatted document name?

The F command displays a file directory of all the files on the logged disk with the extension .FRM. You can change the settings in one of the predefined formats by moving the highlighting bar to its name, pressing Return, and specifying the modifications. However, once you change a predefined format, your new settings permanently replace the original format file unless you go through this process again to change them back.

You'll probably want to create a new format file rather than change an existing one. To do this, type the name of the new file you want to create, using the extension .FRM at the end of the file name to identify it as a format file. That way, the next time you open a document, this new format will be listed on the file directory displayed by the F command.

You can also use the F command to make changes in the format of a document you have already created. When WordStar 2000 asks the name, just type the name of the document whose format you want to change. (It won't be displayed on the file directory, since it's a document file rather than a format file.) However, you can't change the format of a document created with UNFORM.FRM. Instead, you can transfer an unformatted file into a formatted file by creating a new file with the desired format and using ^BI to insert the unformatted file.

Printer Defaults

After you've specified a format or document name, WordStar 2000 asks you two questions:

Font to use?

and

Line height (spacing)?

These settings control the horizontal and vertical spacing of the lines of your text. You choose the answers from a series of choices that work on your printer, such as NON PS 10 for font and 6.00 LPI for line spacing. These format choices are only the defaults that will apply to your document. You can change these settings anywhere inside your document by using the commands ^PF and ^PH. Font and line height options are described in Chapter 10.

The Decisions Screen

After you have answered the font and line height questions, you will see a Decisions screen. At the bottom of this screen, a series of questions appears to determine your page layout and other formatting features. As you answer each question, WordStar 2000 adds a new question line at the bottom, like this:

DECISIONS

Press **Return** to accept current answer, or type new answer over old and press **Return**	**^G**et help
Press **^V** to view all answers Press **^Q** to accept all answers	**Esc**ape

^G means hold down **Control** key and press **G**

How many lines in the top margin?	6
How many lines in the bottom margin?	6
Right margin in what column?	65
Set a tab stop at every n columns—enter a number for n:	5
Number of lines per page?	66
Even-numbered page offset in columns?	10
Odd-numbered page offset in columns?	10
Text Justified or Ragged-right? (J/R)	J
Automatic hyphenation on? (Y/N)	Y
Use form feeds when printing? (Y/N)	Y
Underline between underlined words? (Y/N)	Y
Display page breaks? (Y/N)	Y
Page numbers: Centered, Left, Right, Alternating, or None? (C/L/R/A/N)	C
Press Return to conclude the format.	

Format Decisions Screen

Each question has a default choice, which you can accept by pressing Return. The choices shown here are the defaults for a document created with NORMAL.FRM. (Actually, you won't see all these questions on the Decisions screen at the same time, since the top few will scroll off the screen when you reach the last few. They are shown together here for easy reference.)

Here are some notes to help you with these questions (see Chapter 11 for a description of the commands to use to change your default choices within a document).

- **Top and bottom margins** are the number of blank lines WordStar 2000 will print at the top and bottom of each page. With continuous fanfold paper, you'll need at least a few blank lines so that the printer won't print over the perforated break in the pages.

- The **right margin column** is the number of columns on each line. You can change this setting with the ^TR command.

- **Tab stops** are the interval in columns between the tabs that WordStar 2000 automatically places on the ruler line. You can change these stops in the text with the ^TS and ^TC commands.

- **Lines per page** are the number of lines on each page, including the blank lines in the top and bottom margins. For single spacing on 11-inch pages, you'll want 66 lines per page (11 inches times the line height of 6 lines per inch). For double spacing, you should use 33 lines per page (11 inches times 3 lines per inch). The number of lines actually printed will be this number minus the top and bottom margins.

- The **Page offset** is the number of the column where the printed lines will start, measured from the left edge of the page. With the NON PS 10 font, a 10-character offset will produce a one-inch left margin. You can specify different offsets for odd and even pages, which is useful if you're intending to reproduce the text on the front and back of each sheet of paper.

- **Text justification** is either justified or unjustified (ragged-right) text. Within the text, you can change to the opposite mode with ^OJ.

- **Automatic hyphenation** tells whether you want WordStar 2000 to automatically divide long words at the ends of lines. If you choose hyphenation, you cannot turn this feature off within the text, but you can use ^O- to overrule the automatic hyphenations individually.

- **Form feeds when printing** tells whether you want WordStar 2000 to send a code to the printer at each page break to tell it to skip directly to the top of the new page. If you answer no, the program will space *manually* to the next page by inserting enough blank lines to complete the page. Both choices work equally well on most printers.

- **Underline between words** affects the way ^PU underlines text. Some people like to underline the spaces between underlined words, others prefer to underline only the separate words. Take your pick.

- **Display page breaks** tells whether you want to see the lines of dashes on the screen at the point where each new page begins. This setting affects only the on-screen display, not the printed output—either way, the printed output is still divided into pages.

- **Page numbers** chooses among various styles for printing page numbers at the bottom of each page. You can use ^OF within your text to replace the page numbers with a footer of your own design.

When you've answered all these questions and pressed Return, you'll see a Quit Format menu, with three choices:

- **Save changes** stores your changes as the new format file.

- **Continue formatting** puts you back at the beginning of the format choices, so you can review or change any of your answers.

□ **Abandon changes** takes you back to the Opening menu without storing the new format file.

Boilerplate in Formats

A format file is a text file like any other document. You can open it with the E command on the Opening menu and type text and command tags into it. If you then use ^QS to save the file, the text becomes part of the format file.

If you use this file as the format for another file, the text that you typed will appear when you open the new file. This text therefore becomes a kind of **boilerplate text** that serves as a starting point for every file of that format. Once you begin editing the new file, you can delete or change this boilerplate text just as if you had typed it into that file.

Some of the predefined formats use boilerplate text. MEMOFORM.FRM, for example, includes a few lines of text that serve as a header for a company memorandum. JUSTIFY.FRM uses a different kind of boilerplate that defines a new ruler line at the beginning of the document with different tab stops from the standard ones that are set every five columns (you can see this new ruler line by pressing ^OD). If you don't like these tab settings, you can change them with the Tabs and Margins commands (Chapter 11).

Boilerplate text can be a real time-saver. You might want to define a boilerplate format that automatically creates each file with a standard header and footer. Or, you could design a standard letterhead to go at the beginning of each letter you type. Since the boilerplate text can also include command tags, you can set special print effects, tabs, margins, and options that you want to include in a number of files.

Chapter 17 (MailMerge) describes another kind of boilerplate that you can use in creating repetitive documents.

13

Key Glossaries

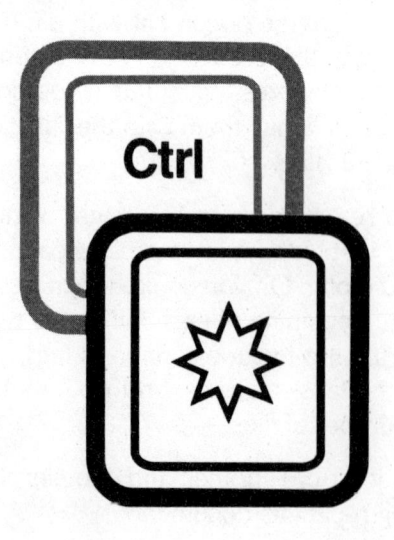

You'll probably find that there are words and commands that you have to type over and over as you're editing a document. WordStar 2000 lets you define **key glossaries** that provide a shorthand way of typing these repetitive keystrokes. A key glossary may contain words, commands, or both.

The key glossary is kept on disk in a special **key file.** You can add or delete abbreviations from this file, and you can switch to another key file to create more than one set of key abbreviations.

Long and Short Forms	A key glossary links a **long form** and a **short form** of the keystrokes. The long form is the entire word or series of control keys that you would normally have to type out. The short form is the abbreviation that you'll use in its place. The abbreviations can be one key or a series of keys, but they must use letter or number keys. You cannot use any special keys, such as function or Alt keys, in a short form.

For example, if you were writing a book about WordStar 2000, you might have to type the phrase *WordStar 2000* countless times. Rather than typing it out each time, you could define a short form, such as *ws,* to serve in its place. Then, every time you needed the phrase, you could just type *ws* and be done with it.

Key glossaries are extremely useful, especially if you combine commands and text into your long forms. You can define an abbreviation to do a whole series of complex commands, such as copy a sentence, read a template file, or set special tabs and margins, and then use the simple abbreviation whenever you need to perform that operation. |

The Key Glossary Menu

The three commands for manipulating key glossaries are found on a special menu:

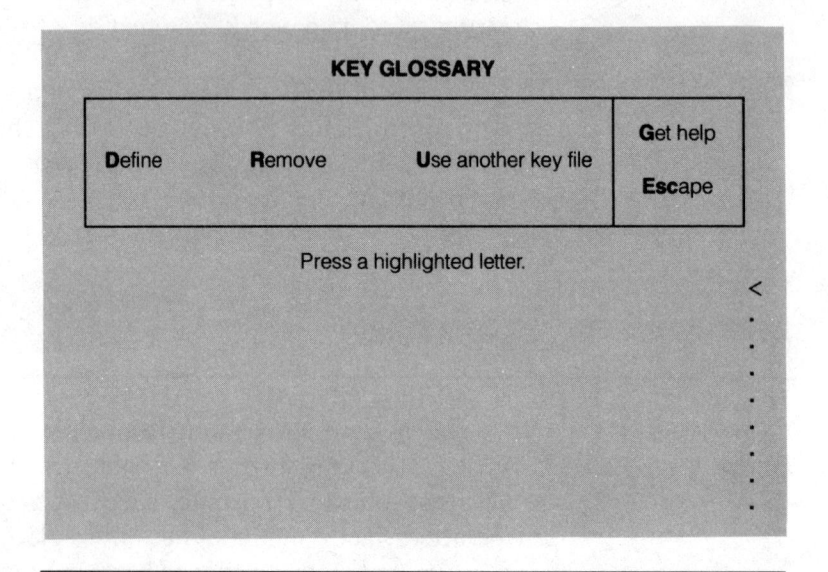

```
                        KEY GLOSSARY
┌─────────────────────────────────────────────┬──────────────┐
│                                             │ Get help     │
│  Define      Remove      Use another key file│              │
│                                             │ Escape       │
└─────────────────────────────────────────────┴──────────────┘
                   Press a highlighted letter.
```

Key Glossary Menu

You can call up the Key Glossary menu from two different places: from the Opening menu by pressing K or from within a document by pressing ^K.

Defining a Short Form

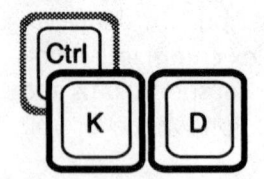

You define a key glossary using the ^**KD** (**Key Define**) (or **KD** from the Opening menu) command. When you give this command, WordStar 2000 asks:

   Short form to define? (Press Esc to cancel)

Beneath this question is a list of the short forms that are already predefined.

Since you're defining a new abbreviation, you'll probably want to type a letter or series of letters that are not on the directory, for example:

ws

Press Return when you're done.

WordStar 2000 will respond with the question:

Long form? (Press ^Q to end)

Now type the full text of the phrase that you want to abbreviate:

WordStar 2000

When you're done, press ^Q. You use a ^Q rather than a Return at the end of the long form so that you can include a carriage return as part of the text you want to abbreviate.

You can also include Control-key commands in your long form. To do this, type the command with a caret symbol, using Shift with the 6 key, rather than actually pressing the Control key. For example, the long form:

^RT.

tells WordStar 2000 to remove text to the next period, or delete from the cursor to the end of the sentence. ^L is one Control-key command that does not work well in a long form; it's best to avoid using ^L in a key glossary.

When you've finished typing the long form, the program goes back and asks you for another short form:

Short form to define? (Press Esc to cancel)

You can go on typing short forms and long forms as long as you want. When you're done defining key glossaries, press the Esc key. Then, WordStar 2000 asks the rather confusing question:

Should these changes be saved? (Y/N)

This actually means, "Should these new keys be stored permanently on the disk?" If you answer N, the keys will go into effect immediately, but they will be remembered only as long as you remain in WordStar 2000 and don't use another key file.

If you answer Y, WordStar 2000 will ask another odd question:

Key file to use?

Since you can have multiple key files, you may type any file name that you want. In most cases, however, you'll just want to add your new keys to the default key file, **WS2.KEY.** Just press Return to accept that choice. Since you're writing the expanded file over an existing key file, WordStar 2000 feels obliged to check with you one more time:

That file already exists — Replace? (Y/N)

When you answer Y, you'll finally get back to the Editing menu (or to the Opening menu if that's where you began the procedure).

Using the Short Form

To use the short form, follow these steps:

1. Position the cursor after a space, at the beginning of a line, or after a command tag. If you don't do this, the program takes the preceding characters to be part of the abbreviation.
2. Type the short form.
3. Press the Esc key.

When you press the Esc key, WordStar 2000 immediately converts the short form into the long form.

You could try out the new abbreviation by typing *ws* and then pressing the Esc key. The program will immediately convert this to the full phrase, WordStar 2000, and the short form will disappear.

Deleting a Short Form

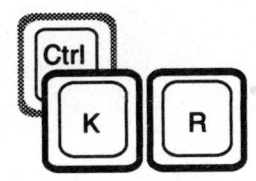

You can delete an abbreviation from your key file by pressing ^**KR** (**Key Remove**) (or **KR** from the Opening menu). WordStar 2000 will show the list of short forms and ask the question:

Short form to remove?

Type the abbreviation you want to delete and press Return. The program repeats the question, in case you want to delete more than one abbreviation. Press the Esc key when you're finished deleting short forms. WordStar 2000 will ask a few more questions to make sure you really want to make the changes. Answer the questions just as you did for ^KD.

Using Another Key File

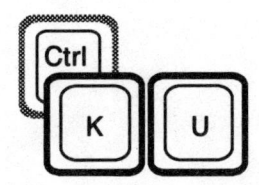

The last command on the Key Glossary menu is ^**KU** (**Key Use another key file**) (or **KU** from the Opening menu) which lets you select a different key file from the one you've been using. When you give this command, WordStar 2000 asks:

Key file to use?

and gives you a choice of available key files. Choose one and press Return. That file becomes the active set of abbreviations until you leave WordStar 2000 or use ^KU again.

You can have no more than 20 entries in any one key file. The total length of all the short and long forms in a file cannot exceed 2000 characters. The maximum length of a short form is 15 characters. The maximum for a long form is 560 characters.

If you find key glossaries useful, you might want to invest in the ProKey program by RoseSoft. You install ProKey before you start WordStar 2000. Then, you can call up that program interactively any time you want to define a meaning for a key on the keyboard. ProKey works even while you're inside WordStar 2000 editing a file. See Appendix B for more information.

14

Files and Windows

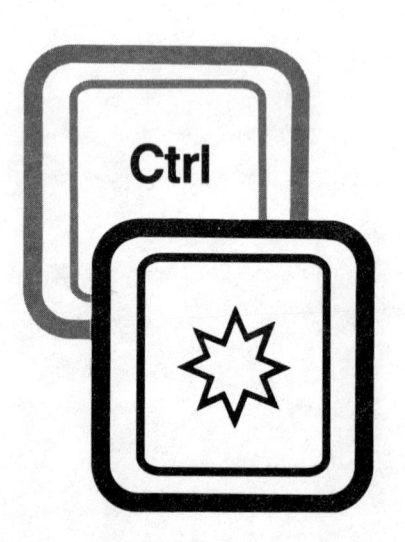

Back in Chapter 5, you learned about the commands that let you save and change the files you've been working on: ^QS, ^QP, ^QC, and ^QA. These commands (except for ^QA) automatically change some of the files on your disk, usually creating a backup file at the same time.

In this chapter, we'll review the other file handling commands in WordStar 2000. You'll also learn how to edit in multiple windows on the screen.

Most of the file handling commands are grouped on the Opening menu. The Opening menu is divided into two screens, but only the first is really important:

```
                    OPENING MENU – 1 of 2

        Edit / create          Print              Get help
        Remove                 Copy               Quit

        Directory / drive      Key glossary
        Move / rename          Typewriter mode
        Spelling correction    Format design

        Press a highlighted letter or Spacebar for more choices.
```

Opening Menu – Screen 1

The commands on the second screen are devoted to special options that are provided only with WordStar 2000+ and to the WordStar-to-WordStar 2000 conversion program described in Appendix C.

You have already used many of the Opening menu commands in previous chapters. For example, E (Edit/create) should be quite familiar by now since you've used it every time you've begun editing a document. F (Format design) was described in

Chapter 12 in connection with format files. K (Key glossary), which lets you create short-form key files, was discussed in Chapter 13. And P (Print) does essentially the same thing as the ^QP command you've been using to print your documents. You'll learn more about printing in Chapter 15.

Using DOS Commands

[Q]

Many of the commands described in this chapter duplicate DOS commands. If you want, you can use the DOS versions instead. Simply choose **Q** (**Quit**) from the Opening menu to exit WordStar 2000. Once you're back at the A> prompt, you can give the equivalent DOS file command. The advantage of using WordStar 2000's commands is that you can avoid the interminable waits of leaving and reentering the program. Also, WordStar 2000 lets you choose files by moving the highlighting bar around the file directory. In DOS, you have to type all file names. (Of course, if you want a DOS command that's not on WordStar 2000's Opening menu, you can't avoid using Q to get out to DOS.)

The Logged Disk Drive

WordStar 2000 starts up assuming you're using the disk drive where the program files are located. This **logged disk drive** will be A: if that's the drive from which you started the program.

You can always specify another drive by adding its drive letter as a prefix to your file names. B:MYFILE.DOC, for example, will tell WordStar 2000 to look for MYFILE.DOC on drive B:. However, if you're doing all of your work on a drive other than the one where your program is located, you'll probably find it easier to change the logged drive and then forget about it.

[D]

To change the logged drive, use the **D** (**Directory/drive**) command. The program will ask you:

Change directory or disk drive to?

Type the letter of the drive you want, followed by a colon. If you want to use the second floppy-disk drive, type:

> B:

WordStar 2000 will change its default disk drive to B: and use that drive whenever you don't specify a drive. Of course, you can still call up a file from another drive by typing its drive letter before the file name.

If you change your logged disk drive, your format and key files will stay on your program disk. When you open a document on a blank work disk, WordStar 2000 won't display a list of format file names when it asks you to choose a format. You have two choices: you can use one of the format files on drive A: by typing the drive letter before its name (A:NORMAL.FRM, for example), or you can copy the format files onto your work disks. To see the list of the formats available on drive A: before choosing one, type A: by itself after you see the Choose a Name screen and then press Return. If you want to see a list of the key files on drive A:, press ^KU, type A:, and then press Return.

The D command also lets you change to another **file directory** on a disk. This is a feature that is handy for hard-disk system users, who can divide the large disk into a number of smaller **subdirectories.** Hard disks and subdirectories are described in Appendix D.

Deleting Files

One of the most important file handling commands is **R** (**Remove**), which deletes files from your disk. When you press R, WordStar 2000 asks you:

> **File to remove?**

Type the name of the file you want to delete, or choose it from the file directory at the bottom of the screen.

If you want to delete a file that isn't shown on the directory, such as a file on a disk other than the currently logged drive, just type the drive name in front of the file name. Even though you can't see the file name disappear, you'll know the command worked if you get back to the Opening menu without an error message.

Copying Files

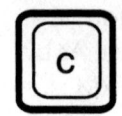

[C key]

Another important file operation is **C** (**Copy**), which makes an exact duplicate of one of the files on the disk. You can use this command either to copy a file onto the same disk or to transfer the file to another disk.

When you press C, WordStar 2000 brings up a file directory and asks:

File to copy from?

Type the name of the file or choose it from the directory. The program will then ask:

File to copy to?

Here you type a name for the duplicate file. It must have a different name from the original, if it is going to be on the same drive. If you want to copy the file to a different drive, type the drive prefix before the file name.

Renaming and Moving Files

[M key]

Very similar to the Copy command is the **M** (**Move/rename**) command. The difference is that M does not produce a second copy of the file; it simply moves the file to a new location.

When you press M, the program asks:

File to move or rename?

Type or choose the old file name. When you press Return, WordStar 2000 asks:

New location or new name?

Type the new file name, including a drive prefix if you want to move the file to another drive.

The Move command is executed differently depending on whether you tell it to put the file on a different drive. If you give a new name on the same drive, WordStar 2000 simply renames the file (like the DOS RENAME command). If you ask for a name on a different drive, the program first copies the file to the new drive, then deletes the old version.

The M command is handy if you want to edit or print the backup version of a document that WordStar 2000 created when you saved a file with one of the ^Q commands. You cannot open a .BAK file, but you can rename it using the M command and then work with it.

Typewriter Mode

The last command on the Opening menu is **T** (**Typewriter mode**). When you give this command, you are opening up a direct line to your printer.

In typewriter mode, you can type one screen line of text, and WordStar 2000 will display it on the screen until you press Return; then it sends the line directly to the printer.

Until you send the line off, you can edit it with a few of the standard editing keys (^S or ← move backwards, Backspace and Del delete characters, and so forth). Once you press Return, however, you cannot go back and make changes before the line is printed.

Typewriter mode can be handy for quick tasks such as typing an envelope because you don't have to open an editing file or figure out spacing.

Disk Full Messages

Because of the way that WordStar 2000 juggles its document files, temporary files, and backup files, it may need three times as much free space on the disk as the document takes up. (You can find out how much space a file is using by exiting to the operating system and giving the DOS DIR command.)

If you push your disk past the limit, you will come up against the dreaded **disk full** message:

> The disk is full – you must delete one or more files to continue, or press Escape to abandon the current document.

Below this message is a directory of all the files on your disk.

In most cases, you can solve the problem just by deleting a few files. Start with all of the .BAK files on the disk. They are old versions of files that you've already changed. While they're good insurance, they aren't necessary. The best file to start with is the backup of the document you're working on. You lose nothing by deleting this old .BAK file because, once you save your current work, it would be replaced by the old version of what you just changed anyway.

If deleting the backup files doesn't solve the problem, you may need to delete some actual files. Check through the file names and see if you can throw any away.

You may have some of the files on other disks. If you're wise, you are making periodic backups of your work disks onto spare **backup disks.** If so, you can even delete some necessary files if you're sure they're on the backup disk. If you have no alternative and your file is on the program disk, you can even try deleting some WordStar 2000 program files, if you know you've got other copies.

If you need to, you can delete the name of the document itself. That doesn't destroy the version of the file you are currently editing. It deletes the previous version—the one that was going to become the new backup file. By deleting that copy, you may be able to make room for the current version you're trying to save.

Only in the most extreme case will you get the disk full message and not be able to get out of it. Then you're stuck—you have to press the Esc key and abandon your changes without saving them.

The moral of this is: **Don't let your disks get too full!** When you've got a long file, save it frequently and keep your disks as clean as you can. Anytime you see the disk full message, take heed and start a new disk.

Multiple Windows

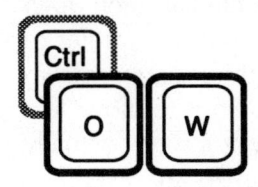

WordStar 2000 lets you have more than one document open at a time. When you do this, the program divides the screen into horizontal **windows,** each of which acts like a full editing screen. You can have up to three windows on the screen.

To open a second window while you're editing a document, press ^**OW** (**Option Window**). WordStar 2000 will respond by asking:

Document to edit or create?

This is the same screen as the one that appears when you press E from the Opening menu to open a document. And that's exactly what you're doing—you're just doing it from inside another document.

Once you choose a file name (and a format, if it's a new file), WordStar 2000 will put you back at the Editing menu. Now, however, the screen is divided by two ruler lines, and you see parts of both documents. If you have your menus on, you may want to turn them off with ^GGN to make more room for the new window.

Within a window, editing commands work just as they do on the full screen. However, you must use ^CW to move the cursor from window to window. The cursor will land at the last position it occupied in the other window.

When you're done using a window, use the regular ^Q commands to store it as a file. ^QS and ^QP, which normally take you back to the Opening menu, simply close the window and leave the cursor in the other document. ^QA closes the window without saving the changes.

Windows are especially useful for transferring text from one document to another. If you mark a block in one document, move the cursor to the other window, and press ^BC, the block will be copied directly into the other document. ^U also works in another window.

You can also open two windows into the same document. In a long file, for instance, you might want to have one window open where you're editing near the end of the file, then open another into the beginning of the file. You could then refer to other parts of the document or copy text without skipping from one part of the file to the other. (If you attempt to *move* text from one part of the file to another in this way, it won't actually disappear from the first part when your changes are saved.)

In general, if you open multiple windows into a document, choose one of them as the window where you'll make all your changes. When it comes time to stop work and save the file, you must choose one of the versions to save, and abandon the other windows with ^QA before you close the document.

When you open a second window on a document, you see it as it was last saved, without any of your current changes. To see the current version, use ^QC before using ^OW.

15

Printing Out

Printing Out 147

WordStar 2000 has a variety of options for printing out your files:

- You can print multiple copies or selected pages only.
- You can have the printer stop at the end of each page.
- You can ask the program to print the command tags in a draft copy of a document.
- You can send the output to a disk file rather than to the printer.
- You can continue editing other files while you're printing a document.

There are two commands for printing a file with WordStar 2000: You can press ^QP to print a file as you save a document from the Editing menu, or you can press P from the Opening menu.

These commands work essentially the same way, except that the P command starts by asking:

Document to print?

^QP from within a file doesn't need to ask this, since it always prints the file you were editing.

The Print Decisions Screen

After you have chosen the file to print, WordStar 2000 brings up a Decisions screen that lets you choose the options you want.

DECISIONS

Press **Return** to accept current answer, or
type new answer over old and press **Return**   ^**G**et help

Press ^**V** to view all answers   **Esc**ape
Press ^**Q** to accept all answers

^**G** means hold down **Ctrl** key and press **G**

Begin printing on what page?	1
Stop printing after what page? (L for Last)	L
Print how many copies?	1
Pause between pages for paper change? (Y/N)	N
Obey page formatting commands? (Y/N)	Y
Print and continue working? (Y/N)	N
Send document to Printer or ASCII Disk file? (P/D)	P

Prepare the printer and press Return.

Print Decisions Screen

If you've read Chapter 12 or created a format file, you've already seen a Decisions screen like this.

For any question, you can either type your own answer, usually a one-letter response, or accept the default answer by pressing Return. The defaults are shown on the screen above.

Your other option is to press ^Q and bypass the Decisions screen. If you do this, WordStar 2000 will use the default settings for all the options. (If you want to look at the default answers all at once before deciding whether to accept them, press ^V.)

Even if you answer some of the questions on the Decisions screen, you can still use ^Q. When you do, WordStar 2000 will use the answers you gave and accept the default answers for the remaining questions. This can be handy if you want to change the first few answers and leave the rest unchanged.

Here are your printing options:

- **Begin and stop printing on what page** lets you limit the printout to certain pages of your document. The default answers print the whole document.

- **Number of copies** lets you print multiple copies of a document, up to 1000.

- **Pause between pages** lets you use individual sheets of paper in your printer, rather than continuous-feed fanfold paper. If you answer Y to this question, the program stops at the end of each page so that you can feed in a new sheet.

- **Obey page formatting** lets you print a draft of your document with command tags spelled out. The output will look like the screen with ^OD on. If you accept the default answer (Y), the command tags will not be printed, but they will be used to format the output.

- **Print and continue working** lets you go back to the Opening or Editing menu and do more work while the file is printing. WordStar 2000 will divide its attention between the printing and your editing. The default answer is No because there are occasional problems with editing while printing. With its attention divided, the program often takes a longer time to react to your commands. It's usually faster and less frustrating just to wait until the printing is done.

- **Printer or disk file** lets you send the output to the printer or to a file on the disk. If you press D to ask for this option, the program asks you for a file name. Disk output can be useful if you just want to preview the output without printing it. Also, it is the best way to convert a formatted file into an unformatted file that can be used by other word processors and programs. You can later print this disk copy of the file, though some of the formatting options may be lost.

Once you've finished answering these questions, WordStar 2000 asks you to:

Prepare the printer and press Return.

When you do, it immediately begins printing and displays the message:

Printing A:*FILENAME*. Press P to interrupt.

Unless you've told it otherwise, the program will continue printing until it has reached the last page.

If you press P while the file is printing, WordStar 2000 puts this message on the screen:

Printing is interrupted. Continue or Abandon? (C/A)

The default response C (Continue) lets you start the printer again if you want to finish printing. A (Abandon) takes you back to the Opening menu and stops the printer where it was.

16

The Spelling Checker

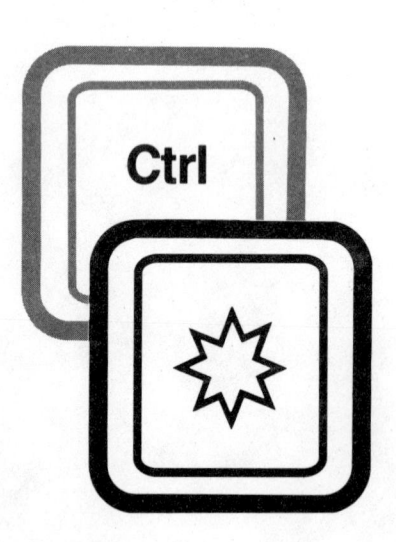

Another important feature built into WordStar 2000 is **CorrectStar,** a module that automatically checks the spelling of words in a document.

When you set CorrectStar to work on a document, the program checks every word against its **dictionary.** Each time it encounters a word that is not among the 65,000 it knows, CorrectStar stops and flags the word as **suspect.** Whenever possible, CorrectStar will then search its dictionary and come up with one or more suggestions for what you might have meant to type.

Not every suspect word is misspelled. Most documents contain some perfectly good words that are not in the CorrectStar dictionary, such as some place names, names of people, technical words, and unusual vocabulary. So, you should use CorrectStar simply as a guide to pick out words that you should double-check.

CorrectStar only catches spelling errors. You can buy other programs that check for mistakes in grammar, style, and usage. Two good ones are *Grammatik* by Wang Electronic Publishing and *Punctuation + Style* by Oasis Systems. Among other options, *Grammatik* can print out a list of how many times you have used each word in your document. You can often catch freak misspellings by scanning through the list of words that occur only once.

Spelling Mistakes

People make all kinds of spelling mistakes in typing documents:

- Good, old-fashioned illiteracies such as *mispel* and *illitericy*
- Simple typos such as *hte* (for *the*) and *compuiter* (for *computer*)

- Incomprehensible gobbledygook like *VpttrvyDyst,* which can easily be the result when your fingers slip on the keyboard

CorrectStar is a good tool for catching these types of spelling errors.

CorrectStar won't catch one special type of spelling mistake: words that you misuse in place of others. You might misspell the word *insure,* for instance:

I ensured my car.

CorrectStar would let this pass because *ensure* is a perfectly good word that unfortunately means something different.

Your Dictionary Disk

CorrectStar checks the spelling of words by comparing them to a large dictionary of common words. With WordStar 2000, this dictionary takes up an entire disk, which comes as a part of your WordStar 2000 package. The CorrectStar dictionary disk contains over 65,000 words, based on the *American Heritage Dictionary* (© The Houghton Mifflin Company, New York, 1984).

The **dictionary disk** is the third disk of the WordStar 2000 package. You must keep this disk on hand and use it every time you run a spelling check.

The first thing you should do is **copy** your dictionary disk if you haven't already done so. Never use the original MicroPro disk for running CorrectStar because there are too many things you might do that could make it irreparably unreadable.

Next, take stock of your disks. On a floppy-disk system, you will need three disks to run CorrectStar:

- The WordStar 2000 program disk, which includes the program information that tells WordStar 2000 how to react to CorrectStar commands.

- The CorrectStar dictionary disk, which is packed full of words and suggested corrections (the dictionary disk contains no program information).
- Your data disk, which must have at least 93,000 bytes of free disk space, in addition to the space needed for your files.

If, like most people, you have a system with only two floppy-disk drives, you will have to stop and swap disks back and forth as part of any spelling operation. Generally, you leave your data disk where it is and exchange the WordStar 2000 program disk and the dictionary disk.

Because of this disk swapping, the program must follow a special procedure for any CorrectStar command:

1. WordStar 2000 prepares itself so that it can let you remove the program disk. WordStar 2000 must always have some of its program information, even while the dictionary disk has replaced the program disk. To preserve this information, the program copies two files from the program disk onto your data disk. These files—WS2.OVR and SPMSG.OVR—take up the 93,000 bytes of space that had to be free. (If the files are already on your data disk, this step is ignored.)

2. WordStar 2000 asks you to remove the program disk and insert your dictionary disk. Once you have swapped the disks, you press the Esc key to continue working. From this point on, the program is running from the two files copied onto your data disk.

3. CorrectStar goes through the entire spelling check, using the dictionary disk.

4. When it's done, CorrectStar asks you to remove the dictionary disk and put back the program disk.

5. WordStar 2000 returns to its normal operation.

You can avoid this disk swapping if you have a hard disk or RAM disk system. With a hard disk, you can normally fit both the WordStar 2000 program and the dictionary on the same disk drive. You generally can't fit both the program and the dictionary into a RAM drive, but if you have 640K of memory you can put the entire WordStar 2000 program in the RAM disk and leave the dictionary in one of the floppy-disk drives as if you had a third disk drive. You still have to press the Esc key when WordStar 2000 asks you to change disks, but you won't have to do any actual swapping. See Appendix B for information about installing WordStar 2000 for these types of systems.

Kinds of Spelling Checks

You can use the CorrectStar program either from the Opening menu or from within a document. From the Opening menu, you can check the spelling of the entire document. From within a document, you can check the spelling of a single word, all the words in a paragraph, or the rest of the document from the cursor to the end (if the cursor is at the beginning of the document, this checks the entire document).

To use CorrectStar, you must always follow the full disk-swapping routine, even if it's just for a single word. For this reason, you'll probably want to use CorrectStar mostly for whole-document checks, rather than to check individual words or paragraphs.

Running a Spelling Check

Let's start by using the spelling command from the Opening menu, which checks an entire document. The spelling commands from within documents work in essentially the same way. We'll get to them later.

The command on the Opening menu is **S** (**Spelling check**). When you press this key, WordStar 2000 will ask:

Document to Spell Check?

You give the name of a file, just as if you were starting to edit the file. In fact, you really are editing the file, using CorrectStar as an aid.

The program then asks you to:

Replace the WS2000 program disk with the dictionary disk. Press Escape.

Swap the disks and press the Esc key to continue.

Choosing a Personal Dictionary

Now CorrectStar asks you:

Personal Dictionary to Use?

A **personal dictionary** is a text file containing an additional set of words that you want CorrectStar to recognize in addition to the words in its main dictionary. These extra words may be special words that you're in the habit of using, or technical terms that are peculiar to your particular document. CorrectStar considers these additional words to be correctly spelled, and accepts them in its spelling check.

If this is your first time using CorrectStar, you probably don't have a personal dictionary. Just press Return to create an empty personal dictionary. CorrectStar checks to make sure this is what you want to do:

Create new Personal dictionary? (Y/N)

Press Y for yes. CorrectStar creates a dictionary with the default name PERSONAL.DCT. (If you press N, you'll just get the *Personal Dictionary to Use?* question again.)

Don't worry that you don't have any words in your personal dictionary. You can do a spelling check without anything in the personal dictionary—CorrectStar does fine with the 65,000 words of its own. As you will see, it is easy to add words to the personal dictionary as you do your spelling check. (Even if you don't plan to add any words, though, you must still go through this procedure.)

If you have done some previous spelling checks, you might already have a personal dictionary. In that case, CorrectStar will display the file name PERSONAL.DCT when it asks for the name of the personal dictionary; you can choose that dictionary just by pressing Return. You can, if you want, also create another personal dictionary with a different name—you may have as many separate dictionaries as will fit on your disks. More on this later.

The Spelling Correction Menu

After you have chosen or created your personal dictionary, you get a new menu—the **Spelling Correction menu**—along with the first part of your document:

SPELL.TXT	Page 1 Line 1 Col 8	Insert Horiz
Add to Dictionary **I**gnore **T**ype correction	**C**orrect all occurrences **N**ext suggestion **P**revious suggestion	**G**et help **Esc**cape

Press **Return** to correct as suggested.

Suspect word: **Speling**
Suggestion: **Spelling**

Speling is hard for many forners. I have a friend from Shanghai who writes very well, but has real trouble speling. I try to help him, but Im not too good at it ether. So I suggested he use CorrectStar to check his speling. . . .

In this case, CorrectStar has flagged the first misspelled word in the document, *Speling,* and is suggesting that you change it to *Spelling.* CorrectStar also highlights the word in the document to show where it is suggesting the change. The menu options describe the keys you will press to make the spelling changes.

Notice that CorrectStar's suggested spelling has the same initial capital as the word you misspelled. If you had typed the word with a lowercase letter, CorrectStar would have suggested you type it *spelling.* If you wanted to change this initial capital, you could make the correction using the T command, which we'll explain later.

If you want to accept CorrectStar's suggestion and have it fix the word in the document, just press Return. The word is corrected in the document, and CorrectStar moves on to the next suspect word.

Another way to accept CorrectStar's correction is to press **C** (**Correct all occurrences**). This does the same thing as the Return key and more—it tells CorrectStar to automatically correct the misspelled word throughout the document.

This is handy for words that you habitually misspell. For example, the writer of the sample document obviously forgot how to spell *spelling,* since the same mistake occurs two more times in the same paragraph. By pressing C, you could tell CorrectStar to make the same change whenever it encounters the word without asking you about it each time. Note that CorrectStar does not change the other occurrences immediately after you press C, but instead waits until it reaches them in scanning the document.

In some versions of WordStar 2000, if you press C to change all occurrences of a capitalized word like *Spelling,* CorrectStar will not automatically change the occurrences that begin with a lowercase *s.* Instead, it suggests that you change them to *Spelling* with an initial capital letter. Use the N command described next to change the suggestion to *spelling,* and press

C again. Once you have done this, all further occurrences will be changed correctly.

So, to accept CorrectStar's correction for only that occurrence of the word, press Return; to accept it for all occurrences, press C.

With the word *speling,* the correction is fairly obvious, and CorrectStar immediately recognizes the word you intended to use. With more bizarre contortions, however, the correction may not be obvious. You may have mangled the word so badly that CorrectStar can only guess which word you meant to spell.

An example of this is the second word that CorrectStar flags in the sample document: *forners.* The writer of this document obviously meant *foreigners,* but missed by a rather wide margin. CorrectStar guesses that the writer might have mistyped the first letter, actually meaning to type *corners.* That's a reasonable guess, but it's wrong.

This is why CorrectStar often gives **multiple suggestions.** In cases where it has no way of guessing what you actually meant, CorrectStar gives a whole series of choices for you to choose from.

Only the most likely suggestion is displayed at first. To see other choices, press **N** (**Next suggestion**). If CorrectStar has another suggestion, it displays it on the suggestion line; if it doesn't, it prints the message:

No more suggestions.

Pressing N in the present case will get you the correct spelling, *foreigners.*

If you press N a third time, you get yet another suggestion, until CorrectStar finally runs out of ideas. For some short words, CorrectStar may have ten or more suggestions. If you pass by the one you want, you can get back to it by pressing **P** (**Previous suggestion**).

When you get to the suggestion that you want to use, press Return or C to accept the new spelling. CorrectStar changes the text to match the suggestion you have chosen, then goes on to the next suspect word.

In any spelling check, CorrectStar will usually flag some words that are actually correct—words that are either too obscure for it to recognize or too specialized to be included in a general dictionary.

Take, for example, the next word CorrectStar stops at in the sample document: *Shanghai*. The dictionary does include some place names, but *Shanghai* isn't one of them. CorrectStar, in fact, finds *Shanghai* to be such a strange word that it doesn't even have a suggested correction. It just leaves the space blank and types the message:

No more suggestions.

In this case, the word is not misspelled, and you don't want CorrectStar to change it. If you press **I** (**Ignore**), CorrectStar will leave the word as it is and continue on to the next suspect word.

CorrectStar keeps no record of the words you tell it to ignore, it simply skips over that occurrence of the word. If you used *Shanghai* again later in the text, CorrectStar will flag it again, and you will have to press I another time to leave the word as it is.

If you plan to use the word *Shanghai* often in your document, you may want to use a different command: **A** (**Add to dictionary**). This command adds the word to the personal dictionary you have chosen. That way, the next time CorrectStar encounters the word *Shanghai*, it will recognize the spelling and continue on without flagging an error.

Make sure that the word is spelled correctly before you add it to the personal dictionary because no matter how you spell it, CorrectStar will treat that version as the correct one and will never catch that misspelling again (unless you remove it from the dictionary).

A has the same immediate effect as I; It tells CorrectStar to accept the suspect word as it is. The difference is that when you press A, you make that word part of CorrectStar's vocabulary.

So, to have CorrectStar leave the suspect word as it is for only that occurrence, press I; to have CorrectStar accept that spelling for all occurrences, press A.

The last letter on the Spelling Correction menu is **T (Type correction)**. T lets you change the suspect word to anything you want by typing in the correction.

Some misspelled words get no suggestions at all—for these you have no choice but to type the correction. Other words get many suggestions, but none of them are right. Even if one of the suggestions is right, you may find it easier just to retype the word rather than scan through the possibilities with the N and P commands.

The misspelled contraction *Im* is an example of a word for which you have to type a correction. CorrectStar actually comes up with nine different suggestions for this word (If, In, Is, It, Am, Aim, Him, Em, and Iamb), but misses the correction you actually need: a simple apostrophe between the I and the m.

Press T. The menu prompt changes to read:

Suspect word: Im

Type correction:

You type the correct word:

I'm

and press Return.

At this point, you might think you have completed the command and changed the word in the text; however, you're not through yet. CorrectStar treats the word you typed as an additional suggestion and returns you to the suggestion line:

>Suspect word: **Im**
>
>Suggestion: **I'm**

You have to press Return again to accept your own suggestion and make the change in the document. You can also use C to change all occurrences of the word to this new spelling. You can even use N and P to go to other suggestions than the one you typed.

Ending the Spelling Check

When CorrectStar finally passes the last suspect word in your document, it returns you to the normal WordStar 2000 editor. On its way back, CorrectStar asks you to:

>Replace the dictionary disk with the WS2000 program disk.
>
>Press **Escape**.

When you get back to WordStar 2000, you will find yourself within the document you were checking, rather than at the Opening menu where you began. This allows you to go back and make any changes that you might not have been able to make while you were locked into the routine of the spelling check. In the document we have been looking at, for example, you might have noticed that *either* was misspelled as *ether*. CorrectStar passed by this word because *ether* is a valid English word. Unfortunately, it is the wrong word, so you'll have to go back now if you want to set it right. To get back to the Opening menu, use ^QS or ^QP.

Spelling Checks From Within Documents

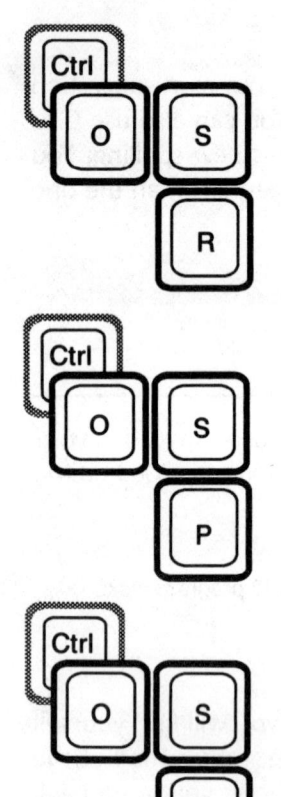

You can also start a spelling check from within a document. There are three commands for this, all beginning with the prefix ^OS (**Option Spelling**):

- ^OSR (**Option Spelling Rest**) checks the spelling of words from the cursor to the end of the document. If the cursor is at the beginning of the document, this command is equivalent to typing S from the Opening menu.
- ^OSP (**Option Spelling Paragraph**) checks the spelling of all words in the paragraph where the cursor is located. This command always checks the whole paragraph, no matter where the cursor is located within it.
- ^OSW (**Option Spelling Word**) checks the spelling of a single word

You use these commands in much the same way as you use S from the Opening menu. You place the cursor where you want it in the document, give the spelling check command, insert the dictionary disk, then follow the same series of directions. You also have the same set of commands for accepting or changing CorrectStar's suggestions: Return to accept, C to change all occurrences, N and P for other suggestions, I to ignore, A to add the word to the dictionary, and T to type your own correction.

When it has checked all the words in the section, CorrectStar asks you to reinsert the WordStar 2000 disk, then lets you continue editing. It leaves the cursor at the end of the section you were checking, or, for ^OSR, at the end of the document.

Selecting a Personal Dictionary

If this is the first spelling check you have run since opening that document, CorrectStar asks for the dictionary name, just as it does from the Opening menu. If, however, you have already run a check on that document, CorrectStar assumes it is using

The Spelling Checker   **165**

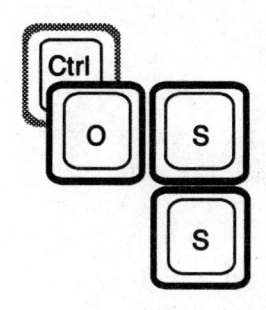

the same dictionary you used the last time and will not ask for the dictionary name.

If you do want to choose a different dictionary from the one that you've been using, press **^OSS** (**Option Spelling Select**) before you start the spelling check. CorrectStar asks you:

Personal dictionary to use?

You can choose any of the personal dictionaries listed on the screen, or create a new one by typing a name that isn't listed. If you type a new name, CorrectStar checks to make sure you want to:

Create new personal dictionary? (Y/N)

Press Y to confirm that you do. (Note that you have to swap your program and dictionary disks even with this command.)

Personal dictionaries are usually stored on the CorrectStar dictionary disk. That disk, however, is quite full even before you start, so you may run out of space quickly if you add a lot of words to your dictionaries. You can avoid this problem by creating personal dictionaries on your data disks. To do this, type the data disk's drive name when CorrectStar asks for the name of the personal dictionary to use. For example, if your data disk is in drive B:, you could type the file name B:MYDICT.DCT to create a special dictionary that you are using only in connection with that particular data disk.

More on Personal Dictionaries

The main CorrectStar dictionary contains general words that are of interest to a wide variety of people. You cannot edit this dictionary. If you try, you will see the following message:

> **WARNING: This file may not be modified or edited by the end user.**
> **If you are seeing this message from an editor or a debugger, abandon the session or the dictionary may be destroyed.**

Don't try it!

You make additions to the main dictionary by adding words to your personal dictionaries. You will typically set up these dictionaries to contain more specialized and technical words that only you are likely to use.

You may want to use just a single personal dictionary as a storehouse for words that are not in the main CorrectStar dictionary. You can create and enlarge this dictionary automatically as you do your spelling checks, simply by pressing A whenever CorrectStar flags a word that you don't want to be asked about. You will gradually build up a personal dictionary that includes most of the special words you commonly use.

If you commonly work on technical documents, you may want to create several special dictionaries devoted to the subjects you are writing about. You can only have one dictionary in effect at a time.

Here are some examples of words that might be included in specialized personal dictionaries:

- For computer manuals: debug, ROM
- For engineering reports: cabletray, exceedance
- For legal documents: encumbrancer, subrogation

If you create a personal dictionary for each type of vocabulary, you can use ^OSS to switch between the dictionaries before you run your spelling checks.

If you have a glossary of specialized words that you intend to use in your documents, you might want to create a personal dictionary before you start your spelling check. Personal dictionaries are standard text files, which you can create and edit with WordStar 2000's unformatted format, UNFORM.FRM. Type the words on separate lines with hard carriage returns between them. You can still use the A command to add other words to these dictionaries as you encounter them in your spelling checks.

Bypassing the Spelling Check

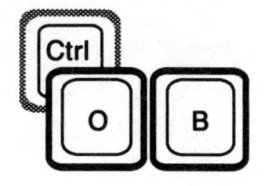

If you have highly technical sections in your documents, you may find it difficult to add all the extra words to your personal dictionaries. In this case, the easiest thing to do is simply to mark the techical blocks of your text so that they will be **bypassed** when you run the spelling check.

You mark the sections to be bypassed while you are editing the document, before you run the spelling check. Press ^**OB** (**Option Bypass**) at the beginning and end of the section that you want CorrectStar to skip. WordStar 2000 will place a command tag at the beginning and end of the marked section. For example, computer manuals are full of phrases such as this:

[BYPASS SPELLING CHECK ON]
   The minimum configuration is an IBM PC with 256K bytes of RAM.
[BYPASS SPELLING CHECK OFF]

Without the bypass commands, running CorrectStar on this kind of text could take a lot more time than you want to spend.

17

MailMerge

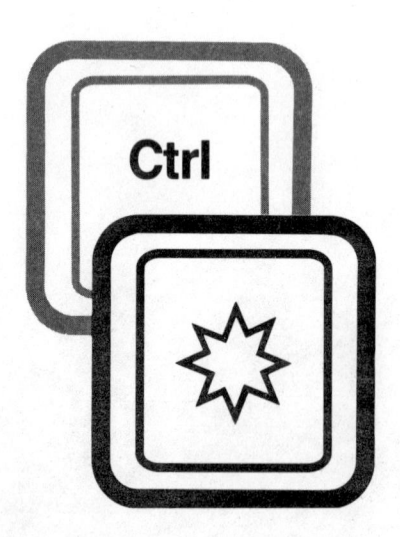

MailMerge is the part of the WordStar 2000 program that lets you print **repetitive documents.** With MailMerge, you can print many copies of a single document, making small changes in each copy as you send it to the printer.

Customized form letters are the most common use for MailMerge. You might have a single letter that you want to send to a variety of people. You want to keep the letter the same, while you vary the name, address, and a few other pieces of information.

This **boilerplate** idea has many other uses as well. You might want to include certain paragraphs in a report when you send it to some people, but not when you send it to others. In a legal contract, you might have special clauses that apply only to certain people. You can even create a short MailMerge document that serves as a template for mailing labels. You could use the same mailing list to print both letters and envelopes.

You can also use MailMerge to print several files in a single operation—as when you have chapters of a book that you want to print all at once. You can have MailMerge number the pages consecutively, and you don't necessarily have to begin each chapter on a new page. You simply include MailMerge commands in your text that explain which files WordStar should put together as it prints out the document.

First, we'll explain how MailMerge works.

Merging Documents   MailMerge takes two documents and **merges** them together as it prints them. You start by creating a single **master document** that stays the same every time you print it. You then create a **data file** that contains the changing information. MailMerge simply combines the two, inserting the changing data from the data file into the blanks in the master document.

The master document contains the basic text of the document and some command tags that tell MailMerge how to do the printing. These command tags might include information about:

- The name of the data file you want to use in printing the document

- The number of times you want to repeat the printing

- The **variables** that you want to have filled in differently each time you print the document

- Conditions that have some part of the document printed only if they are fulfilled

- Other files that you want included in the printed output

Variables are the key to MailMerge. In your master document, you include **variable fields** to tell MailMerge where to insert the information from your data file. For a form letter, your variable fields might be the recipient's first name, last name, address, city, state, and zip code. You don't type any actual names or addresses in the master document. Instead, you type in a name for each variable and enclose each one with ampersands (for example, &address&). The ampersands mark the word as a blank, or variable field, that will be filled in during printing.

After you've finished your boilerplate document, you create the data file with all the names and addresses. Each entry in this data file will have a series of fields that correspond to the variable fields in the master document. Each entry in the data file produces one copy of the document—if you have 100 names and addresses, you will get 100 different letters, all personalized for the particular recipient.

Creating a Form Letter

Suppose, for example, that you are writing cover letters to apply for jobs. You want each one to sound very personal, but you don't want to type the same basic letter over and over. This letter, then, is a good candidate for MailMerge. You'd start something like this:

June 12, 1985

&Mr-Ms& &FirstName& &LastName&
&Title&
&Company&
&Street&
&City&, &State& &Zip&

Dear &Mr-Ms& &LastName&:

   I was delighted to hear of your opening for the position of &JobName&. I have spent many years as a successful &JobName& and I feel I could add greatly to your organization in that capacity.

Yours truly,

Horatio Jobhunter

This form letter has ten different variables, three of which are used twice.

Variable Names

Your selection of variable names is governed by a few rules:

1. The name must not be longer than 31 characters.
2. It must be made up only of letters, numbers, and hyphens, and it must begin with a letter. It cannot contain any other punctuation marks—not even a space.
3. It may not consist of the words *and, or,* or *not.*

MailMerge treats capital and lowercase letters the same: *JobName, JOBNAME,* and *jobname* are all the same variable as far as it's concerned.

The variable name *Mr-Ms* is legal, because it starts with a letter and includes only a hyphen as a special symbol. You couldn't use *Mr/Ms,* though, because it contains a slash. *Mr Ms* is also out—spaces are illegal. And you couldn't use *1stWord,* because it doesn't begin with a letter.

Be careful about what you put between the variable fields in the master document, since anything outside the ampersands will be printed as part of the final document. In the above letter, *&City&* and *&State&* are separated by a comma outside the ampersands because the comma should appear in the final letter; no other fields have any punctuation between them.

MailMerge also lets you include different types of variable names, called **system variables,** that show specific details on your repetitive documents. System variables include the date, time, page, line, and file name. These variable names are preceded by a percent sign rather than enclosed in ampersands. For example, if you include *%date* on your master document, WordStar 2000 will automatically fill in the current date during printing (the date you entered when you booted up the system).

The Data File

The purpose of the data file is to supply **values** to fill into the blanks or variable fields in the master document. (We're using the word *values* in its broadest sense—to WordStar 2000 it means any string of characters.)

The data file will typically consist of a series of **records** that supply values for each of the variables in turn. Each record has a series of fields separated by **commas.**

To create a data file using WordStar 2000, open a file using the UNFORM.FMT (Unformatted Format) command. Type the fields in the order that you want to use them. Don't put any extra characters or spaces in the lines because they slow down the processing and they might end up in your letter by mistake.

If you want to include a comma in a field, enclose the whole field in quotes. The quotes tell MailMerge that the comma is part of the field and not a mark that separates fields (the quotes do not appear in the master document). You also need to put quotes around the field if it contains a quotation mark.

You *must* type each record as a single line (a *line* to WordStar 2000 is any continuous text without a hard carriage return) in the data file, no matter how long it is. A hard carriage return separates each different record in the data file.

You might type a record such as the following:

Ms.,Celeste,Ward,Tour Director,"Sky-High Travel, Inc.",   +
100 Sirius Ave.,Alpha Centauri,CA,94703,astronaut

In practice, this record will appear as one long line in your unformatted data file. For practical reasons, we have to break these long lines in this book, so we'll use a + sign at the right to mark the continuation. Don't type these plus signs.

If you were to use this record with the master document for the sample form letter, each field's value would be inserted in place of the appropriate variable name, like this:

June 12, 1985

Ms. Celeste Ward
Tour Director
Sky-High Travel, Inc.
100 Sirius Ave.
Alpha Centauri, CA 94703

Dear Ms. Ward:

I was delighted to hear of your opening for the position of astronaut. I have spent many years as a successful astronaut and I feel I could add greatly to your organization in that capacity.

Yours truly,

Horatio Jobhunter

Simply by adding other records to the data file, you could apply for other jobs at other companies.

If you want to leave a field blank in the data file, just type two commas in a row. That field will be included in the text as a **null string,** which contains no characters, not even a space. However, if, for example, you left out Ms. Ward's title in the data file, you would get a blank line between her name and her company because the variable field &Title& in the master document appears on a line of its own. Later in this chapter, we will describe a way to avoid this added blank by using conditional commands.

If you plan to use MailMerge often, you might want to use the MailList utility, one of the advanced features included in WordStar 2000+. MailList automatically creates a data file in the form that MailMerge can read.

Creating a Master Document

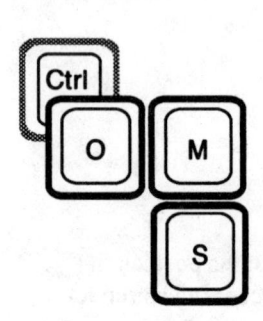

So far, we haven't filled in our master document with any of the commands that tell MailMerge how to complete its task. All MailMerge commands begin with ^**OM (Option MailMerge)**. A special sequence of ^OM commands is required, so let's take them in order.

The first thing you need to do is **select** the data file that you want to use in filling out the master document. You do this by going to the beginning of your master document and pressing ^**OMS (Option MailMerge Select)**. WordStar will ask you:

Data file to use?

You type the name of the file, such as JOBS.LST, and press Return. WordStar will insert a command tag at the place where you are in the file—you may need to type ^OD (Option Display) to see the tag:

[SELECT DATA FILE JOBS.LST]

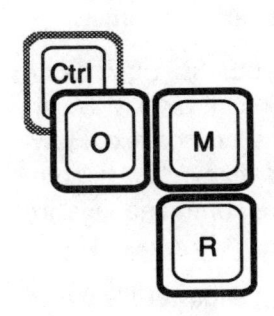

You can use any valid file name for your data file. If you don't name a disk drive, MailMerge assumes the file is on your current logged disk. If you name another drive before the file name, MailMerge will look for the data file on that disk.

The second step is to specify the number of times you want to **repeat** the printing. Press ^**OMR** (**Option MailMerge Repeat**). WordStar 2000 will respond:

Repeat how many times? (Return for end of data)

In most cases, you simply want to have MailMerge keep repeating until it reaches the last record in the data file, so you should just press Return in response to this question. WordStar 2000 will put the following command tag into your document:

[REPEAT UNTIL END OF DATA]

If you do want to limit the number of times the document will be printed, type the number before you press Return.

The third step in creating your master document is to tell MailMerge which variables you are going to **load** in. For this, you use the command ^**OML** (**Option MailMerge Load**).

In the example above, you enclosed ten different variables in ampersands. All ten of these must be read in so that they can be inserted in the appropriate place in the text. The ^OML command tells MailMerge which variables correspond to which fields in the data file.

The ^OML command is tied directly to the data file. You must arrange the variable names in the master document in exactly the same order as they appear in each record of the data file. Each variable name then takes on the value of the corresponding spot in the data record —the whole string of letters between two commas.

When you press ^OML, you get the message:

Variables to be loaded? (separate with commas)

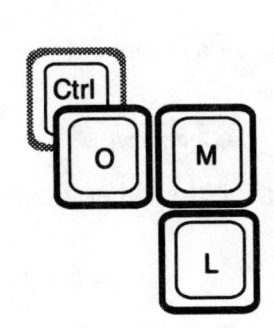

As the message says, you separate all your variable names with commas, just like the fields in the data file. But, in your answer, don't type the ampersands as a part of the variable names.

You are limited to 64 characters in your list of variable names—that's the most that WordStar 2000 can display as part of the [LOAD DATA] command tag it inserts into the text. However, you can get around this by using as many ^OML commands as you need; variables in successive command tags are treated as if they were continuations of the first list.

For an example, let's go back to the sample master file we've been using. The list of ten variables is too long to fit on a single line, so divide it into two lines. Type the first five as your response to your first ^OML command:

   Mr-Ms,FirstName,LastName,Title,Company

When you press Return, WordStar 2000 shows a command tag for the variables:

   [LOAD DATA Mr-Ms,FirstName,LastName,Title,Company]

Then give another ^OML command for the other five variables:

   Street,City,State,Zip,JobName

When you're done, you should have a total of four command tags at the top of your master document:

   [SELECT DATA FILE JOBS.LST]
   [REPEAT UNTIL END OF DATA]
   [LOAD DATA Mr-Ms,FirstName,LastName,Title,Company]
   [LOAD DATA Street,City,State,Zip,JobName]

The variables in the [LOAD DATA] command tags do not have to be in the same order as they appear in the text; they just have to match the order in the data file you are using. You can even include some variables that are never used in the text (as long as they correspond to data fields that also won't be used). Many people start their data records with a dummy record number field such as RecNum, which simply numbers the entries in the data file. For example:

[LOAD DATA RecNum,Mr-Ms,FirstName,LastName,Title,Company]
[LOAD DATA Street,City,State,Zip,JobName]

would be quite all right, as long as you included an extra field at the beginning of every line in your data file:

1,Ms.,Celeste,Ward,Tour Director,"Sky-High Travel, Inc.",   +
100 Sirius Ave.,Alpha Centauri,CA,94703,astronaut

Think of these three MailMerge commands as a unit: ^OMS to select a data file, ^OMR to tell how many times to repeat the printing, and ^OML to specify the variables that you're going to use from the data file. Place all these commands at the beginning of your master document, before any text that uses variables. Then, type the main body of your master text, including any variables that you want to fill in from your data file.

Ending a Master Document

At the end of your master document, you add a few more commands to tell MailMerge how to set up the document pages and print more copies.

Page Numbers

Page numbers are the first concern. If you're writing a form letter, you will probably not want page numbers at all. In that case, you should create your master document with a format such as JUSTIFY.FRM that does not produce page numbers or revise the format to eliminate them (see Chapter 12).

If you do want page numbers, you'll probably want them to be the same for all copies of the document. If you don't do anything special, MailMerge will add one to the page number on each successive copy. To avoid this, use ^OA (Option Assign) to set the page number back to 1 (see Chapter 11). This places a command tag:

[PAGE NUMBER 1]

to show that MailMerge will reset the page number each time it prints that page of the document.

Page Breaks

You usually will want to start each copy on a new page. To do this, use ^OP (Option Page Break) command (see Chapter 11). The page break will be marked with the following tag:

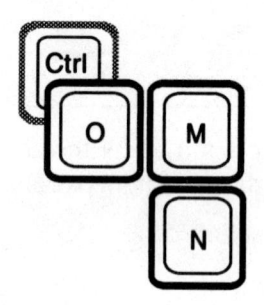

[PAGE]-------------------------P

Remember that this starts a new page for the next copy, rather than for the remainder of the existing document.

The final step is to give a command that sends MailMerge back to start the **next** copy of the master document. The command for this is ^OMN (**Option MailMerge Next**), and it places the following tag in your document:

[NEXT COPY]

This command simply tells MailMerge that this is the place where you want it to go back and begin the process all over. MailMerge uses the next record in the data file to fill in the blanks in the next copy of the master document.

The entire block of text, including command tags, between your ^OMR and ^OMN commands is repeated over and over. Any line before [REPEAT] or after [NEXT COPY] would be printed only once.

Printing Out

You print a MailMerge file (the master document) just like any other WordStar 2000 document: either press P (Print) from the Opening menu or ^QP (Quit and Print) from within your master document.

When you give the print command, you get the same Decisions screen as the one that appears for regular printing:

Begin printing on what page?	1
Stop printing after what page? (L for LAST)	L
Print how many copies?	1
Pause between pages for paper change? (Y/N)	N
Obey page formatting commands? (Y/N)	Y
Print and continue working? (Y/N)	N
Send document to Printer or Disk file? (P/D)	P

You can accept the default answers or choose other answers, just as you do for normal printing. Only two questions are different for MailMerge:

- **Print how many copies?** refers to the number of copies of each variation printed from the master document. If you have ten names and addresses in your data file and a one-page document, a single copy will yield ten pages of output—one for each record in the data file. If you ask for ten copies, you will get ten copies for each record, or a hundred pages in all. You will usually want only one copy for each record in the data file.

- You must answer N (no) to the question **Print and continue working?** because you cannot continue editing while you are printing out a file that contains MailMerge commands.

Messages

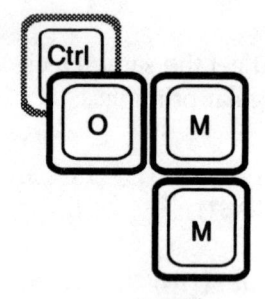

As it begins printing, WordStar 2000 clears the screen so that it can display messages about how it is printing the file. For the moment, you can ignore most of what you see on this screen.

If you want, however, you can place a command tag inside your master file that displays a message on screen at the time you print the file. Press ^OMM (**Option MailMerge Message**) at the place where you want the message to be printed. WordStar 2000 responds:

Message to be displayed? (maximum 79 characters)

Type your message and press Return. The command tag appears at the appropriate place in your text:

[MESSAGE This is the message you just typed**]**

When you print the document, MailMerge displays this message every time it encounters the tag. If you place the message tag in the repeated section of the document, the message will be displayed on screen for each copy of the document.

You can include variable names in your messages:

[MESSAGE &Company& had better give me a job!]

produces the message:

Sky-High Travel had better give me a job!

when you print its letter.

Note that you can also use ^OU (Option Unprinted comment) to insert comments in the editing text that will not appear when the file is printed (see Chapter 11).

When it has finished printing, MailMerge announces itself with a final message:

Please review the messages and press any key to continue.

MailMerge 181

Samples   Let's see how this all fits together. Here is a full master document, its associated data file, and the two pages of output it produces (a third sample—for applying for the job of astronaut—appears earlier in this chapter).

Master Document   The file name of the sample master document is COVER.LTR.

[SELECT DATA FILE JOBS.LST]
[REPEAT UNTIL END OF DATA]
[LOAD DATA RecNum,Mr-Ms,FirstName,LastName,Title,Company]
[LOAD DATA Street,City,State,Zip,JobName]

                    June 12, 1985

&Mr-Ms& &FirstName& &LastName&
&Title&
&Company&
&Street&
&City&, &State& &Zip&

Dear &Mr-Ms& &LastName&:

 I was delighted to hear of your opening for the position of &JobName&. I have spent many years as a successful &JobName& and I feel I could add greatly to your organization
in that capacity.

Yours truly,

Horatio Jobhunter
[PAGE] –P
[NEXT COPY]

Data File   The file name of the sample data file is JOBS.LST. Each record occupies only one line in the actual file.

  2,Mr.,Augustus,Barnacle,Bureaucrat Supreme,Circumlocution +
  Office,1 Government Way,Washington,DC,20001,paper pusher

3,Mr.,Joachim of,Fiore,Chief Visionary,Millennium Books,   +
1260 Eschaton Parkway,World's End,CA,94117,prophet

Output   The sample output is produced by printing the COVER.LTR file.

June 12, 1985

Mr. Augustus Barnacle
Bureaucrat Supreme
Circumlocution Office
1 Government Way
Washington, DC 20001

Dear Mr. Barnacle:

  I was delighted to hear of your opening for the position of paper pusher. I have spent many years as a successful paper pusher and I feel I could add greatly to your organization in that capacity.

Yours truly,

Horatio Jobhunter

* * * * * * * *

June 12, 1985

Mr. Joachim of Fiore
Chief Visionary
Millennium Books
1260 Eschaton Parkway
World's End, CA 94117

Dear Mr. Fiore:

  I was delighted to hear of your opening for the position of prophet. I have spent many years as a successful prophet and I feel I could add greatly to your organization in that capacity.

Yours truly,

Horatio Jobhunter

Asking for Values

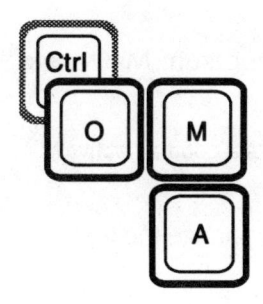

MailMerge gives you a way to enter information directly from the keyboard rather than through a data file. This might be useful in cases where you have only a few words to change in your document and have no need to store the alternatives for the future. You could also use this feature for changing a minor word in a form letter at the time you print it out.

To have MailMerge **ask** for values, use ^**OMA** (**Option MailMerge Ask**). MailMerge prompts you with three questions. First, it asks:

> Variable name to ask for?

If you wanted to be able to supply an adjective other than *delighted* in the first sentence of the sample cover letter, you might type:

> Adjective

MailMerge then asks you:

> Question to display when asking?

You should type a suitable **prompt** to remind yourself what you need to type:

> What's a good adjective?

You don't have to supply a prompt. If you just press Return, MailMerge will merely prompt you with the variable name.

Finally, MailMerge asks you to type the maximum number of characters it should accept as that field:

> Maximum characters in response? 10

The number 10 appears here as the default—the number MailMerge will use if you just press Return. If you type another number, it will replace the 10. You can use any number from 1 to 40.

The reason for this final question is to allow for **data checking.** If you want the variable to represent a state's abbreviation, for instance, you might want to limit the responses to two characters. That way, if you make a mistake and type too many letters, MailMerge can detect the error and make you type the word again.

When you finish answering this final question, MailMerge creates a new command tag:

> [ASK FOR Adjective WITH PROMPT What's a good adjective? +
> MAXIMUM LENGTH 10]

Within your master file, you'll also want to change the text so it uses this new variable:

> I was &Adjective& to hear of your opening for the position of &JobName&. I have spent many years as a successful &JobName& and I feel I could add greatly to your organization in that capacity.

When you print this file, MailMerge will stop before it prints each copy of the letter, displaying the prompt you suggested:

> What's a good adjective?

You then type whatever word you think is most likely to impress your boss-to-be: *happy, thrilled,* or some other adjective. MailMerge inserts the adjective into the appropriate place:

> I was thrilled to hear of your opening for the position of . . .

You can ask for as many variables as you want. In some cases, you may want to use ^OMA for all your variables, doing away with the data file completely.

In general, you will want to place your [ASK FOR] command tag between the [REPEAT] and [NEXT COPY] tags, so that MailMerge asks for the information each time it prints a copy. If you put the [ASK FOR] tag before [REPEAT], you will be asked only once for the information, and MailMerge will use that one response for all copies of the file.

If you decide to use [ASK FOR] tags instead of a data file, you must supply a number in response to the ^OMR question:

Repeat how many times?

You cannot use [REPEAT UNTIL END OF DATA] without a data file. If you don't know how many repetitions you are going to need, give some huge number like 1729. Then, after you've printed your last copy, press the Esc key to stop the endless printing loop.

Conditional Expressions

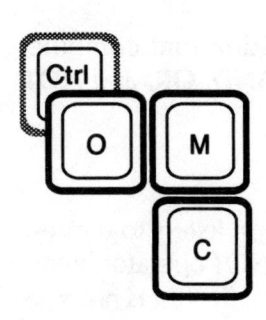

There are many times when you want to include a piece of text only when a certain **condition** is fulfilled. You might, for example, want to add a special paragraph to all the cover letters you send for a particular job title.

The ^**OMC** (**Option MailMerge Condition**) command lets you mark a part of your master document to be printed only in some cases. When you give this command, WordStar 2000 asks you:

Condition to be evaluated? (maximum 64 characters)

You type the test that you want MailMerge to perform— a **relation** between a variable and a value it might hold. For example:

JobName = "President"

marks a block to be printed only in letters that you send to companies looking for a new president. Note that you don't put ampersands around the variable, but you do include quotes around the value.

You can use any of six relational expressions to compare a variable to the values it must satisfy:

=	equal to
< >	not equal to
<	less than
< =	less than or equal to
>	greater than
> =	greater than or equal to

If you're wondering how one piece of text can be *greater than* another, here's the answer: MailMerge follows the standard computer convention that a word is *less than* another if it precedes it in alphabetical order. So:

JobName < = "G"

would be true for *Accountant, Bureaucrat,* and *Garbage Collector,* but not for *Handyman.*

You can also create a **complex condition** that combines several different tests with the **operators AND, OR,** and **NOT.** The condition:

City = "Philadelphia" OR State = "NJ"

would print the marked block of text only in letters to the residents of Philadelphia and New Jersey. The NOT operator before a test tells MailMerge to print the text only if the test is not true. You can use NOT either by itself:

NOT JobName = "Salesman"

or as a shorthand for *and not:*

State = "CA" NOT City = "Los Angeles"

You can combine as many tests as you want into a complex condition. To prevent confusion, use parentheses to group the pair of operations you want to perform first:

City = "Berkeley" OR (Zip >"94100" AND Zip<"94200")

would include the marked section in letters to Berkeley or to any address with a zip code between 94100 and 94200.

When you press return to finish typing your condition, WordStar 2000 places a command tag in your master document:

[CONDITION JobName = "President"]

This tag marks the beginning of the conditional block. To finish marking the block, move the cursor to the end of the section, and press ^OME (**Option MailMerge End Condition**). WordStar 2000 will insert another command tag:

[END CONDITION]

to mark the end of the block. Every [CONDITION] tag must be balanced with an [END CONDITION] tag.

MailMerge also allows an **otherwise** block that is executed only when the condition is false. Usually, you will use this only when you have an *either-or* condition, in which you want to include one thing if the condition is true and another thing if it is not.

To use the otherwise feature, press ^OMO (**Option MailMerge Otherwise**) somewhere between the [CONDITION] and [END CONDITION] tags. Another command tag will appear, splitting the conditional block into two parts, for example:

[CONDITION JobName = "President"]
   I am applying for this position because I like to
lead people.
[OTHERWISE]
   I am applying for this position because I like to
follow other people's leadership.
[END CONDITION]

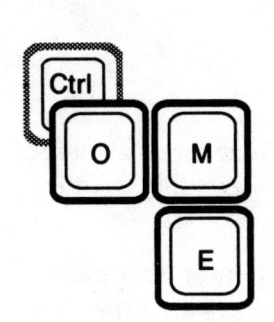

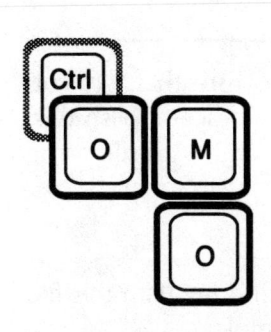

Only one of these sentences will be printed in any particular letter.

You can use conditional blocks for many purposes. You can use a condition to eliminate the blank space that might appear if you are missing a piece of information from your data file. For example, you could use the following condition in the letter's address:

[CONDITION Title<>""]
&Title&
[END CONDITION]

That way, if the Title field is empty in the data file, MailMerge would simply omit the line for the addressee's title from the document.

If you enclose the entire repeating portion of your master document in a conditional block, you will get copies of the letter only for those records that satisfy your condition.

Merging Whole Files

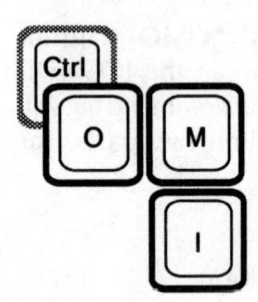

MailMerge has one other important feature that lets you **insert** entire files into another document. To accomplish this, press **^OMI** (**Option MailMerge Insert**) and give the file name when the program asks:

Document to be inserted?

As usual, WordStar 2000 inserts a command tag with this file name into your master document, for example:

[INSERT DOCUMENT CHAIN.DOC]

When WordStar 2000 prints the document, it simply inserts the other file at that point as if it were part of the same text.

This insertion feature is handy for patching standard paragraphs into other documents. You might, for example, work for a company that requires a confidentiality statement at the top of every document. Just type the statement into a file, then put an insertion tag at the beginning of each document you write.

Command Files

There is no reason why your master document needs to have any text at all. It could easily be just a series of MailMerge commands that call up other files and link them together. Such a file is called a **command file.**

The most common use for command files is **chain printing,** in which you print a series of separate documents. To print the first three chapters of a book, you could create a command file such as this:

[INSERT DOCUMENT CHAPTER1]
[INSERT DOCUMENT CHAPTER2]
[INSERT DOCUMENT CHAPTER3]

Then press ^QP (Quit and Print) to print this master file. The three chapters will come out of the printer, with page numbers running consecutively from page 1 through the end of Chapter 3.

With the command file shown, the chapters will be printed without starting each file on a new page. If you want page breaks, add them to the command file with ^OP commands.

Mailing Labels

You can also create a MailMerge command file to print mailing labels. The following file would work for narrow strips of labels that have only one label on each line:

[SELECT DATA FILE ADDRESS.LST]
[REPEAT UNTIL END OF DATA]

[LOAD DATA Name,Company,Street,City,State,Zip]

&Name&
&Company&
&Street&
&City&, &State& &Zip&

[NEXT COPY]

Be sure to type the blank lines where they are indicated here: standard mailing labels are exactly the length of six lines on a printer.

You must create this file with a special format that does not add blank lines at the top and bottom of each page, or WordStar 2000 will add a series of blank lines on labels each time it gets to a place it thinks a page should end. To avoid this, set the top and bottom margins to zero. (See Chapter 12 for information on creating formats.)

If you have the MailList advanced feature of WordStar 2000+, you can use it to print mailing labels more easily.

Alternating Letters and Envelopes

You can use one final MailMerge trick to print letters and envelopes at the same time. The following command file asks you to alternate between sheets of paper and envelopes:

[SELECT DATA FILE ADDRESS.LST]
[REPEAT UNTIL END OF DATA]
[LOAD DATA FirstName,LastName,Street,City,State,Zip]
[MESSAGE Insert a piece of paper]
[PAUSE]

July 26, 1985

&FirstName& &LastName&
&Street&
&City&, &State& &Zip&

Dear &FirstName&,

   I know this is the first letter I've written you in seventeen years, but I've been thinking of you constantly . . .

Sincerely,

Errant Letterwriter
[PAGE]-------------------------P
[MESSAGE Insert an envelope]
[PAUSE]
                    &FirstName& &LastName&
                    &Street&
                    &City&, &State& &Zip&

[PAGE]-------------------------P

[NEXT COPY]

   Use ^PP (Print Pause) to insert the [PAUSE] command tags. These tell MailMerge to stop the printer and give you a chance to put in a piece of letterhead or an envelope. The [MESSAGE] commands, which you insert with ^OMM, remind you which type of stationery you need to insert.

A

Summary of WordStar 2000 Commands

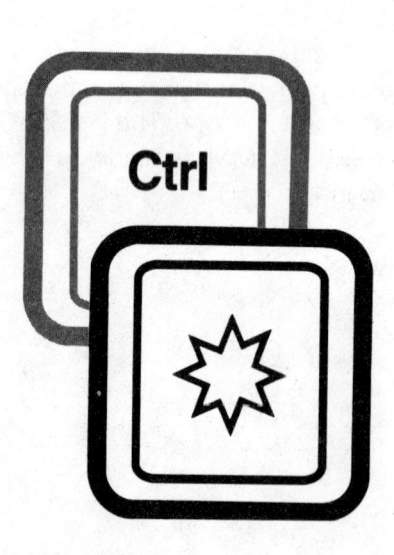

All the commands in this appendix are accessed from the Editing menu unless otherwise stated. You can use capital or lowercase letters to type any of the commands. For those commands with default settings, the default is shown in capital letters:

(ON/off) means that ON is the default setting for this command

(on/OFF) means that OFF is the default setting for this command

The pointing hand shows function-key alternatives for giving each command.

This summary is organized as follows:

Moving the Cursor	194
Scrolling the Screen	200
Scrolling Directories	
Viewing Menus	202
Removing Text	203
Restoring Deleted Text	
Moving Text	
Saving Files	206
Abandoning File Changes	
Getting Help	207
Working with Blocks	208
Moving the Cursor to a Block	
Locating Text	211
Cursor Markers	
Replacing Text	213
Printing	214
Print Enhancements	
Printing Features	
Immediate Printing	

Formatting Your Text	218
Resetting Margins	
Setting Tab Stops	
Formatting Options	
Inserting a Blank Line	
File Handling	224
Windows	225
Using Key Glossaries	226
Checking Spelling	228
Using MailMerge	231
Choosing a Name	234
Decisions Screens	236
Accessing Add-on Programs	237
File Conversion	238

Moving the Cursor

You use the cursor to move around in your document. To move to the nearest character, word, or line, you can use either the cursor diamond keys or the arrow keys.

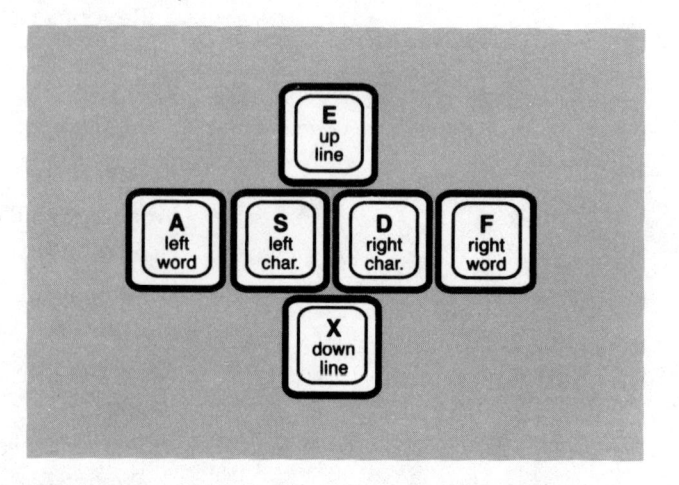

The cursor movement diamond

Appendix A – Summary of WordStar 2000 Commands   195

Arrow keys and cursor diamond keys

These keys . . .

Move the cursor . . .

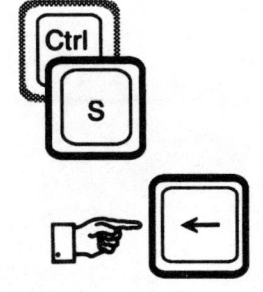

Ctrl S ←

Left one character.

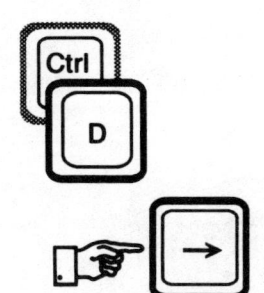

Ctrl D →

Right one character.

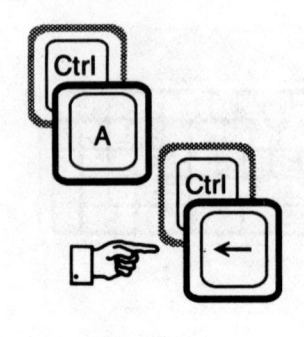

Ctrl-A or **Ctrl-←** Left one word.

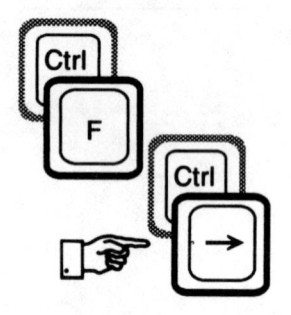

Ctrl-F or **Ctrl-→** Right one word.

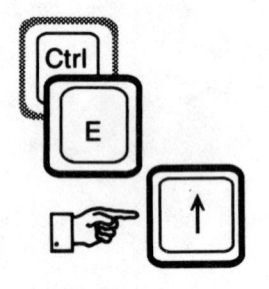

Ctrl-E or **↑** Up one line.

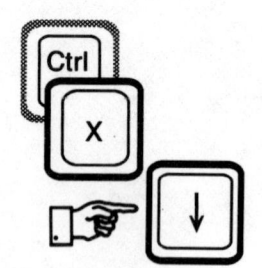

Ctrl-X or **↓** Down one line.

Appendix A — Summary of WordStar 2000 Commands   197

Use the following commands to move the cursor farther:

These commands . . .   *Move the cursor to . . .*

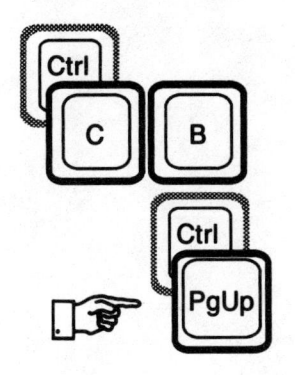

Ctrl C B

Ctrl PgUp   The **B**eginning of the document.

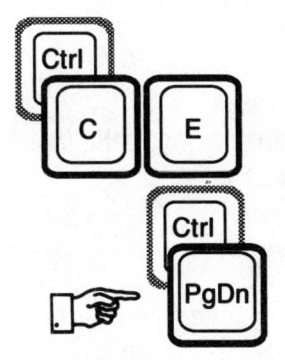

Ctrl C E

Ctrl PgDn   The **E**nd of the document.

Ctrl C L

Ctrl Home   The **L**eft end of the line.

Ctrl + R

The **R**ight end of the line.

Ctrl + End ☞

Ctrl + P

A **P**age number. Give the command, then type the page number you want to move to.

Ctrl + N

A foot**N**ote. Give the command, then type the footnote number you want to move to.

Ctrl + T

A character. Give the command, then type the character you want to move to.
(*Note:* You can also use this command to find a tab character.)

Ctrl + H

Home ☞

The upper-left of the screen.

Appendix A – Summary of WordStar 2000 Commands 199

Ctrl-C X ☞ **End** The lower-left of the screen.

Scrolling the Screen

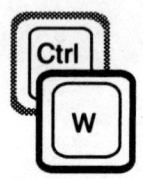

Ctrl + W — To view one more line at the top of the screen.

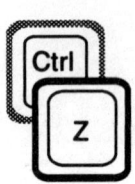

Ctrl + Z — To view one more line at the bottom of the screen.

Ctrl + C ☞ **PgUp** — Scroll the screen **U**p one page.

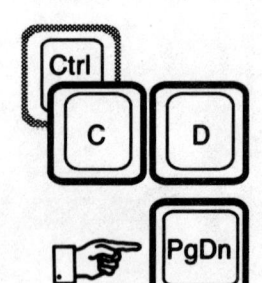

Ctrl + C ☞ **PgDn** — Scroll the screen **D**own one page.

Scrolling Directories

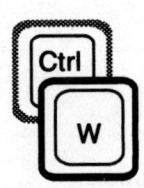

Ctrl W   To view one more row at the top.

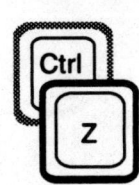

Ctrl Z   To view one more row at the bottom.

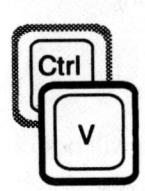

Ctrl V   **V**iew directory (ON/off).

Viewing Menus

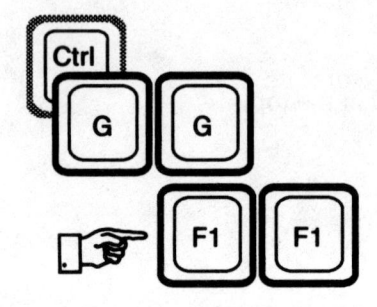

Ctrl-G G F1 F1   Set menu display level. You have three options:

A   Display **A**ll menus. This is the default setting.

S   Display **S**ubmenus only. The Editing menu will not be displayed, allowing you to view more of your document at one time.

N   Display **N**o menus.

Appendix A – Summary of WordStar 2000 Commands   203

Removing Text

These commands all **R**emove (delete) text from your document:

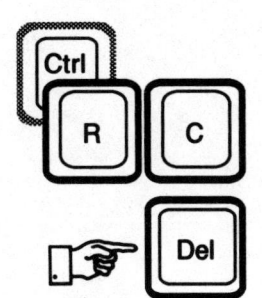

Ctrl + R + C

☞ **Del**

The **C**haracter the cursor is on.

←

The character to the left of the cursor.

Ctrl + R + W

☞ **F6**

The **W**ord the cursor is on.
(*Note:* You can also use this command to delete a block of space. Position the cursor anywhere in the block of space and give the command.)

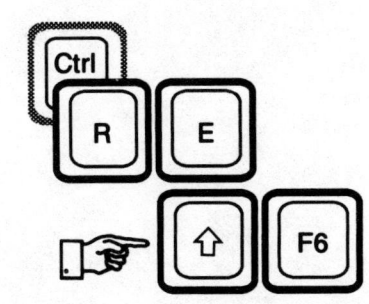

Ctrl + R + E

☞ **⇧ + F6**

The **E**ntire line the cursor is on.

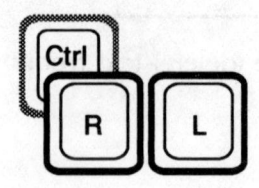

Ctrl + R, L The line to the **L**eft of the cursor.

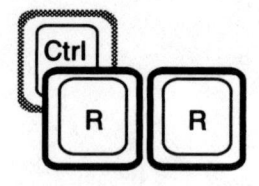

Ctrl + R, R The line to the **R**ight of the cursor.

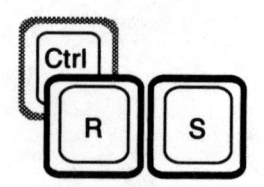

Ctrl + R, S The **S**entence the cursor is on.

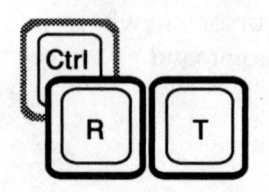

Ctrl + R, T The text up **T**o a character you specify. Give the command, then type the character up to which you want to delete text.

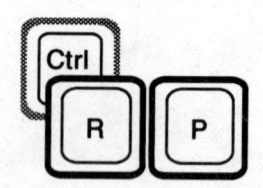

Ctrl + R, P The **P**aragraph the cursor is in.

Restoring Deleted Text

If you change your mind after any Remove command other than ^RC or Backspace, press:

Ctrl U ☞ **F2**

To **U**ndo the last deletion and restore the text.

Moving Text

You can also use the Remove commands to move text. For example, to move a paragraph, give the command:

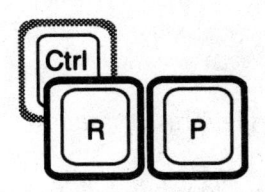

Ctrl R P

To remove the paragraph.

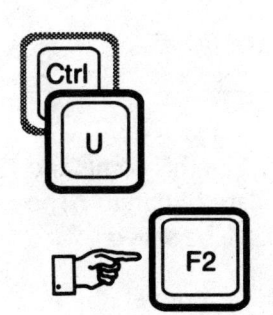

Then move the cursor to the new location for the paragraph and press:

Ctrl U ☞ **F2**

To move the text to its new location.

Saving Files

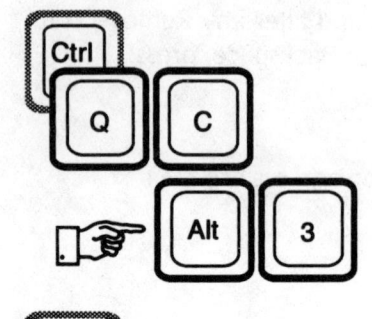

Ctrl Q C / **Alt 3** — Save your changes and then **C**ontinue editing.
(*Note:* Use this command frequently to avoid losing data.)

Ctrl Q S / **Alt 1** — **S**ave your changes and return to the Opening menu.

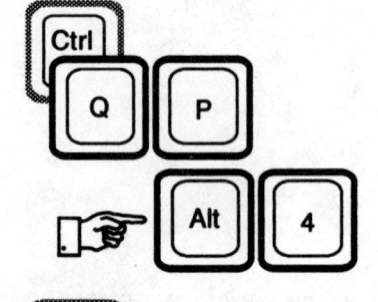

Ctrl Q P / **Alt 4** — Save your changes and **P**rint the file. This command returns you to the Opening menu.
(*Note:* If you are printing another file while editing, this command is used to stop printing.)

Abandoning File Changes

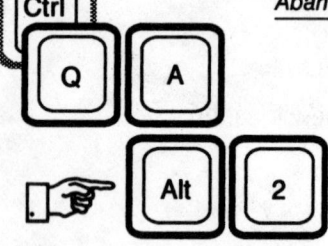

Ctrl Q A / **Alt 2** — **A**bandon latest version of the file. Use this command if you do not want to save your latest changes. The previous version of your file will still be saved.

Getting Help

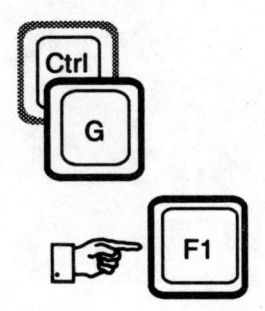

Ctrl G

F1

Get helpful information about the menu or screen you are using.

Esc

When you are done reading the help screens.

Working with Blocks

Once you mark a piece of text as a block, you can move, copy, or delete it easily. You can also sort and perform arithmetic on blocks.

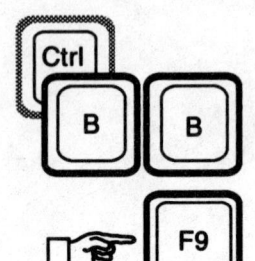

Ctrl B B

Mark the **B**eginning of a block.

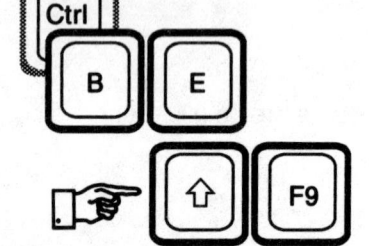

☞ **F9**

Ctrl B E

Mark the **E**nd of a block.

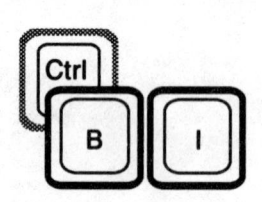

☞ **⇧ F9**

Ctrl B I

Insert a copy of a file into your document. This command treats a whole file as a block. Move the cursor to the place where you want the file inserted, then give the command. Move the highlighting bar to the file you want to insert and press Return.

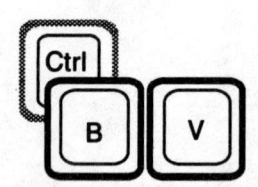

Ctrl B V

Vertical block mode (on/OFF). Use vertical mode to mark a column as a block.
(*Note:* You must mark the end of a column block at a point far enough to the right to include the longest item.)

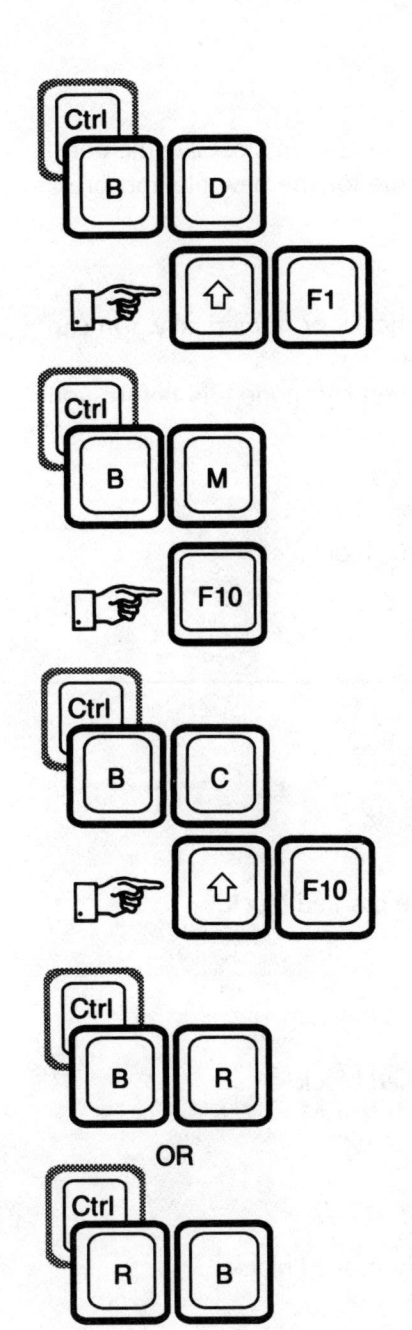

Appendix A – Summary of WordStar 2000 Commands **209**

Ctrl B D

☞ **⇧ F1**

Display marked block (ON/off). Turning display OFF will remove the highlighting from the block. The other block commands work only when ^BD is ON.

You must have a block marked before you give any of the following commands:

Ctrl B M

☞ **F10**

Move a block. Move the cursor to the new position for the block, then give the command.

Ctrl B C

☞ **⇧ F10**

Copy a block. Move the cursor to the place where you would like a copy to appear, then give the command.

Ctrl B R

OR

Ctrl R B

Remove (delete) a block.

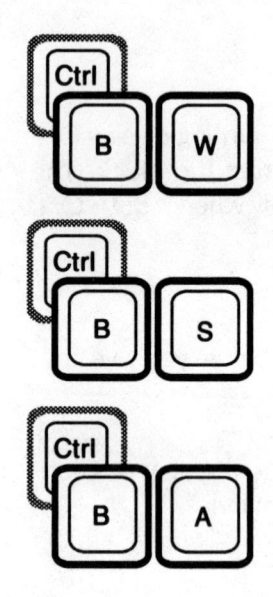

Ctrl B W — Save a copy of a block in its own file. Give the command, then type a name for the new file and press Return.

Ctrl B S — **S**ort a block—alphabetically or numerically. You can sort a maximum of 150 lines.
(*Note:* You must turn vertical mode ON before you give this command.)

Ctrl B A — Perform **A**rithmetic on a block.

Moving the Cursor to a Block

These commands . . .   Move the cursor . . .

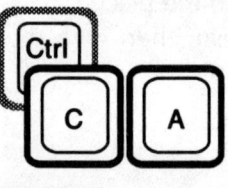

Ctrl C A — To the beginning of the marked block.

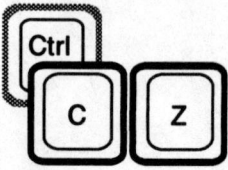

Ctrl C Z — To the end of the marked block.

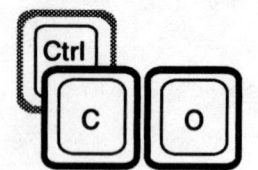

Ctrl C O — To the **O**ld position of a moved block.

Locating Text

Ctrl + L

Locate text. Type the text you want to search for, being sure to include punctuation and spaces if they appear. Press Return. Use the Del or Backspace key to correct typing errors. When your text is correct, press Return.

L

To specify locating without replacing text. Press Return. (For replacing text see below.)

Now you can choose one or more of the following options for the search:

C

To find an exact **C**ase match. Will locate only a piece of text where the case (capital or lowercase) matches exactly the way you typed it.

W

To find **W**hole words only. Choose this option to locate a whole word only, and not places where the word occurs as part of another word.

B

To search **B**ackwards through the file. (If you don't choose this option, the program will always search forward in the file from the cursor position.)

n

(Where n is any number). To search for the nth occurrence of the locate text.

Ctrl + N

When using Locate to search for the next occurrence of your locate text, use:

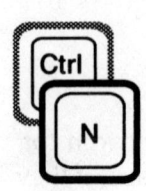

To find the **N**ext occurrence of the text when a search has stopped at the first location.

Note: You can also locate command tags, tab characters, and end-of-paragraph markers.

Cursor Markers

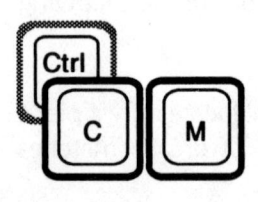

Ctrl + C, M

To **M**ark a place in your document. Give the command then choose a number from 0 through 9.

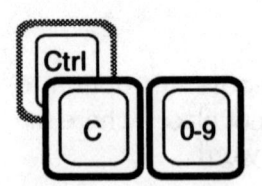

Ctrl + C, 0-9

Move the cursor to a place previously marked with ^CM.

Replacing Text

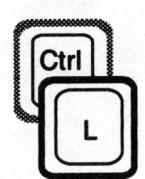

Ctrl + L — **L**ocate and replace text. Type your locate text and press Return.

R — To specify locating *and* **R**eplacing text. Type your replacement text and press Return.

Now you can choose any of the four options for locating text (*n* specifies how many occurrences you wish to replace) plus one or more of these options:

P — **P**reserve case of the replacement text (even if it differs from the case of the located text).

D — **D**on't ask approval. Replaces each occurrence of your locate text automatically (without asking your approval each time).

S — **S**how each replacement on the screen as it is made. (*Note:* This option can only be used together with the D option.)

Printing

[P]

Print a file (from the Opening menu). Move the highlighting bar to the name of the file you want to print and press Return. Answer each question that appears.

[Ctrl]+[Q]

Press Return to accept a default answer or:
To accept all of the remaining default answers.

[P]

If you want to stop printing at any time, press:
Stop printing

[C]

To **C**ontinue

[A]

To **A**bandon the printing attempt.

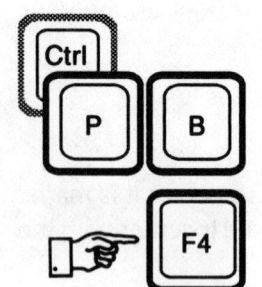

Print Enhancements

[Ctrl]+[P]+[B] ☞ [F4]

While you are editing your document, you can mark parts of it to print in a variety of special ways. The print enhancement commands that follow must be used in pairs, before and after the text to be enhanced:

Boldface (on/OFF).

Ctrl + P + U (or **Ctrl + P + Shift + F4**)

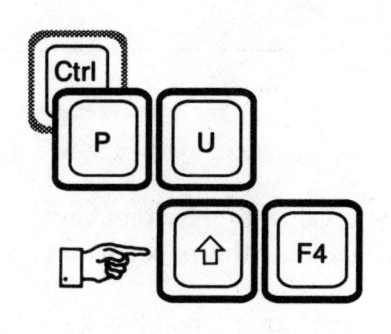

Underline (on/OFF).
(Note: The format you chose for your document determines whether underlining will print between characters.)

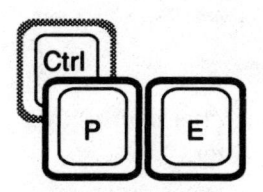

Ctrl + P + E

Emphasis (on/OFF). Emphasized print is darker than regular print but lighter than boldface.

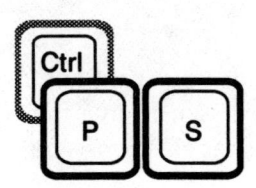

Ctrl + P + S

Strikeout (on/OFF). Text is struck through with hyphens (for parts of legal documents, for example).

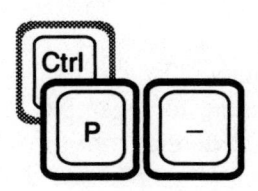

Ctrl + P + −

Subscript (on/OFF).

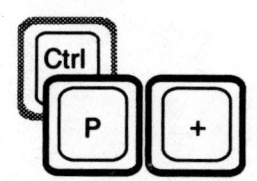

Ctrl + P + +

Superscript (on/OFF).

Printing Features

Ctrl-P N

No new line. The line you flag with this command will overprint the previous line—the paper won't advance.
(*Note:* You can use this command for underlining.)

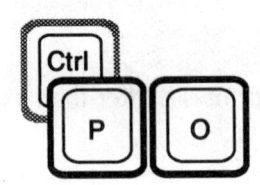

Ctrl-P O

Overstrike. Will print the following character in the same space as the preceding character.

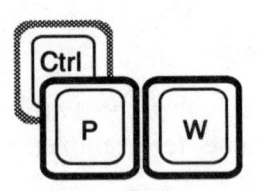

Ctrl-P W

Mark a space between two **W**ords you want kept together when printed. Type one word, give the command (instead of typing a space), then type the second word.

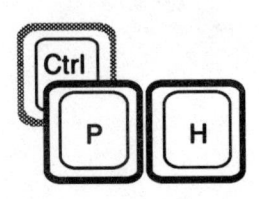

Ctrl-P H

Change **H**eight of lines (line spacing). To alternate between single- and double-spacing, for example, or to choose any line spacing that differs from the format you chose for the document.

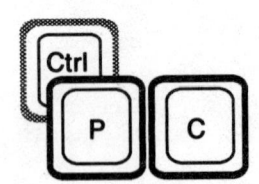

Ctrl-P C

Change **C**olor of print.

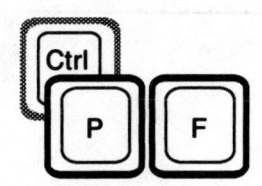

Ctrl P F — Change **F**ont (change typeface or size).

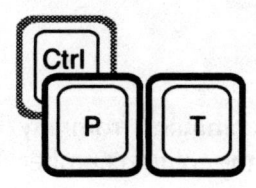

Ctrl P T — Change printer **T**ray. Enables you to change to a different kind of paper if your printer is equipped for this.

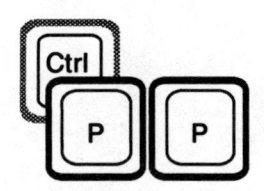

Ctrl P P — **P**ause printing. (To change the daisy wheel, for example.)

Immediate Printing

T — Access **T**ypewriter mode from the Opening menu. Prepare your printer. Each line of text you type will print when you press Return. This enables you to go back and edit each line before printing it.

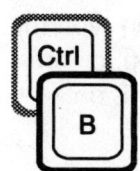

Ctrl B — If your printer allows, this command turns off the print buffer, so that the text you type will print immediately, without waiting for you to press Return.

Formatting Your Text

Resetting Margins

Ctrl-T L ☞ **F7**

Reset the **L**eft margin. Give the command from any position in your document. Type the column number you want and press Return.

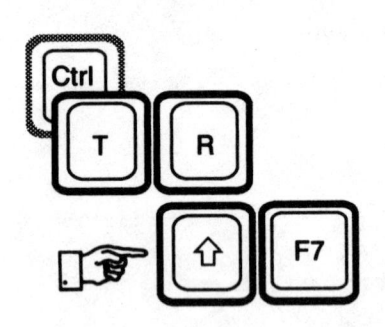

Ctrl-T R ☞ **⇧ F7**

Reset the **R**ight margin (as above).

Setting Tab Stops

Ctrl-T S ☞ **F8**

Set a **T**ab **S**top. Give the command, then type the column number you want for the tab stop, or press Return to choose the column your cursor is on.

Ctrl-T D

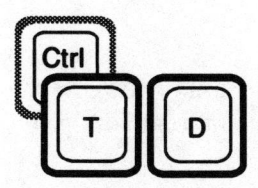

Set a **D**ecimal tab stop (as above). Numbers you subsequently type will align on the decimal points.

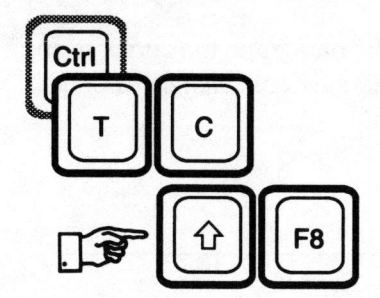

Ctrl-T C ☞ ⇧ F8

Clear one or all tab stops. Give the command, then type the column number of the tab you want to clear; type A to clear **A**ll tab stops; press Return to clear the tab stop at the column your cursor is on.

Ctrl-T I ☞ F5

Indent the left margin one tab stop from the current margin. Position the cursor on the current left margin, then give the command. ^T Tab is a third form of this command.

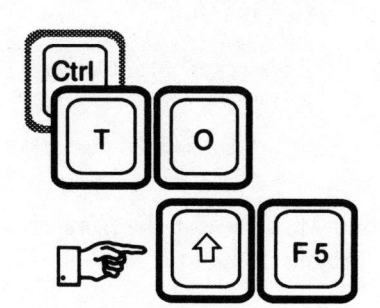

Ctrl-T O ☞ ⇧ F5

Move indented left margin **O**ut one tab stop. Give the command with the cursor at the current left margin if you want to move the text on your current line.

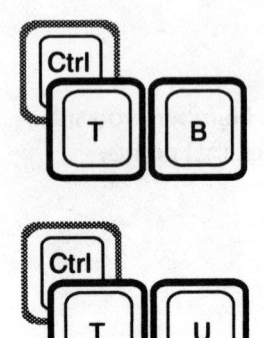

Ctrl + T + B — Indent **B**oth margins one tab stop. Position the cursor at the beginning of the line you want to indent, give the command, and press Return.

Ctrl + T + U — **U**ndo all indentation. The paragraph the cursor is on will reform within the margins, cancelling all indents.

Formatting Options

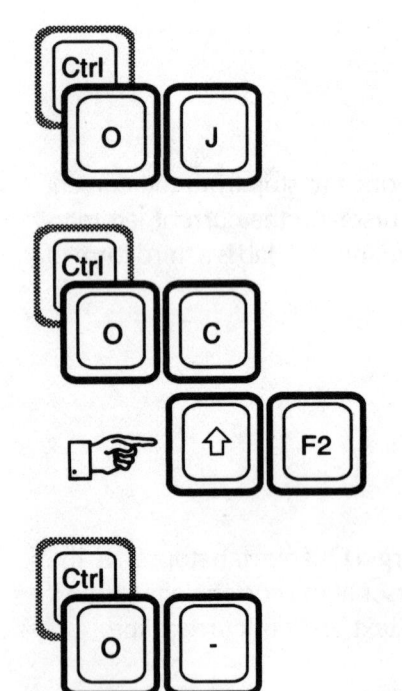

Ctrl + O + J — **J**ustify text (on/off). The default depends on the format you are using. Use this command to alternate between justified and ragged-right text within the same document.

Ctrl + O + C (or ⇧ + F2) — **C**enter text. Give the command with the cursor anywhere on the line to be centered. Give the command again to move the text to the left margin.

Ctrl + O + - — Insert hyphen. The hyphen will appear in the printed document only if the word falls at the end of a line.

Ctrl + O, O ☞ **Ins**

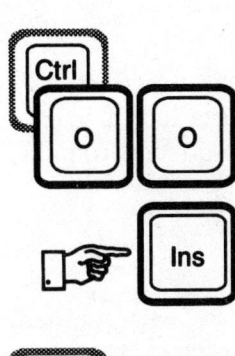

Overtype mode (on/OFF). Text you type with overtype ON will type over and replace existing text.

Ctrl + O, R

Repeat next key. Precedes a command or text that you would like to repeat.
(*Note:* This command is useful with cursor-movement and screen-scrolling commands.)

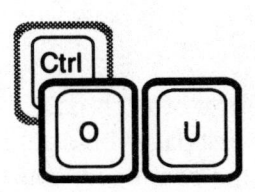

Ctrl + O, U

Unprinted (nonprinting) comment. Give the command, then type your comments between the tags. Your comments will be displayed on the screen any time that document is opened but will not appear in the printed document.

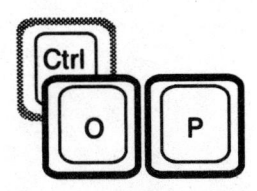

Ctrl + O, P

Force a **P**age break. Move the cursor to where you want the page to break and give the command. The next text you type will be on a new page.

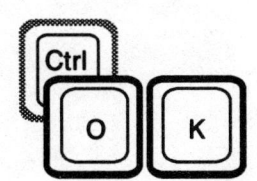

Ctrl + O, K

Keep lines together (do not break the page between these lines). Give the command on the first line of a group you want to print on the same page. Type the number of lines you want to keep together and press Return.

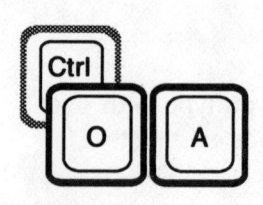

Ctrl O A — **A**ssign a page number to a page. Give the command, type a number for the page and press Return. Subsequent pages will be numbered in sequence from the page number you designate.

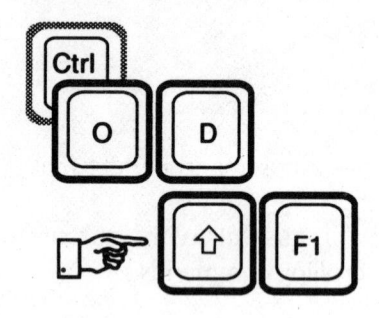

Ctrl O D / ⇧ **F1** — **D**isplay command tags, tab characters, markers, footnotes, and comments (on/OFF).
(*Note:* You cannot delete command tags when the option display is OFF unless they are part of deleted text.)

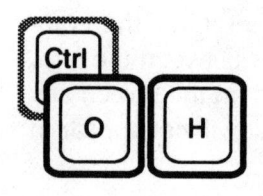

Ctrl O H — Define a **H**eader to print at the top of each page. Move the cursor to the top of the first page you want to print with a header and give the command. You are given these choices:

O — **O**dd pages only

E — **E**ven pages only

B — **B**oth odd and even pages

Appendix A – Summary of WordStar 2000 Commands **223**

Ctrl O F

Type the text you want to appear as a header between the tags. When you are done, move the cursor out of the header.

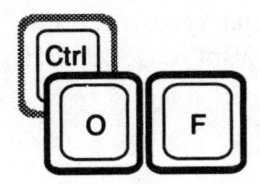

Define a **F**ooter to print at the bottom of each page. The procedure and options are the same as for the Header, above.

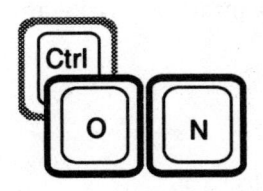

Ctrl O N

Type a foot**N**ote. Move the cursor to the in-text reference, then give the command. Type the footnote between the tags. When you are done, move the cursor out of the footnote. A superscripted number will appear beside the reference when the document is printed.

Inserting a Blank Line

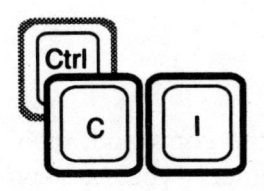

Ctrl C I

Insert a Return. The cursor stays in place while any text to the right of it drops to the next line.

File Handling

Note: File handling commands are all accessed from the Opening menu.

[R] **R**emove a file. Give the command, then move the highlighting bar to the file you want to delete and press Return.

[C] Make a **C**opy of a file. Give the command, then move the highlight to the file you want to copy. Type a new name for the copy unless you want to overwrite an existing file.

[Q] **Q**uit WordStar 2000 and return to DOS.

[D] Change **D**rive or directory. Give the command, then type B: to change the default drive to B, or C: to change the default drive to C.

[M] **M**ove or rename a file. Give the command, then move the highlight to your choice. Type the new drive or the new name for the file and press Return.

Windows

While working in one file, you can display another file on your screen in a second window. You can have a maximum of three windows open at one time.

Ctrl + O W (☞ F3)

Open a **W**indow. Give the command, then move the highlighting bar to the file you want to display (or type a new file name to open a window on a new file) and press Return.

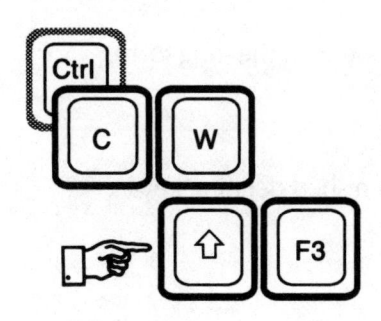

Ctrl + C W (☞ ⇧ F3)

Move the **C**ursor into a **W**indow. Give the command again to move the cursor into the next window (if you have another window open).

Using Key Glossaries

Key glossaries enable you to store a long string of text or commands for incorporating into any open document by typing a shorthand version of it. For example, you might store boilerplate paragraphs as key glossaries.

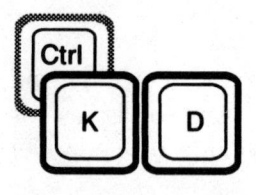

Ctrl K D

Define or edit a glossary entry. Give the command, type the short form and press Return. Type the long form.

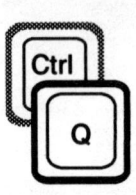

Ctrl Q

Press when you are done with the long form.

Esc

Press when you have finished defining keys.

Y

Choose to save your new or edited key glossary, and then choose a key file to save the entry in.

Y

Type to overwrite an existing key file with your new version. You can add entries to key files up to a maximum of 20 entries per file.

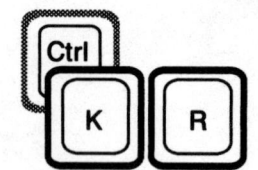

Ctrl K R

Remove (delete) a glossary definition. Move the highlighting bar to the entry you want to delete and press Return.

[Y] Press to *Save the changes* (i.e., to finally delete your chosen entries).

[N] Press to change your mind.

[Esc] Press when you are done deleting entries.

[Ctrl]+[K]+[U] Use a key file. Give the command, then move the highlighting bar to the key file you want to use, or type a new name and press Return.

Checking Spelling

S

To access the Spelling Correction menu (CorrectStar) from the Opening menu.

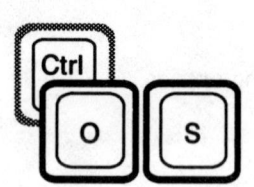

Ctrl O S

To access the Spelling Correction menu (CorrectStar) from the Editing menu.

CorrectStar will check spelling in your document against its own dictionary. You can't add words to its dictionary, but you can create personal dictionaries, and add and delete entries in those. Proper names, technical terms, and legal or medical terms are examples of words you might choose to enter in your personal dictionaries.

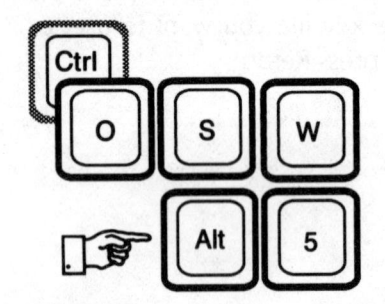

Ctrl O S W
☞ **Alt 5**

Check the spelling of the **W**ord the cursor is on.

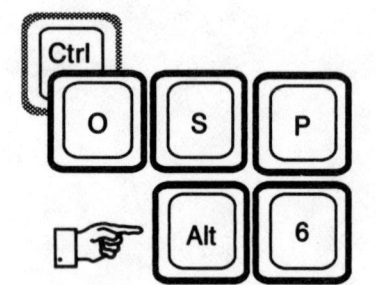

Ctrl O S P
☞ **Alt 6**

Check the spelling in a **P**aragraph. Give the command with your cursor anywhere in the paragraph.

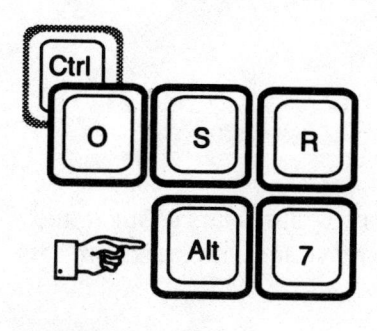

Ctrl + O S R / **Alt 7** Check the spelling in the **R**est of the document, following the cursor position.

Ctrl + O S S **S**elect a new personal dictionary. You can either select an existing dictionary from the directory or create a new one.

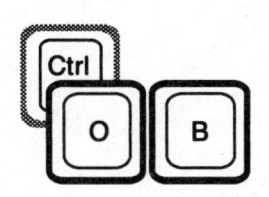

Ctrl + O B **B**ypass spelling correction (on/OFF). Use this command to mark a portion of your text to be bypassed during spelling checks. Give the command again with the cursor where you will want the program to resume checking spelling.

You have these choices to tell CorrectStar what to do with a word the program finds misspelled:

A **A**dd to Personal Dictionary.

↵ Correct as suggested.

C **C**orrect all occurrences. Replace misspelled word with CorrectStar's suggestion globally from the highlighting to the end of the document.

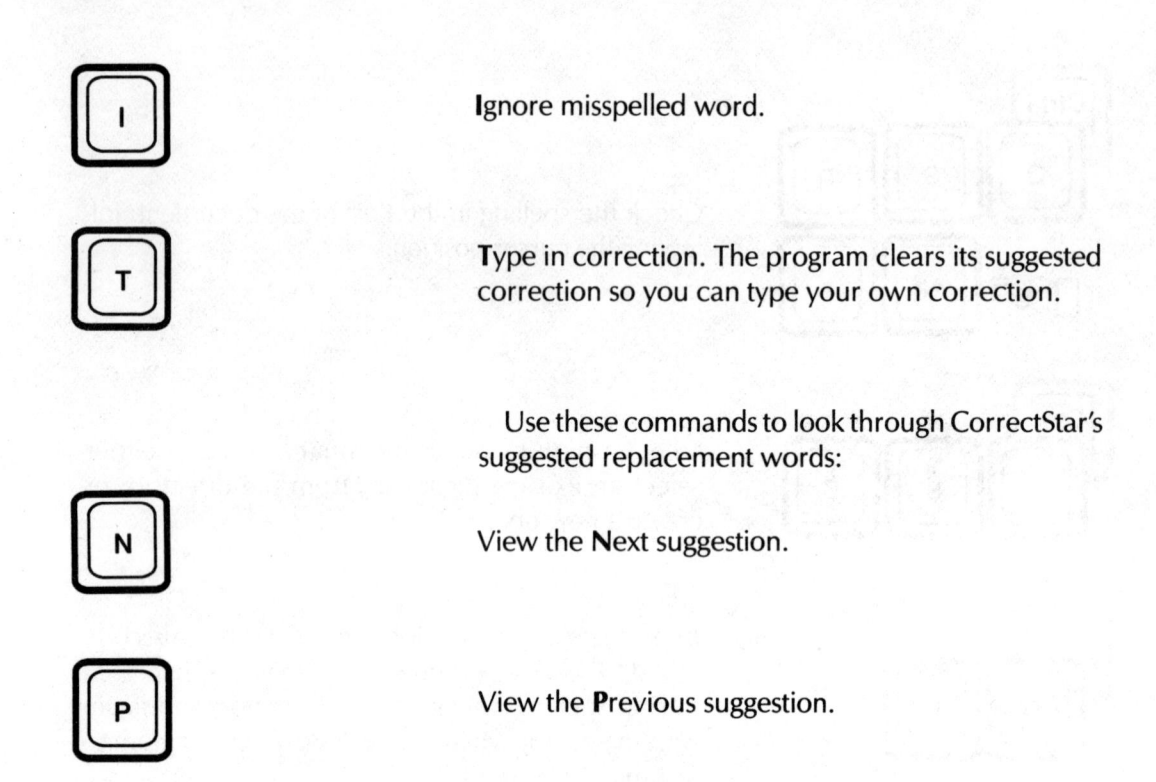

[I] **I**gnore misspelled word.

[T] **T**ype in correction. The program clears its suggested correction so you can type your own correction.

Use these commands to look through CorrectStar's suggested replacement words:

[N] View the **N**ext suggestion.

[P] View the **P**revious suggestion.

Using MailMerge

MailMerge commands allow you to print mailing labels and create form letters using boilerplate paragraphs that you can use over and over in different documents. It takes study and practice to use MailMerge, so read Chapter 17 carefully and use this MailMerge command summary only for quick reference.

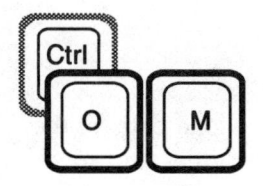

Ctrl + O + M

To access the MailMerge submenu.

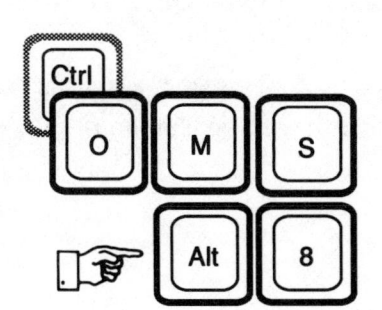

Use the following four commands in this order to print form letters or mailing labels:

Ctrl + O + M + S
☞ **Alt + 8**

Inserts [SELECT DATA FILE] tag.
To use MailMerge, you first name, then supply data in, a data file (as opposed to a document file). This command tells the program which data file to use.

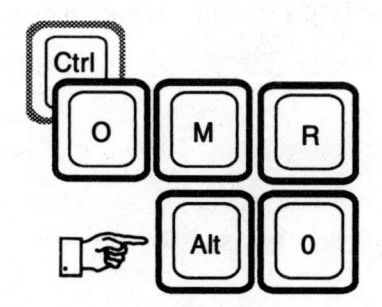

Ctrl + O + M + R
☞ **Alt + 0**

Inserts [REPEAT] tag.
Print all or part of your master document over again. You will usually choose to have the procedure **R**epeat until the end of the data records.

^OML (Ctrl+O, M, L) ☞ Alt+9

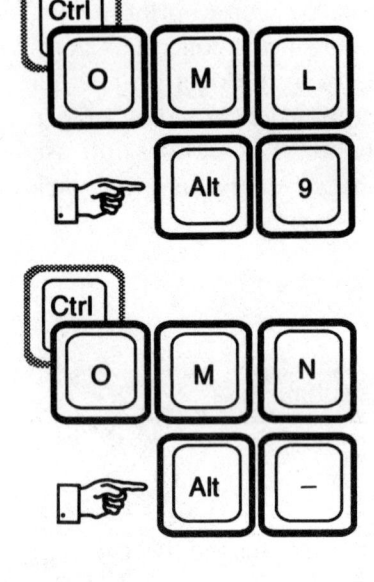

Inserts [LOAD DATA] tag.
This command tells the program which variables correspond to which fields in the data file, and thus which fields to load from the data file into the master document.

^OMN (Ctrl+O, M, N) ☞ Alt+−

Inserts [NEXT COPY] tag.
This command tells the program to load data for the next letter or label however many times you specified with ^OMR.

^OMM (Ctrl+O, M, M)

The following commands are for features you can use with MailMerge:

Display a **M**essage on the screen for the user while printing. The message can have a maximum of 79 characters.

^OMA (Ctrl+O, M, A)

Ask user to enter data. You can specify questions to ask the user (printing will stop until the question is answered, i.e., the data is supplied).

^OMC (Ctrl+O, M, C)

Specify a **C**ondition. You can specify text to be included only for certain records, e.g., those within a zip code range.

^O M O — Otherwise (condition). You can specify text to be included only when the ^OMC condition is not met.

^O M E — End condition. Mark the place in the text to resume printing for all records.

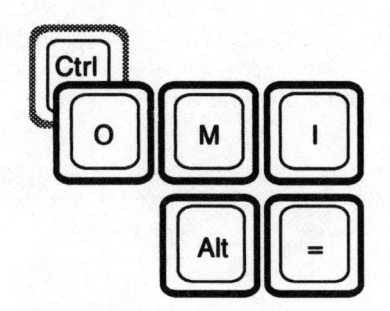

^O M I (Alt =) — Insert an entire document into your master document, or request that another document print immediately following your master document (chain printing).

^O M U — Use specific value for data. Designate a specific value for MailMerge to use for a field (instead of a variable value).

Choosing a Name

↵ — Choose the highlighted name.

Ctrl-T — **T**ransfer the highlighted name to the answer line. Begin typing the file name on the answer line. When the highlighting moves to that file name, give the command.

← — Remove the character to the left of the cursor.

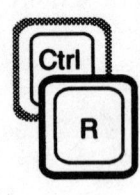

Ctrl-R — **R**emove the answer from the answer line.

These commands . . .   Move the highlighting . . .

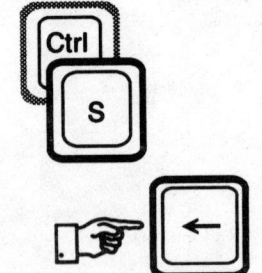

Ctrl-S   ☞ **←**   Left one name.

Ctrl + D → Right one name.

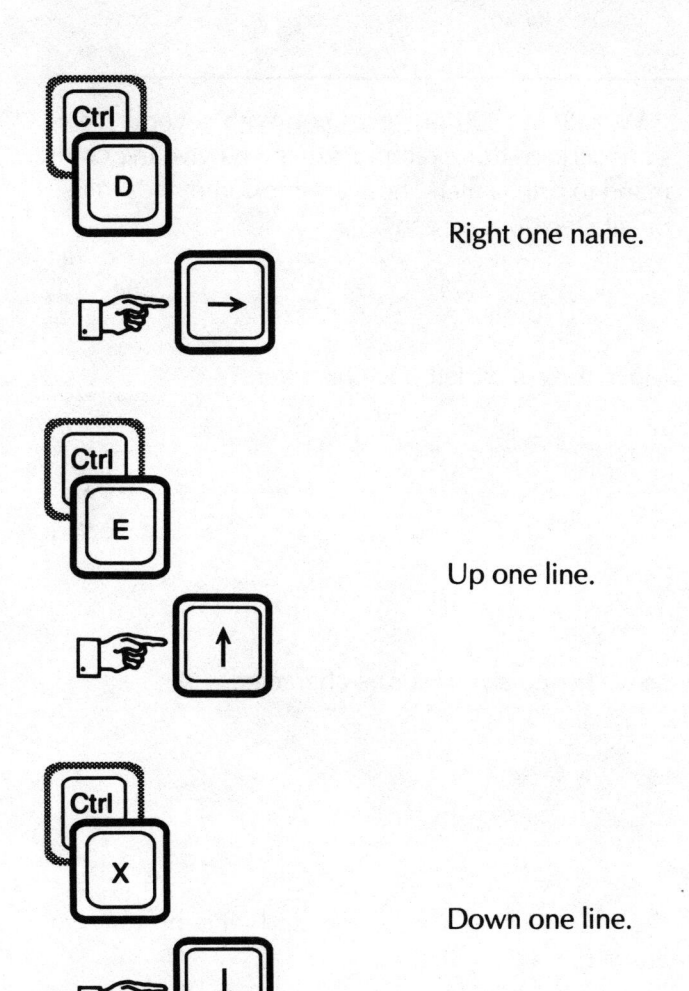

Ctrl + E ↑ Up one line.

Ctrl + X ↓ Down one line.

Decisions Screens

WordStar 2000 presents you with several Decisions screens (for example, when you give the command to print a file). These are the commands to use on all Decisions screens:

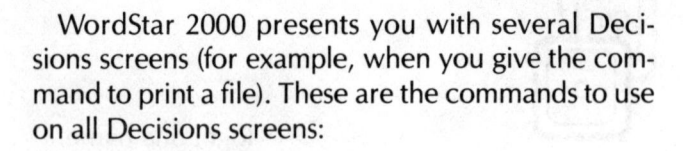

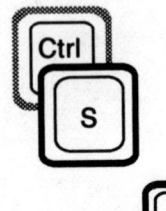

Ctrl S

Move the cursor left one character.

**← **

Ctrl D

Move the cursor right one character.

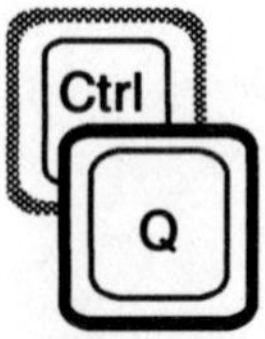

→

Ctrl Q

Quit answering questions and accept current answers.

Del

Remove the character the cursor is on.

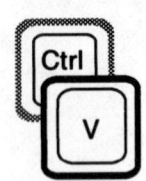

Ctrl V

View all questions and default answers (on/OFF).

Accessing Add-on Programs

Add-on programs do not come with WordStar 2000; they must be purchased separately.

[A] Access TelMerge from the Opening menu. TelMerge enables you to send and receive electronic mail.

[L] Access MailList from the Opening menu. MailList is a data base program for use with MailMerge.

[I] Access StarIndex from the Opening menu. StarIndex is a program that creates indexes and tables of contents from WordStar 2000 files.

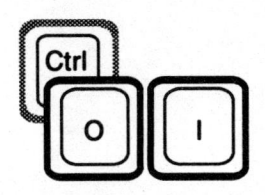

[Ctrl][O][I] Access StarIndex from the Editing menu.

File Conversion

[W] **W**ordStar/WordStar 2000 file conversion. Give this command to use the conversion program (WS-CONVRT.EXE) to convert WordStar files to WordStar 2000 files and vice versa. You can convert only one file at a time. Neither program can read the other's files until they are run through this conversion program.

B

Installing WordStar 2000

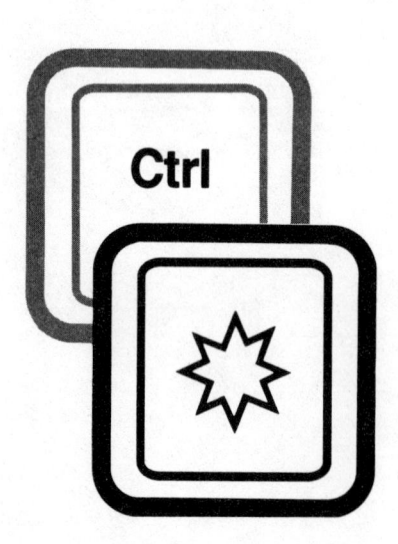

Installation is a necessary evil of programs such as WordStar 2000. It would be nice if MicroPro could just sell you a plain, vanilla program that you could put directly into your system and run. Unfortunately, that isn't possible because such a program could not take advantage of any of the special features you might have attached to your system.

When you install WordStar 2000, you tailor the program to fit your specific system, which may include:

- A special graphics card or color monitor
- A printer with special features
- A hard-disk drive
- A RAM disk

During installation, you can also reprogram some of the preset features of WordStar 2000, such as the start-up settings for command tag and menu displays.

The installation programs take care of most of the work; you just answer questions about the equipment that you have attached to your particular system.

What Are All Those Disks?

Your WordStar 2000 package is imposing at first blush. It contains a minimum of six disks—seven if you've bought WordStar 2000+ with Advanced Features. Let's take an inventory:

1. **The installation disk** contains the installation programs and specialized files that will be automatically transferred to your disks as you install them.

2. **The program disk** contains the WordStar 2000 program and format files.

3. **The dictionary disk** is used by CorrectStar whenever you ask for a spelling check.

4. **Tutor disk A** contains tutorial programs that explain basic WordStar 2000 functions.

5. **Tutor disk B** contains tutorial programs for special functions such as MailMerge and CorrectStar.

6. **The Advanced Features disk,** which comes with WordStar 2000+, contains special programs that work with WordStar 2000: StarIndex, TelMerge, and MailList.

7. **The conversion disk** contains a program for converting files from WordStar 3.3 to WordStar 2000 and back. This disk also contains a text file called README with the latest news on WordStar 2000 and tips for setting it up.

These seven disks don't seem so overwhelming when you realize that you need only the first two to get WordStar 2000 running. The others are tutorials and special programs that you can investigate later.

Copy Those Disks!

The first thing you should do is copy all of the MicroPro disks. This is important because you never want to do any real work with the original disks—one mistake can cost you $500!

To do the copying and the installation, you need to use one other disk: the IBM DOS disk that you got with your computer. You'll need this disk for starting up your system and for running several utility programs.

Follow these steps carefully to duplicate your disks:

1. Buy a full box of 10 blank double-sided, double-density disks. You'll need them all.

2. Put write-protect tabs on all seven of the MicroPro disks so you won't accidentally write over them.

3. Start up your system with the DOS disk (none of the MicroPro disks can start your system).

4. Copy your DOS disk and all seven of the MicroPro disks. To do this, type:

    DISKCOPY A: B:

    with your DOS disk still in the drive. Then, when DOS asks you to insert source and target disks, remove the DOS disk and put the MicroPro disk in drive A: and a blank disk in drive B:. Then press Return again. (There is no danger of erasing the MicroPro disk as long as you have covered the write-protect notch with a tab.) The computer formats the blank disk and copies the program information onto it. When it finishes, it asks if you want to copy another. Type Y to keep copying until you have duplicated all of your disks.

5. Put the MicroPro disks away in a safe place. Use the duplicates from now on for all operations.

A Quick Tour of DOS

You should also copy your DOS disk because you will need it every time you start your system. This copy becomes your **boot disk,** which you'll use for start-up and for special DOS commands.

You can delete most of the files that DOS copies onto this boot disk, but you should keep a few of them:

- The **COMMAND.COM** file contains a program that holds part of IBM's disk operating system. Sometimes when you exit from WordStar 2000, the computer may ask you to reinsert the boot disk so it can read this file back in because the information is necessary for continued work.

- The **FORMAT.COM** file contains a program that lets you format blank disks.
- The **DISKCOPY.COM** file contains a program that lets you duplicate disks to use as backups of your work disks.
- The **CHKDSK.COM** file contains a utility program that verifies a disk and tells you how much space remains on it. This command also tells you how much memory you have free in your system—often a useful thing to know.
- **CONFIG.SYS** is a *configuration file* that specifies default parameters for DOS. If this file is missing, the installation procedure creates it.
- **Hidden files,** which you duplicated when you copied the DOS disk, contain the information DOS needs as it starts up the system. The files are not listed on the disk directory, but they take up roughly 20K of disk space.

You must have the boot disk in the disk drive when you give a DOS command such as **FORMAT, DISKCOPY,** or **CHKDSK,** and when you reboot your system.

You can also use a variety of **resident DOS commands** that are in your system whenever you have loaded DOS. The most important of these have the following functions:

- The **COPY** command transfers files between disks.
- The **RENAME** command changes the names of files.
- The **DIR** command lists the disk directory (names of all files).

Once you've loaded DOS, you can always use these commands (you don't need to keep the boot disk in the system). See your DOS manual for further details.

Basic Installation: Floppy-disk Systems

Now that you've got your boot disk set up, it's time to run the installation procedure. MicroPro has designed a pair of **auto-install** programs that handle most of the details. You just follow the steps as the programs explain them on the screen.

The first phase of the installation involves the installation disk and your boot disk. Place the copy of the installation disk in drive A: and your boot disk in drive B:. Then type:

    ins-1 floppy

Ins-1 is the name of the first half of the WordStar 2000 installation program.

The first phase of the installation is pretty much automatic. The only thing this procedure really does is alter (or create) the CONFIG.SYS file on your boot disk so that certain parameters are set up for WordStar 2000. When the first phase is finished, you can take a look at this file by typing:

    type config.sys

DOS will display the contents of the CONFIG.SYS file, something like this:

    FILES = 20
    BUFFERS = 6

The important line here is the second; if the CONFIG.SYS file has FILES set to less than 20, some WordStar 2000 operations will crash the system. You don't have to do anything beyond creating this file—DOS loads it automatically when it boots the system.

The second phase of the installation is more involved, because that is where you set up your program disk to work on your system. Leave the installation disk in drive A: and put your program disk in drive B:. The program disk is the copy you made of the second MicroPro disk. Don't run the installation program on the original program disk!

To start the second part of the installation, type:

   ins-2 floppy

The computer first asks you:

   On which drive are your WordStar 2000 files?

The answer is presumably *B:*, if you've been following our suggestions. This question does not affect the drive in which you will run the installed program. You can run the installed WordStar 2000 from either drive.

There are three major questions you must answer in the course of the installation. The first is easy enough:

   Do you have a color monitor?

If you answer *Y* for yes, the installation program will set up the WordStar 2000 program so it displays block markers, boldfacing, and underlining in different colors on the screen. (Even if you answer no, you can still use the program on a color monitor, but the block markers, boldfacing, and underlining will not appear in different colors.) If you answer *N* for no, you are asked:

   Does your computer have a special graphics card?

Type *Y* if it does or *N* if it doesn't.

The second major question may seem a little odd:

   Will you be using WordStar 2000 with a hard disk?

If you're installing WordStar 2000 for a floppy-disk system, you probably don't have a hard disk. It is conceivable, however, that you might have a reason for running the program from a floppy disk even if you have a hard disk—space might be very tight on your hard disk, for example. If that is the case, answer *Y*, otherwise type *N*.

The third decision you have to make concerns the printer you will be using. For this decision, the installation program gives you an extensive **Printer menu,** which is actually nine separate menus that include virtually every printer sold in this country. Keep pressing the numbers from 1 to 9 to change menus until you reach the one that lists your printer. The names are in alphabetical order. When you choose a name, the installation program will work for quite a while, creating a customized **printer driver** so that WordStar 2000 can use your printer's special features.

What if your printer isn't on the menu? You've got a problem because WordStar 2000 has no provision for custom installation of printers. Your best bet is to read your printer's manual. Chances are that your printer can be made to emulate one of the other common printers on the list, such as an Epson MX-80 or IBM Graphics Printer. If it can't, check with your MicroPro dealer. There are usually things that can be done to make any printer work.

Advanced Modifications

Once you've answered the third question, you are shown a menu of four choices:

QUIT INSTALLATION MENU

A Save the choices you've made and exit from the installation program.
B Answer the installation questions again.
C Abandon the choices you've made and exit from the installation program.
D Continue to the Advanced Modifications Menu.

Press **A-D** to choose an action

Advanced modifications are special options that you can select to customize WordStar 2000 to your taste. Some of these enhancements are quite useful. If you're interested, press D for "advanced modifications". You'll get another menu:

ADVANCED MODIFICATIONS MENU

- **A** Submenu delay
- **B** Beep on error
- **C** Initial directory display
- **D** Display [COMMAND TAGS]
- **E** Initial overtype mode
- **F** Numeric representation
- **G** Menu display levels
- **H** Reprogram function keys
- **I** Change colors on color monitor
- **X** Exit

The options you're most likely to find useful are:

- **B** (**Beep on error**)—If, like most people, you object to computer programs that mock your errors by beeping at you, you can fight back by turning the beep off.

- **D** (**Display [COMMAND TAGS]**)—When you use print enhancements and other formatting commands, WordStar 2000 places command tags in your document; however, it does not display these tags unless you press ^OD. D reverses this so that the tags are displayed unless you press ^OD to turn them off.

- **G** (**Menu display levels**)—WordStar 2000 is preprogrammed to display all menus. You can speed up the program considerably by turning some or all of the menus off.

- **H** (**Reprogram function keys**)—You can change WordStar 2000's preset function key definitions using this option.

Here's a set you may want to try (commands are shown as they are displayed on the H option screens):

<Ctrl-C>E	**F1**	**F2**	<Ctrl-P>B
Cursor to End of file			*Print Boldface*
<Ctrl-A><Ctrl-R>W	**F3**	**F4**	<Ctrl-R>W
Remove Word left of cursor			*Remove Word*
<Ctrl-C>L	**F5**	**F6**	<Ctrl-C>R
Cursor to the Left side of line			*Cursor to Right side of line*
<Ctrl-A>	**F7**	**F8**	<Ctrl-F>
Cursor left one word			*Cursor right one word*
<Ctrl-Q>C	**F9**	**F10**	<Ctrl-R>S
Quit, save, and Continue			*Remove Sentence*

The changes aren't difficult to make—you just follow the instructions on the screen. When entering <Ctrl>, use the Control key with a letter, not the caret.

When you're done with your modifications, return to the final menu and choose *Save the Choices you've made and exit from the installation program.* Don't worry about getting the installation perfect. You can reinstall a program disk by running Ins-2 on it again, and you can always go back and make new copies of your original MicroPro disks.

Basic Installation: Hard-disk Systems

Hard disks are becoming quite popular on the IBM PC, especially with the introduction of the PC-XT and PC-AT models. If you have a hard-disk system, you'll probably want to install WordStar 2000 to take advantage of the faster disks. A hard disk makes WordStar 2000 a much better program because it eliminates many of the aggravating delays involved in reading sections of the program from a floppy disk.

To install WordStar 2000 on a hard disk, you must have at least 2150K bytes free on your disk (the number is no mistake: that's 2.1 megabytes). The reason for this is that the installation program insists on copying all the files on all six (or seven) disks into a single directory on your hard disk. You can delete many of these files immediately because there's no need to keep tutorial and information files on your hard disk. You can trim your disk files down to less than 1 megabyte—perhaps to as little as 350K if you can do without CorrectStar and the Advanced Features.

The hard-disk installation follows the same two-step procedure as for floppy disks, except that its first phase has a different function. Instead of setting up your boot disk, the Ins-1 program creates a directory on your hard disk with the name WS2000, then copies the contents of all six (or seven) program disks into it. The command to start the installation is:

   ins-1 hard ws2000 6

If you have WordStar 2000+ and want to install the Advanced Features, replace the 6 with a 7. When you're done with the first part, start the second part of the installation with the command:

   ins-2 hard ws2000 6 (or 7)

Answer the three basic questions, just as with floppy disks, and you're done.

You'll need the following files to run WordStar 2000:

- **WS2.BAT** (roughly 31 bytes) is a small **batch file** that gives a few special DOS commands as it starts up the WordStar 2000 program. When you type *ws2*, you are running this batch file, which in turn starts the WordStar 2000 program. You can add other DOS commands to this file if you wish.

- **WS2000.EXE** (164,592 bytes) is the **executable** code of the WordStar 2000 program. This entire file is loaded into the computer's memory when you start WordStar 2000 and is continually being reloaded as you give commands. You must keep it in one of your disk drives while you run the program.

- **WS2.OVR** (86,496 bytes) is an **overlay file** that contains parts of the WordStar 2000 program that are not included in the main program file. Whenever WordStar 2000 needs these parts of the program, it automatically loads the appropriate section of the overlay file. You must keep this file in one of your disk drives.

- **WS2MSG.OVR** (64021 bytes) is another overlay file that contains all the printed messages you see on the screen: menus, instructions, and error messages. If this file is missing, WordStar 2000 will crash as soon as it needs to display a message on the screen.

- **PD.OVR** (varies, usually around 20,000 bytes) is the **printer driver** that tells WordStar 2000 what special codes your printer expects for underlining, boldface, and superscripts. You must have this file in your system when you start up and when you print, but you can remove it at any other time.

The required files add up to about 330K bytes, which is very close to the capacity of a double-sided floppy disk. This means that there is no room on the program disk for anything else, not even COMMAND.COM and the hidden DOS files that let a disk start up the system. This means that you cannot make your program disk a boot disk. You need to use a separate disk to boot your system.

One trick is to copy the system files onto your work disks, then use them to boot the system. This takes away roughly 30K from your disk capacity, but it eliminates that extra boot disk. You can even leave your work disk in drive A: and run WS2 from drive B:. If you make your work disks bootable, make sure you copy the CONFIG.SYS file onto them from the installed boot disk. That file is necessary.

Another consequence of the full program disk is that certain operations require you to insert a third disk in a floppy-disk system. When this is necessary, WordStar 2000 will ask you to swap this extra disk with the WordStar 2000 program disk, then swap the program disk back when you're finished. This disk-swapping can become quite tedious with two of the programs in this book: CorrectStar and the WordStar/WordStar 2000 conversion program.

RAM disks

One way to reduce disk-swapping and to speed up the program is to install a **RAM disk.** A RAM disk is a program that fools DOS into thinking that part of the main memory is actually a third disk drive (usually named C:). You can copy disk files into this imaginary drive and run them just as if they were actually being loaded from a disk. The difference is that the reading takes only a fraction of a second, and other files can be put in the physical disk drives. (RAM-disk software is usually provided along with memory expansion boards—see your dealer if you need a program.)

Running WordStar 2000 from a RAM drive is a real pleasure. It takes less than two seconds to start the program and roughly a second to open a document. Most editing commands are almost instantaneous, even if you leave the menus on.

The only problem is that RAM disks require a lot of memory— generally 640K bytes for WordStar 2000—because in addition to the large chunk devoted to the electronic disk, you must keep enough memory to run the program. WordStar 2000 requires a minimum of 256K bytes for program storage, above and beyond what you devote to a RAM disk. If you have less free memory than that, the program may not load or may crash inexplicably. Note that this 256K is required even if you have copied the program files into the RAM drive.

If you have 640K bytes, create a RAM disk by all means. Create a full double-sided drive (360K bytes), and copy all the files to it from your program disk, using a command such as:

```
copy a:*.* c:
```

You can then switch to drive C: and start the WS2 program just as if it were a normal disk. When running spelling checks, you can simply leave the dictionary disk in one of the physical drives.

If you have 512K bytes or less, you can't create a RAM disk big enough to hold all the program files. You may, however, still be able to speed up the program considerably by using a smaller RAM disk and copying some of the program files, such as WS2.OVR and WS2MSG.OVR. Or, you can use the RAM disk to hold a small extra program such as the WordStar/WordStar 2000 conversion utility, so that you don't have to keep swapping disks.

If you create a RAM disk, you'll have to make a small modification to the WS2.BAT file. To do this, just open the file and add the symbols shown in boldface:

```
echo = off
path = a:;c:
ws2000 %1 %2
```

Then, press ^QS to save your corrections. This addition to the Path command tells DOS to check first in drive A:, then also in drive C: if it can't find the file it is looking for. Without this change, the WordStar 2000 program may not be able to find necessary files.

C

WordStar 2000 for Former WordStar Users

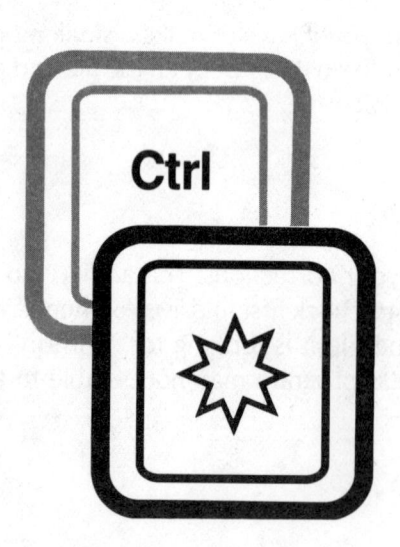

WordStar 2000 follows in the footsteps of an older brother, the plain old WordStar that has dominated the word processing market for years. This appendix is designed to help WordStar users become familiar with WordStar 2000 and to give some hints on translating files.

There are some significant differences between WordStar and WordStar 2000. The most important is the addition of **format files,** which control the page layout of a printed document. Also, many of the commands for print formatting work in different ways, and most of the commands have been given new control-key names in WordStar 2000.

The two programs are different enough that neither can read a file created by the other. You can open a WordStar document as an unformatted WordStar 2000 file, but you will see bizarre graphics characters in places where you'd expect simple print codes.

To translate files from one program to the other, run the WordStar/WordStar 2000 conversion program by typing **W** from the Opening menu of WordStar 2000. You must give the name of the file to be converted and the format and name of the file that will receive the result. If you have a floppy-disk system, your screen will turn black and you will see the message:

Can't find WSCONVRT.EXE.
Insert the disk containing WSCONVRT.EXE
or type the correct disk/directory name. Then press Return.
Or press **Esc**ape to leave.

Don't let this throw you. Just exchange the conversion disk with the WordStar 2000 program disk, type the drive name, and press Return. The rest of the conversion is automatic.

The conversion program does pretty well, but it doesn't take care of everything. Because WordStar 2000 has a different formatting system, there are bound to be differences between the documents. Also, some WordStar print enhancements and dot commands have no equivalent in WordStar 2000, and these commands are simply marked off as unprinted comments by the translation program.

The tables in this appendix are merely a guide for old WordStar users learning the new program. The commands in the two columns are not always identical. WordStar 2000 commands inside parentheses are only approximate equivalents. The word *auto* in parentheses means that WordStar 2000 performs the function automatically. The word *format* means that these commands are incorporated in WordStar 2000's format file.

Opening Menu

Most of the commands on the Opening menu have different names, but they generally work the same way. WordStar 2000 displays the file directory only when you're choosing a name. You can choose a file name in WordStar 2000 by moving the cursor around the file directory, then pressing Return. WordStar 2000 does not let you run an external DOS program.

Command	WordStar	WordStar 2000
Edit a document	D	E
Edit in non-document mode	N	E (UNFORM.FMT)
Change logged disk drive	L	D
File directory on/off	F	V
Set help level	H	GG
Print a file	P	P
Rename a file	E	M
Copy a file	O	C
Delete a file	Y	R
Run another program	R	—
Print a MailMerge document	M	P
Spelling check	S	S
Exit to DOS	X	Q

Command	WordStar	WordStar 2000
Format design	—	F
Key glossary	—	K
Typewriter mode	—	T
Restore previous name	^R	(^T)

Cursor Movement and Scrolling

Within a document, WordStar and WordStar 2000 use the same basic commands for moving the cursor and scrolling the screen. The most important cursor-movement keys are arranged in a diamond on the keyboard: ^E is up, ^X is down, ^S is left, and ^D is right. You can also use the arrow keys in both programs.

The WordStar Quick menu is generally replaced by WordStar 2000's Cursor menu. WordStar commands starting with the ^Q prefix are often ^C commands in WordStar 2000.

Command	WordStar	WordStar 2000
Up		
Line up	^E or ↑	^E or ↑
Top of screen	^QE or Home	^CH or Home
Page up	^R or PgUp	^CU or PgUp
Beginning of file	^QR	^CB
Scroll up one line	^W	^W
Scroll up continuously	^QW	—
Down		
Line down	^X or ↓	^X or ^DA
Bottom of screen	^QX or End	^CX or End
Page down	^C or PgDn	^CD or PgDn
End of file	^QC	^CE
Scroll down one line	^Z	^Z
Scroll down continuously	^QZ	—

Command	WordStar	WordStar 2000
Left		
Character left	^S or ←	^S or ←
Word left	^A	^A or ^←
Left end of line	^QS	^CL
Right		
Character right	^D or →	^D or →
Word right	^F	^F or ^→
Right end of line	^QD	^CR
Other		
Move to beginning of block	^QB	^CA
To end of block	^QK	^CZ
To position of last search or move	^QV	^CO
To last cursor position	^QP	—
To temporary markers 0 through 9	^Q0–9	^C0–9
To page number	—	^CP
To character	—	^CT
CorrectStar: next misspelled word	^QL	(auto)

Deleting Text

WordStar 2000 has changed the functions of the Backspace and Del keys, so that they delete characters left and right, respectively. This fits with the current standards of word processing software.

Most of the other delete commands have been grouped into a new Remove menu. Several new commands have been added to WordStar 2000, including Remove Sentence, Remove Paragraph, Remove To character, and the useful Undo command.

Command	WordStar	WordStar 2000
Delete previous character	Del	Backspace
Delete character under cursor	^G	Del
Delete word	^T	^RW
Delete line	^Y	^RE
Delete to end of line	^QY	^RR
Delete to beginning of line	^Q Del	^RL
Delete block	^KY	^RB or ^BR
Remove sentence	—	^RS
Remove paragraph	—	^RP
Remove to character	—	^RT
Undo deletion	—	^U

Locate and Replace

The find and replace operation has been combined into a single command, but the general idea remains the same.

Command	WordStar	WordStar 2000
Locate	^QF	^L
Locate and replace	^QA	^L
Repeat search	^L	^N

Miscellaneous Editing

An important difference between the two programs is that WordStar 2000 automatically reformats paragraphs in all documents with word-wrapped formats. WordStar waits until you press ^B before it reformats a paragraph.

Command	WordStar	WordStar 2000
Reformat paragraph	^B	(auto)
End paragraph with carriage return	Return	Return
Insert carriage return after cursor	^N	^CI
Insert mode on/off	^V or Ins	^OO or Ins
Interrupt command	^U... Esc	Esc
Repeat next key or command	^QQ	^OR

Footnotes and Windows

WordStar 2000 has added commands to arrange footnotes automatically and to open multiple windows on the screen. When two windows are open, cursor commands operate on the window, not on the entire screen.

Command	WordStar	WordStar 2000
Footnote	—	^ON
Move to footnote number	—	^CN
Open another window	—	^OW
Move to other window	—	^CW

Help System (J Menu)

WordStar 2000 has a more extensive help system, which is linked directly to commands. You can always get help by pressing ^G, even after you have pressed one or two prefix keys.

Command	WordStar	WordStar 2000
Get help	^J	(^G)
Set help level	^JH	^GG

Block Commands (K Menu)

The WordStar Block menu has a variety of commands for marking, moving, and deleting blocks. Most of these commands have different names in WordStar 2000. Two new commands have been added for block arithmetic and sorting.

Command	WordStar	WordStar 2000
Mark beginning of block	^KB	^BB
Mark end of block	^KK	^BE
Hide/display marks	^KH	^BD
Move block	^KV	^BM
Copy block	^KC	^BC
Delete block	^KY	^BR or ^RB
Vertical/horizontal block	^KN	^BV
Set temporary markers 0 through 9	^K0-9	^CM0-9
Read a file	^KR	^BI
Write a block as a file	^KW	^BW
Block arithmetic	—	^BA
Block sort	—	^BS

File commands (K Menu)

WordStar users may be disappointed to discover that WordStar 2000 does not let you give DOS file commands from within a document. To give these commands, you must save the document and exit to the Opening menu.

Command	WordStar	WordStar 2000 (from Opening Menu)
Print a file	^KP	P
Rename a file	^KE	M
Copy a file	^KO	C

Command	WordStar	WordStar 2000 (from Opening Menu)
Delete a file	^KY	R
Change logged disk drive	^KL	D
File directory on/off	^KF	D

Saving the Document (K Menu)

The two programs have most of the same commands for saving a document. The differences are that the Save and Continue command in WordStar 2000 returns the cursor to its previous position rather than to the beginning of the document and WordStar 2000 does not allow you to save and exit to DOS without going through the Opening menu.

Command	WordStar	WordStar 2000
Save and continue	^KS	^QC
Save and return to Opening menu	^KD	^QS
Save and exit to DOS	^KX	—
Quit without saving	^KQ	^QA
Save and print	—	^QP

Formatting (O Menu)

Many of the commands on WordStar's On-screen menu have no direct equivalent in WordStar 2000; they are either automatic or incorporated into the format file. Many of these commands are only approximate equivalents, since the two programs have different ways of arranging tabs, margins, and justification.

Command	WordStar	WordStar 2000
Set left margin	^OL	^TL
Set right margin	^OR	^TR
Margin release	^OX	—
Set tab or decimal tab	^OI	^TS or ^TD
Clear tab	^ON	^TC
Indent paragraph to tab	^OG	^TI
Use text line as ruler line	^OF	(auto)
Center text	^OC	^OC
Line spacing	^OS	format
Justification on/off	^OJ	^OJ
Vari-tabs on/off	^OV	—
Word wrap on/off	^OW	format
Hyphen help on/off	^OH	format
Soft hyphens on/off	^OE	(^O-)
Page break display on/off	^OP	—
Print control display on/off	^OD	^OD
Ruler line on/off	^OT	format
Indent both margins	—	^TB
Left margin out	—	^TO
Undo all indentation	—	^TU

Print Enhancements (P Menu)

The most important WordStar print enhancements have direct equivalents in WordStar 2000. However, some of the more specialized functions, generally those used to print special characters or to change printer type styles, are not included. Many of these commands can be handled in other ways in WordStar 2000 format files. Commands that are not translated in the WordStar/WordStar 2000 conversion program are printed in italics.

Introduction to WordStar 2000

Command	WordStar	WordStar 2000
Boldface	^PB	^PB
Doublestrike	^PD	^PE
Underline	^PS	^PU
Superscript	^PT	^P+
Subscript	^PV	^P-
Strikeout	^PX	^PS
Change ribbon color	^PY	^PC
Overprint previous character	^PH	^PO
Overprint previous line	^P Return	^PN
Alternate pitch	*^PA*	*(^PF)*
Normal pitch	*^PN*	*(^PF)*
Pause while printing	^PC	^PP
Non-break space	^PO	^PW
"Phantom space" character	*^PF*	—
"Phantom rubout" character	*^PG*	—
User patch 1	*^PQ*	—
User patch 2	*^PW*	—
User patch 3	*^PE*	—
User patch 4	*^PR*	—
Change paper tray	—	^PT

Dot Commands

WordStar uses dot commands to mark special print features; WordStar 2000 replaces them with command tags displayed inside brackets. You cannot edit text within command tags as you can WordStar dot commands. Many WordStar dot commands for page layout features have no equivalents in WordStar 2000 because they are incorporated into the format design. Dot commands (including MailMerge dot commands) that are not translated on the WordStar/WordStar 2000 conversion program are printed in italics.

Appendix C – WordStar 2000 for Former WordStar Users

Command	WordStar	WordStar 2000
Page Layout		
Line height	.lh	^PH or format
Page length	.pl	format
Margin at top	.mt	format
Margin at bottom	.mb	format
Subscript/superscript roll	.sr	format
Character width	.cw	(^PF)
Page offset	.po	format
Microjustification on/off	.uj	—
Bidirectional printing	.bp	—
Unprinted comment	.. or .ig	^OU
Pagination		
New page	.pa	^OP
Conditional page	.cp	^OK
Page number	.pn	^OA
Page number column	.pc	format
Omit page number	.op	format
Headers and Footers		
Header	.he	^OH
Footer	.fo	^OF
Header margin	.hm	—
Footer margin	.fm	—

MailMerge Dot Commands

MailMerge is smoother and better integrated into the WordStar 2000 package than it is with WordStar. A MailMerge file in WordStar 2000 is just a normal text file and can be printed with the same print commands as normal documents.

Command	WordStar	WordStar 2000
Select data file	.df	^OMS
Read data	.rv	^OML
Ask for value	.av	^OMA
Set value	.sv	^OMU
Insert a file	.fi	^OMI
Message while printing	.dm	^OMM
Clear screen	.cs	—
Repeat	.rp	^OMR
Begin condition	.if	^OMC
Begin negative condition	.ex	—
End condition	.ef	^OME
Otherwise condition	—	^OMO
Next copy	—	^OMN

CorrectStar

WordStar 2000's CorrectStar is an improvement over WordStar's spelling checker, SpellStar. CorrectStar makes only one pass through the document and suggests new spellings rather than just asking you to retype the words. CorrectStar's command structure bears little resemblance to SpellStar.

D

Hard-Disk Systems

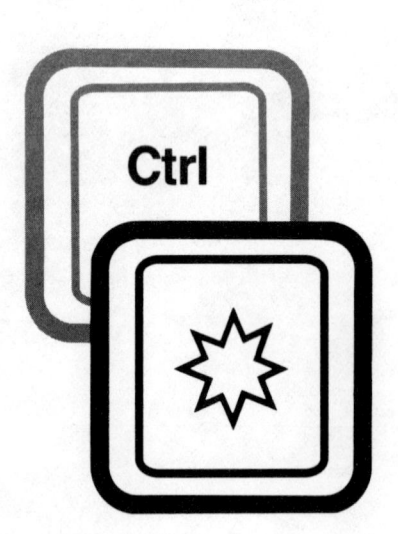

The descriptions in this book have been directed toward normal PCs with floppy disks. If you have a hard-disk drive, you're in luck, because WordStar 2000 is much faster and more flexible when run from this type of system.

Directories are the major difference between a hard-disk system and a floppy-disk system. On a hard disk, you'll probably want to store so many files that you'll need to split them up to keep them straight. To do this, you create smaller directories, or subdirectories, within your hard disk.

You can think of the subdirectories as a series of branches extending down from a main **root directory** (the one you're using before you specify another directory below it). You specify a file as a **pathname** that tells DOS how to get down from the disk's root directory to the specific file. IBM's DOS uses backslashes (\) as a prefix to directories, so the pathname:

C:\WS2000\WS2.EXE

refers to the file WS2.EXE inside the directory \WS2000 on disk C:. The pathname:

C:

refers to the disk's root directory.

When you install WordStar 2000 on a hard-disk system, the installation program creates a \WS2000 directory to hold the program files. It's best just to leave the program files in that directory, since that is where the program automatically looks for the overlay files as it is running.

You can set up your system so that you can run WordStar 2000 from within any other directory. To do this, create or modify an AUTOEXEC.BAT file so it includes the following statement:

PATH C:\;C:\WS2000

Your PC executes the instructions in the AUTOEXEC.BAT file at the time it starts your system. This command tells DOS to look first in the root directory, and then in the \WS2000 directory any time it can't find a file elsewhere. See Appendix B for more hints on installing WordStar 2000 on a hard disk.

With a hard disk, you use WordStar 2000 just as you would with a floppy disk, except that you can use a full pathname whenever you specify a file. If you want to open the file NEEDMONY in the directory \LETTERS, you could press E on the Opening menu and type the name:

C:\LETTERS\NEEDMONY

From then on, editing works exactly the same.

Most of the file commands on the Opening menu adapt easily to hard-disk subdirectories. For example, the D command lets you name a subdirectory in addition to the letter of a drive. If you type:

C:\LETTERS

WordStar 2000 will use that subdirectory as its **logged directory.** You can specify a file within that subdirectory just by typing its file name. If you want a file in another directory, type its full pathname.

The Delete, Copy, Move, and Print commands all work well with subdirectories. You can use Copy, for example, to make a duplicate copy of a file in another directory. Anywhere Chapter 14 refers to a *drive,* you can substitute the words *subdirectory inside a drive.*

A hard disk is a real advantage when using CorrectStar, the spelling checker. With floppy disks, you have to swap the program and dictionary disks in and out of a drive each time you run a spelling check. With a hard disk, you can easily fit the entire program and dictionary files into the same drive and avoid all disk-swapping.

The one thing you cannot do from within WordStar 2000 is **create** a new directory. To do that, you must exit to DOS and use the MKDIR command (or its abbreviation MD). Then you can go back into WordStar 2000 and add files to that directory in any way you wish.

Command and Symbol Index

All commands are accessed from the Editing menu, unless otherwise noted. Default settings are shown in capitals (ON/off or on/OFF). The boldfaced page number indicates where the command is most fully explained.

←	Move cursor left one character, **33**, 195
←	Move highlighting bar left one name (Choose a Name screen), 234
^←	Move cursor left one word, 196
→	Move cursor right one character (Choose a Name screen), **33**, 195
→	Move highlighting bar right one name, 235
^→	Move cursor right one word, 196
↑	Move cursor or highlighting bar up one line, **38**, 196, 235
↓	Move cursor or highlighting bar down one line, **38**, 196, 235
⟵	Remove character to the left of the cursor, **2**, 203
A	Access TelMerge (from the Opening menu), 237
^A	Move cursor left one word, **35**, 196

Alt-key commands

Alt –	End repeat (MailMerge), 232
Alt 0	Repeat procedure (MailMerge), 231

Command and Symbol Index

Alt 1	Quit and save changes, then return to the Opening menu, 206
Alt 2	Quit editing and abandon latest changes, 206
Alt 3	Quit to save changes, then continue editing, 206
Alt 4	Quit, save changes, then print the file, 206
Alt 5	Check spelling of a word, 228
Alt 6	Check spelling in a paragraph, 228
Alt 7	Check spelling in the rest of the document, 229
Alt 8	Select a data file (MailMerge), 231
Alt 9	Load data (MailMerge), 232
Alt =	Insert a file into the open document (MailMerge), 233
^B	Access **B**locks menu, 48, 65
^BA	Perform **A**rithmetic on marked **B**lock, **71-74,** 210
^BB	Mark the **B**eginning of a **B**lock, **66,** 208
^BC	**C**opy marked **B**lock, **68,** 209
^BD	**D**isplay **B**lock markers (ON/off), **67,** 209
^BE	Mark the **E**nd of a **B**lock, **66,** 208
^BI	**I**nsert a copy of a file into a document, **68,** 208
^BM	**M**ove marked **B**lock, **67,** 209
^BR	**R**emove marked **B**lock, **67,** 209
^BS	**S**ort marked **B**lock, **69-70,** 210
^BV	**B**lock **V**ertical mode (on/OFF), **69,** 208
^BW	Copy marked **B**lock to a new file, **68,** 210
C	Make a **C**opy of a file (from the Opening menu), **140,** 224
^C	Access **C**ursor menu, 48, 53-54
^C0-9	Move **C**ursor to the marker (0-9) you marked with ^CM, **58,** 212

^CA   Move Cursor to the beginning of marked block, **57, 68,** 210
^CB   Move Cursor to the Beginning of the document, **55,** 197
^CD   Scroll the screen Down one page, **56,** 200
^CE   Move Cursor to the End of the document, **55–56,** 197
^CH   Move Cursor to the upper-left of window, **54–55,** 198
^CI   Insert a blank line, **59,** 223
^CL   Move Cursor to the Left end of a line, **54,** 197
^CM   Set a Marker (0–9), **58,** 212
^CN   Move Cursor to a footNote reference, **57–58,** 198
^CO   Move Cursor to the Old position of a moved block, **57,** 68, 210
^CP   Move Cursor to a Page you specify, **57,** 198
^CR   Move Cursor to the Right end of a line, **54,** 198
^CT   Move Cursor To a character you specify, **58,** 198
^CU   Scroll the screen Up one page, **56,** 200
^CW   Move Cursor into a Window, **59,** 144, 225
^CX   Move Cursor to the lower-left of window, **54–55,** 199
^CZ   Move Cursor to the end of marked block, **57,** 68, 210

D   Change Drive or directory (from the Opening menu), **138–139,** 224
^D   Move cursor right one character, **33,** 195
^D   Move highlighting bar right one name (Choose a Name screen), 235
Del   Remove the character the cursor is on, **37,** 61, 203, 236

E   Edit or create a document (from the Opening menu), **25**
^E   Move cursor or highlighting bar up one line, **38,** 196, 235
End   Move cursor to the lower-left of a window, 199
^End Move cursor to the right end of a line, 198

Command and Symbol Index

F	Edit or create a **F**ormat (from the Opening menu), **122**
^F	Move cursor right one word, **35,** 196

Flag column symbols

<	End-of-paragraph marker (Return), 39
P	Page break (set with ^OP), 110
C	Unprinted (nonprinting) comment (set with ^OU), 116
F	Footer (set with ^OF), 114
H	Header (set with ^OH), 112
N	Footnote (set with ^ON), 115
–	The first of two lines that will overprint (set with ^PN), 92

Function key commands

F1	Get help with the menu or screen you are using, 207
Shift F1	Display command tags, tab characters, footnotes, headers, footers, and unprinted comments (on/OFF), 209, 222
F1F1	Set menu display level, 202
F2	Undo last Remove command, 205
Shift F2	Center text, 220
F3	Open a window, 225
Shift F3	Move cursor into a window, 225
F4	Boldface text (on/OFF), **88,** 214
Shift F4	Underline text (on/OFF), 215
F5	Indent left margin one tab stop, 219
Shift F5	Move indented left margin out one tab stop, 219
F6	Remove the word the cursor is on, **61,** 203

Shift F6	Remove the entire line, 203
F7	Reset the left margin, 218
Shift F7	Reset the right margin, 218
F8	Set a tab stop, 218
Shift F8	Clear tab stops, 219
F9	Mark the beginning of a block, 208
Shift F9	Mark the end of a block, 208
F10	Move a block, 209
Shift F10	Copy a block, 209
G	**G**et help (from the Opening menu), 25
^G	**G**et help with the menu or screen you are using, 207
^GG	Set menu display level, **44,** 202
^GGA	display **A**ll menus, **45,** 202
^GGN	display **N**o menus, **45,** 202
^GGS	display **S**ubmenus only, **45,** 202
Home	Move cursor to the upper-left of a window, 198
^Home	Move cursor to the left end of a line, 197
I	Access **I**ndexing menu (from the Opening menu), 237
Ins	Overtype mode (on/OFF), **36,** 50, 221
K	Access the **K**ey Glossary menu (from the Opening menu), 130
^K	Access the **K**ey Glossary menu, 49, 130
^KD	**D**efine or edit a glossary entry, **130–132,** 226
^KR	**R**emove a glossary definition, **133,** 226
^KU	**U**se a key file, **133,** 227

Command and Symbol Index   277

L		Access MailList (from the Opening menu), 237
^L		Locate or locate and replace text, 47, **77,** 211–213
	B	search **B**ackwards through the file, **78,** 211
	C	locate exact **C**ase match, **79,** 211
	D	**D**on't ask approval for replacement, **83,** 213
	L	**L**ocate only, **78,** 211
	P	**P**reserve case of replacement text, **83,** 213
	R	locate and **R**eplace, **81–82,** 213
	S	**S**how each replacement on the screen, **83,** 213
	W	locate **W**hole words only, **79,** 211
	n	locate nth occurrence of the text, **78,** 211
	n	replace first n occurrences, **82**

M   Move or rename a file (from the Opening menu), **140–141,** 224

^N   Find **N**ext occurrence of last text located, 47, **79,** 212

^O   Access the **O**ptions menu, 49
^O-   Insert end-of-line hyphen, 80, **109–110,** 220
^OA   **A**ssign a page number to a page, **111,** 178, 222
^OB   **B**ypass spelling correction (on/OFF), **167,** 229
^OC   **C**enter text, **108,** 220
^OD   **D**isplay command tags, tab characters, footnotes, headers, footers, and unprinted comments (on/OFF), 40, 102, 222
^OF   Define a **F**ooter, **114,** 223
^OFB   **B**oth odd and even pages, **114**
^OFE   **E**ven pages only, **114**
^OFO   **O**dd pages only, **114**

^OH	Define a Header, **112,** 222	
^OHB	**B**oth odd and even pages, **113,** 222	
^OHE	**E**ven pages only, **113,** 222	
^OHO	**O**dd pages only, **113,** 222	
^OI	Access the **I**ndexing menu, 49, 237	
^OJ	**J**ustify text (on/off – default depends on the format), **109,** 220	
^OK	Mark lines to **K**eep together on a page when printed, **111,** 221	
^OM	Access the **M**ailMerge menu, 49, 231	
^OMA	**A**sk user to enter data, **183–185,** 232	
^OMC	Specify a **C**ondition, **185–187,** 232	
^OME	**E**nd condition specified with ^OMC or ^OMO, **187,** 233	
^OMI	**I**nsert a file into your document, **188,** 233	
^OML	**L**oad data, **175–177,** 232	
^OMM	Define a **M**essage to display, **180,** 232	
^OMN	**N**ext copy (end repeat), **178,** 232	
^OMO	Specify an **O**therwise condition, **187–188,** 233	
^OMR	**R**epeat procedure, **175,** 231	
^OMS	**S**elect a data file, **174,** 231	
^OMU	**U**se a specific value for a variable, 233	
^ON	Define a foot**N**ote, **115,** 223	
^OO	**O**vertype mode (on/OFF), **50,** 221	
^OP	Mark a **P**age break, **110,** 178, 221	
^OR	**R**epeat commands or text that follows, **50–51,** 221	
^OS	Access **S**pelling Correction menu, 49, 228	
A	**A**dd to personal dictionary, **161–162,** 229	
C	**C**orrect all occurrences (to the end of the file), **159,** 229	
I	**I**gnore misspelled word, **161,** 230	
N	view **N**ext suggestion, **160,** 230	

Command and Symbol Index 279

P	view **P**revious suggestion, **160–161,** 230
T	Allow user to **T**ype correction, **162–163,** 230
^OSP	Check spelling in a **P**aragraph, **164,** 228
^OSR	Check spelling in the **R**est of the document, **164,** 229
^OSS	**S**elect a new Personal Dictionary, **165,** 229
^OSW	Check spelling of a **W**ord, **164,** 228
^OU	**U**nprinted (nonprinting) comment, **116,** 221
^OW	**O**pen a **W**indow, **143,** 225
P	**P**rint a file (from the Opening menu), 147, 214
A	**A**bandon printing, 150, 214
C	**C**ontinue printing, 150, 214
P	stop **P**rinting, 150, 214
^P	Access **P**rint enhancements menu, 48, 87
^P+	Superscript (on/OFF), **91,** 215
^P−	Subscript (on/OFF), **91,** 215
^PB	**B**oldfaced **P**rint (on/OFF), **88,** 214
^PC	**C**hange color of **P**rint, **95,** 216
^PE	**E**mphasized **P**rint (on/OFF), **90,** 215
^PF	Change **F**ont, **96–97,** 217
PgDn	Scroll the screen down one page, **56,** 200
^PgDn	Move cursor to the end of a document, 197
PgUp	Scroll the screen up one page, **56,** 200
^PgUp	Move cursor to the beginning of a document, 197
^PH	Set **H**eight of lines (line spacing), **93–94,** 216
^PN	**N**o new line (overprint on previous line), **92,** 216
^PO	**O**verprint character on preceding character, **91,** 216
^PP	Mark a printing **P**ause, **94,** 191, 217
^PS	**S**trikeout (hyphens over text) (on/OFF), **90,** 215

^PT   Change printer **T**ray, **95–96,** 217
^PU   **U**nderline (on/OFF), **89,** 215
^PW   Mark **W**ords to keep together on a line when printed, **92,** 216

Q   **Q**uit WordStar 2000 and return to DOS (from the Opening menu), 41, **138,** 224
^Q   **Q**uit answering questions (decisions screens), 22, 148, 214, 236; access Quit menu, 46
^QA   **Q**uit and **A**bandon changes, **47,** 206
^QC   **Q**uit and save changes, then **C**ontinue editing, 41, **46,** 206
^QP   **Q**uit and save changes, then **P**rint the file, 22, **46–47,** 206
^QS   **Q**uit, **S**ave changes and return to the Opening menu, 41, **46,** 206

R   **R**emove a file (from the Opening menu), **139–140,** 224
^R   Access the **R**emove menu, 61
^R   **R**emove an answer from an answer line (Choose a Name screen, ^L screen), 234
^RB   **R**emove marked **B**lock, **62–63,** 209
^RC   **R**emove **C**haracter the cursor is on, **61,** 203
^RE   **R**emove **E**ntire line, **62,** 203
^RL   **R**emove line to the **L**eft of the cursor, **62,** 204
^RP   **R**emove **P**aragraph, **62,** 204
^RR   **R**emove line to the **R**ight of the cursor, **62,** 204
^RS   **R**emove **S**entence, **62,** 204
^RT   **R**emove **T**ext up to a chosen character, **62–63,** 204

Command and Symbol Index **281**

Ruler-line symbols

			margin markers, 105
▼	tab stop, 102
#	decimal tab stop, 104

Ruler-line tag symbols (inserted ruler line)

L	left margin, 106
R	right margin, 106
!	tab stop, 106
#	decimal tab stop, 104
^RW	Remove the **W**ord the cursor is on, **61,** 203

S	Access **S**pelling Correction menu (from the Opening menu), **157–158,** 228
^S	Move cursor left one character, **33,** 195
^S	Move highlighting bar left one name (Choose a Name screen), 234

Symbols, flag column. *See* Flag column symbols

Symbols, ruler line. *See* Ruler line symbols

T	Access **T**ypewriter mode (from the Opening menu), **141,** 217
^B	turn off printer **B**uffer, 217
^T	**T**ransfer the highlighted name to the answer line (Choose a Name screen), **30,** 234
^T	Access **T**abs and Margins menu, 49, 101

^TB	Indent **B**oth margins one tab stop, **107,** 220
^TC	Clear **T**ab stops, **105,** 219
^TD	Set a **D**ecimal **T**ab stop, **104,** 219
^TI	**I**ndent the left margin one tab stop, **107,** 219
^TL	Reset the **L**eft margin, **105,** 218
^TO	Move indented left margin **O**ut one tab stop, **107,** 219
^TR	Reset the **R**ight margin, **105,** 218
^TS	Set a Tab **S**top, **103–104,** 218
^TU	**U**ndo all indentation, **107,** 220
^U	Undo last Remove command, 47, **48,** 61, 205
^V	**V**iew all questions and default answers (on/OFF) (decisions screens), 148, 236
^V	**V**iew directory (ON/off) (Choose a Name screen), **28,** 201
W	**W**ordStar/WordStar 2000 file conversion (from the Opening menu), 238
^W	Scroll the screen up one line, **39,** 200
^W	Scroll the directory up one row (Choose a Name screen), 29, 201
ws2	Access **W**ordStar 2000 from the DOS prompt, **20,** 25
^X	Move cursor or highlighting bar down one line, **38,** 196, 235
^Z	Scroll the screen down one line, **39,** 200
^Z	Scroll the directory down one row (Choose a Name screen), 29, 201

Subject Index

Boldfaced page numbers indicate where the entry is most fully explained.

^ (Caret symbol), 15
\ (Backslash symbol), 10

A

AUTOEXEC.BAT, 269
Advanced Features disk, 242
Alt key, **16,** 34
American Heritage Dictionary, 154
Arithmetic, 71. *See also* Blocks, arithmetic
Arrow keys, 33, 38
   on Choose a Name screen, **28**
Auto-install program, 19, 245
Auto-repeat feature, 32

B

.BAK files, 11, 141
Backslash symbol (\), 10
Backspace key, 37
Backspace key reflex, 2
Backup
   disks, 142
   files, 11
   hard disk, 10

Blocks
   and windows, 144
   arithmetic, 71
   arithmetic (vertical), 73
   copying, 68
   copying to new file, 68
   displaying, 67
   highlighting, 66
   horizontal, 69
   inserting entire file, 68
   length, 65
   marking, 66,
   menu, 65
   moving, 67
   removing, 67
   sorting, 69
   Starter Set commands, 75
   vertical, 69
Boilerplate text, 127
Boldface, 88
Boot disk, 243
   using work disk as, 251
Booting up, 19, 25

C

Caret symbol (^), 15
Carriage returns, 39
   inserting, 59
   locating, 80

Centering text, 108
Choose a Name screen, 26
Command tags, 102
    double, 113
    header tags, 112
    locating, 80
    printing, 149
    ruler-line tags, 106
    stand-alone, 94
    variable, 94
COMMAND.COM, 243
Commands
    function key, 34, 56
    letter-key, 15, 34, 43
Comments (unprinted), 116
CONFIG.SYS, 252
Control key, **15,** 34
Conversion disk, 242
Converting old-WordStar files, 255
Copying
    between windows, 144
    blocks, 68
    disks, 242
    files, 140
    with Undo, 61
CorrectStar, 153. *See also* Spelling check
Cursor, 14
Cursor diamond, 38. *See also* Cursor movement
Cursor movement (to)
    auto-repeat, 35
    beginning of block, 57
    beginning of file, 55
    block's old position, 57
    bottom left of screen, 54
    cursor movement diamond, 38
    down, 38
    down one screen, 56
    end of block, 57
    end of file, 55
    Home (top left of screen), 54
    inserting carriage return (blank line), 59
    left end of line, 54
    menu, 53
    next window, 59, 144
    right end of line, 54
    setting placemarkers, 58
    specified character, 58
    specified footnote reference, 58, 115
    specified marker, 58
    specified page, 57, 111
    Starter Set, 59
    up, 38
    up one screen, 56
    word by word, 35

D

DATE and TIME questions, 19
Del key, 37
Deleting text, 61. *See also* Removing text
Dictionary disk, 242
Directory
    Format, 31
    highlighting, 28
    scrolling, 29
    viewing, 28
Discretionary hyphens, 109
    locating, 80
Disk, 9
    floppy, 9
    hard, 10
Disk drive, 9
    logged (default), **28,** 138
    specifying, 27
Disk full message, 55, 142
Displaying command tags, 113

DOS, 138, **244**
    commands 244
    disk, 242
    prompt, 20
    resident commands, 244
Double spacing, 93. *See also*
    Line height
Doublestrike text, 90
    produced by overprinting, 92

E

Editing menu, 32, **47**

F

File handling, 137
File name, 26
    default name, 28
    entering, 28
    extension, 26
Files, 10
    backup, 11
    chain printing, 188
    copying, 140
    length, 11
    loading, 11
    moving, 140
    removing, 139
    renaming, 140
    saving, 11
    unformatted, 68
Footers, 114
Footnotes, 115
Form feeds, 126
Format files, 119
Formats
    choosing, 30
    creating, 122
    Decisions screen, 123
    directory, 31
    modifying, 122

    of inserted file, 68
    predefined, 120
    predefined (chart), 121
Formatting options, 108
Function keys, reprogramming, 54, 61
Function keys, **16,** 34, 56

G

Grammatik, 153

H

Hard carriage returns, 39. *See also* Carriage returns
Hard disk, 269
    and installation, 246
    and spelling check, 156
    AUTOEXEC.BAT file, 269
    creating directories, 270
    logged directory, 270
    pathname, 269
    root directory, 269
    subdirectories, 269
Hard spaces, 35
    displaying, 67
Hardware, 7
Headers, 112
    removing, 113
Help screens, 45
Horizontal mode, 69
Hyphens
    automatic hyphenation, 109, 120, 126
    discretionary, 109

I

IBM PC, 7
    PC-AT, PC-XT, 10

Subject Index 287

Indents, 106
    both margins in, 108
    left margin in, 107
    left margin out, 107
    undoing all, 108
Insert mode, 35
Installation, 19, **241**
    Advanced modifications, 248
    Beep on error, 248
    display command tags
        default, 248
    hard disk, 246, **249**
    Menu display default, 248
    monitor, 246
    PATH command, 253
    printer, 247
    Quit Installation menu, 247
    RAM disk, 252
    reprogramming function
        keys, 248
    reprogramming function
        keys (suggestions), 249
    special graphics card, 246
Installation disk, 241
Italics, 95

J

JUSTIFY.FRM, 120
Justifying text, 108, 109, 120, 125

K

Keeping lines together, 111
Key Glossary menu, 130
Key files, 129 *See also* Key
    glossaries
Key glossaries 129
    deleting entries, 133

    long forms, 131
    menu, 130
    short forms, 130
    using, 132
    using another key file, 133
Keyboard, 14

L

Line height, **93,** 123, 125
    and type font, 99
    double spacing, 93
    lines per inch, 93
    single spacing, **93**
Lines per page, 125
Locating text, 77
    Next occurrence (^N), 79
    carriage returns, 80
    command tags, 80
    find *n*th occurrence, 78
    inserted page breaks, 80
    locating [R], [T], [?], [#],
        and \, 81
    matching case only, 79
    options menu, 78
    search string, 77
    searching backwards, 78
    spaces and hyphens, 79
    tab characters, 80
    whole words only, 79
    wild cards (for letters and
        numbers), 81
    See also Replacing text
Logged disk drive, changing, 138

M

MailMerge, 169
    alternating letters and
        envelopes, 190

asking for values, 183
chain printing, 188
command files, 189
complex conditions, 186
conditional printing, 185
creating master document, 174
data checking, 184
data files, 172
data file (sample), 181
displaying messages, 180
ending a condition, 181
ending master document, 177
form letter, 171
form letters, 169
form letters (samples), 182
loading variables, 175
mailing labels, 189
master document, 169
master document (sample), 181
merging whole files, 188
next copy, 178
null string, 174
number of copies, 179
number of repetitions, 175
otherwise condition, 187
page breaks, 178
page numbers, 177
printing out, 179
records, 172
relational expressions, 186
selecting data file, 174
system variables, 172
variable fields, 170
variable names, 171
variables, 170
Main directory, 10
Margins
   and ruler line, 105
   and type fonts, 98
   limitations on, 105
   right, 125
   setting, 105
   temporary, 106
   top and bottom, 125
   See also Indents; Tabs and Margins menu
MEMOFORM.FRM, 120
Memory, 1, 11
   minimum required, 9
Menu display level, 44
   and headers, 113
   setting, 44
   strategies, 45
Menus, 43
   submenu delay, 45
Monitor
   and installation, 246
   color, 8, 89
   monochrome, 8
Moving
   blocks, **67**
   files, 140
   with Undo, **61**
MS-DOS, 8
MSCRIPT.FRM, 120

N

Non proportional spacing, 97
NORMAL.FRM, 120
Numeric keypad, 14, 34, 56
NumLock key, **14**

O

On-screen formatting, 2
Opening menu, 25, 137
Operating system, 8
Options for on-screen formatting, 108
   Starter Set, 116

Options menu, 49
Overprinting, 91
Overtype mode, 36
    and Return key, 41
    and Tab key, 41

P

Page breaks, 110
    and line spacing, 41
    conditional, 111
    displaying, 41, 126
    inserted page breaks, 110
    locating inserted page breaks, 80
Page numbers
    and MailMerge, 177
    assigning, 111
    screen page numbers, 57, 111
    where printed, 126
    within footer, 114
Page offset, 125
Paragraphs
    breaking into two, 59
    joining, 63
Pausing printing, 94
PC-DOS, 8
PD.OVR, 251
PERSONAL.DCT, 157
Placemarkers, 58, 67
Print color, 95
Print enhancements, 87
    and specific printers, 88
    boldface, 88
    changing colors, 95
    changing paper tray, 95
    color-coding on screen, 89
    combined effects, 89
    deleting tags, 88
    displaying command tags, 88
    doublestrike, 90
    emphasis (doublestrike), 90
    italics, 95
    line height, 93
    menu, 87
    overprinting characters, 91, 92
    overprinting lines, 92
    pausing printing, 94
    print font, 96
    stand-alone command tags, 94
    Starter Set, 99
    strikeout printing, 90
    subscripts, 90
    superscripts, 91
    underlining, 89
    variable command tags, 94
    word grouping, 92
Printers
    and type fonts, 96
    dot-matrix, 8
    letter-quality, 8
    pausing to change print elements, 94
    paper tray, 95
    sheet feeder, 95
Printing
    abandoning, 150
    chain printing, 188
    command tags, 149
    Decisions screen, 147
    files, 147
    interrupting, 150
    mulitple copies, 149
    page formatting, 149
    pause between pages, 149
    selected pages, 149
    to disk file, 149
    while editing, 149
ProKey, 133
Program, 7
Program disk, 241

Proportional spacing, 97
   and status-line column
      indicator, 97
"Punctuation + Style", 153

Q

Quitting WordStar 2000, 41
Quitting editing, 46
   and abandoning changes, 47
   menu, 46
   saving and continuing, 46
   saving, and printing, 46

R

RAGGED.FRM, 120
RAM disk, 252
   and spelling check, 156
RAM, 9. *See also* Memory
Removing
   block markers, 67
   carriage return, 63
   command tags, 88
   end of paragraph, **63**
   end of sentence, **62**
   entire line, **62**
   files, 139
   headers, 113
   left side of line, **62**
   marked block, 62
   paragragh, **62**
   placemarkers, 58
   previous word, **61**
   right side of line, **62**
   sentence, **62**
   single character, 61
   spaces, **61**
   Starter set, 63
   stand-alone command tags, 94
   to specified character, **62**

   with Locate and Replace, 84
   word, **61**
Repeat Option, 50
Replacing text, 81
   deletion throughout file, 84
   displaying each
      replacement, 83
   from cursor to beginning of
      file, 82
   matching case only, 82
   preserving case of
      replacement string, 83
   replacement options menu,
      82
   replacement string, 81
   replacing *n* occurrences, 82
   replacing with command
      tags, 82
   replacing with wild cards,
      not permitted, 82
   whole words only, 82
   without approval, 83
Restoring deleted text, 61. *See
   also* Undo
Return key, 20
   in overtype mode, 41
Ruler line, 40
   and margins, 105
   in boilerplate text, 127
   inserted ruler-line tags, 106

S

Saving a file, 46. *See also*
   Quitting editing
Saving files, 41
Screen, 8. *See also* Monitor
Scrolling
   directory, 29
   text, 39
Searching for text, 77. *See also*
   Locating text

Subject Index

Sheet feeder, 95
Shift key, 34
Single spacing, 93. *See also* Line height
Software, 7
Sorting, 69
Spelling check, 153
    Add word to dictionary, 161
    and RAM disk, 156
    and hard disk, 156
    by paragraph, 164
    by word, 164
    bypassing marked text, 167
    Correct all occurences, 159
    creating personal dictionary, 165
    dictionary disk, 154
    ending, 163
    Ignore suspect word, 161
    Next suggestion, 160
    personal dictionaries, 157
    Previous suggestion, 160
    rest of document, 164
    selecting personal dictionary, 164
    space required on data disk, 155
    suggested corrections, 160
    suspect words, 153
    Type correction, 162
    typos, 153
SPMSG.OVR, 155
Starter Set commands, 55
    Block commands, 75
    Cursor commands, 59
    Formatting Options commands, 116
    Print Enhancement commands, 99
    Remove commands, 63
    Tabs and Margins commands, 116
Starting up, 19, 25
Status line, 39
    cursor tracking, 39
    horizontal/vertical block mode, 40
    insert/overtype mode, 40
Strikeout printing, 90
Subdirectories, 139
Subscripts, 90
Superscripts, 91

T

Tab characters, 40, 102
    displaying, 40
    locating, 80
Tab key, 40
    in overtype mode, 41, 103, 125
Tab stops, 40, 102, 125
    and type fonts, 99
    clearing, 105
    decimal, 74,
    setting, 103, 104
Tables, 102, 103
    and vertical block mode, 69
Tabs, 102
    and type fonts, 99
Tabs and Margins menu, 101
Temporary margins, 106. *See also* Indents
The Tiger (William Blake), 33, 66
Toggle command, 28
Tutor disks, 242
Type fonts, 123
    and line height, 99
    and margins, 98
    and tabs, 99
    changing manually, 94
    characters per inch, 97
    non proportional, 97
    type faces, 96
    type sizes, 97

Typewriter mode, 141
Typos, 153

U

Underlining, 89
　between words, 126
　produced by overprinting, 92
Undo, 61
　and windows, 144
　to move and copy text, **61**
Unformatted files, 121
UNFORM.FRM, 121
Unprinted comments, 116

V

Variables, 114

Vertical mode, 69

W

WS2.BAT, 250
WS2.KEY, 132
WS2.OVR, 155, 251
WS2000.EXE, 250
WS2LIST.FRM, 120
WS2MSG.OVR, 251
WordStar 2000, 2
　features, 3
Windows, 143
Word grouping, 92
Word processor, 1, **7**
Word wrap, 2
WordStar (old version)
　compared to WordStar 2000, 256
　converting files, 255

Selections from The SYBEX Library

Integrated Software

MASTERING SYMPHONY™
by Douglas Cobb
763 pp., illustr., Ref. 0-244
This bestselling book provides all the information you will need to put Symphony to work for you right away. Packed with practical models for the business user.

SYMPHONY™ ENCORE: PROGRAM NOTES
by Dick Andersen
325 pp., illustr., Ref. 0-247
Organized as a reference tool, this book gives shortcuts for using Symphony commands and functions, with troubleshooting advice.

JAZZ ON THE MACINTOSH™
by Joseph Caggiano
400 pp., illustr., Ref. 0-265
The complete tutorial on the ins and outs of the season's hottest software, with tips on integrating its functions into efficient business projects.

MASTERING FRAMEWORK™
by Doug Hergert
450 pp., illustr., Ref. 0-248
This tutorial guides the beginning user through all the functions and features of this integrated software package, geared to the business environment.

ADVANCED TECHNIQUES IN FRAMEWORK™
by Alan Simpson
250 pp., illustr., Ref. 0-267
In order to begin customizing your own models with Framework, you'll need a thorough knowledge of Fred programming languages, and this book provides this information in a complete, well-organized form.

ADVANCED BUSINESS MODELS WITH 1-2-3™
by Stanley R. Trost
250 pp., illustr., Ref. 0-159
If you are a business professional using the 1-2-3 software package, you will find the spreadsheet and graphics models provided in this book easy to use "as is" in everyday business situations.

THE ABC'S OF 1-2-3™
by Chris Gilbert and Laurie Williams
225 pp., illustr., Ref. 0-168
For those new to the LOTUS 1-2-3 program, this book offers step-by-step instructions in mastering its spreadsheet, data base, and graphing capabilities.

MASTERING APPLEWORKS™
by Elna Tymes
250 pp., illustr., Ref. 0-240
Here is a business-oriented introduction to AppleWorks, the new integrated software package from Apple. No experience with computers is assumed.

SYBEX Computer Books are different.

Here is why . . .

At SYBEX, each book is designed with you in mind. Every manuscript is carefully selected and supervised by our editors, who are themselves computer experts. We publish the best authors, whose technical expertise is matched by an ability to write clearly and to communicate effectively. Programs are thoroughly tested for accuracy by our technical staff. Our computerized production department goes to great lengths to make sure that each book is well-designed.

In the pursuit of timeliness, SYBEX has achieved many publishing firsts. SYBEX was among the first to integrate personal computers used by authors and staff into the publishing process. SYBEX was the first to publish books on the CP/M operating system, microprocessor interfacing techniques, word processing, and many more topics.

Expertise in computers and dedication to the highest quality product have made SYBEX a world leader in computer book publishing. Translated into fourteen languages, SYBEX books have helped millions of people around the world to get the most from their computers. We hope we have helped you, too.

For a complete catalog of our publications:

SYBEX, Inc. 2344 Sixth Street, Berkeley, California 94710
Tel: (415) 848-8233 Telex: 336311